WAR COMES AGAIN

GETTYSBURG CIVIL WAR INSTITUTE BOOKS
published by Oxford University Press
Edited by Gabor Boritt

Why the Confederacy Lost
Lincoln, the War President:
The Gettysburg Lectures
Lincoln's Generals
War Comes Again:
Comparative Vistas on the Civil War and World War II

Other books by Gabor Boritt

Lincoln and the Economics of the American Dream
The Lincoln Image
(with Harold Holzer and Mark E. Neely, Jr.)
The Confederate Image
(with Mark E. Neely, Jr., and Harold Holzer)
The Historian's Lincoln
The Historian's Lincoln, Rebuttals:
What the University Press Would Not Print

By late June it is usually warm,
even hot in Gettysburg.
In the night at our farm,
the fireflies glow in the dark,
fleeting specks illuminating the woods and
turning Marsh Creek into a pageant.
In the daytime along the side of the road,
orange tiger lilies proclaim their eternal message.
My heart overflows;
it is time to see old friends again,
time to make new ones.
It is the time for
the Gettysburg Civil War Institute.

Gabor S. Boritt

WAR

Comparative Vistas on the

Edited by
GABOR BORITT

Preface by
DAVID EISENHOWER

COMES AGAIN

Civil War and World War II

Essays by

Stephen E. Ambrose
Michael C. C. Adams
Ira Berlin
Robert V. Bruce
D'Ann Campbell and Richard Jensen
Don E. Fehrenbacher
Howard Jones
Gerald F. Linderman
Peter Maslowski
Arthur M. Schlesinger, Jr.
Russell F. Weigley

New York • *Oxford*
Oxford University Press • *1995*

Oxford University Press

Oxford   New York
Athens   Auckland   Bangkok   Bombay
Calcutta   Cape Town   Dar es Salaam   Delhi
Florence   Hong Kong   Istanbul   Karache
Kuala Lumpur   Madras   Madrid   Melbourne
Mexico City   Nairobi   Paris   Singapore
Taipei   Tokyo   Toronto

and associated companies in
Berlin   Ibadan

Published by Oxford University Press, Inc.,
200 Madison Avenue, New York, New York 10016

Oxford is a registered trademark of Oxford University Press

Library of Congress Cataloging-in-Publication Data
War comes again : comparative vistas on the Civil War and World War II/
edited by Gabor Boritt ; preface by David Eisenhower ;
essays by Stephen E. Ambrose . . . [et al.].
p. cm.
"Gettysburg Civil War Institute Books
published by Oxford University Press"—P. ii.
Includes bibliographical references.
ISBN 0-19-508845-X
1. United States—History—Civil War, 1861-1865.
2. World War, 1939-1945—United States.
I. Boritt, G. S., 1940- .
II. Ambrose, Stephen E.
III. Title: Gettysburg lectures published by Oxford University Press.
E649.W23   1995   973.7—dc20   94-36511

1 2 3 4 5 6 7 8 9

Printed in the United States of America
on acid-free paper

DEDICATED TO THE
AMERICAN SOLDIER
OF
WORLD WAR TWO

Preface

It is very good to return to Gettysburg and the Civil War Institute that has grown to national fame since its founding barely more than a decade ago. I have spoken in some forty-two states over the last few years, and the happy news about the CWI and its director, Gabor Boritt, is everywhere. I last spoke here on the 125th Anniversary of the Battle of Gettysburg, in 1988, on "Dwight D. Eisenhower's Civil War." A good deal has changed since then. Most important for our purposes, World War II has become a true historical subject. The war's sad continuation symbolized by the Berlin Wall is gone, and the war's memory reached the mature age of fifty, the span of two generations. We can now look at the Second World War dispassionately, and so we can, at last, compare it with authority to that other earth-shattering American experience, the Civil War.

Dwight D. Eisenhower, one of the subjects of this book, the Supreme Allied Commander in Europe during World War II, began to make such comparisons soon after moving to Gettysburg in the 1950s, if not sooner. Indeed as I look back upon my teenage years in Gettysburg, I feel that perhaps my grandfather spoke to me continuously about the Civil War and World War II—though rarely about the later war directly. I think that when he talked about the Civil War, he was in fact often reflecting on his own experiences in World War II. The same was perhaps true when he wrote about the Civil War in his memoirs.

But then Dwight D. Eisenhower spoke as a participant of the Second World War who lived on the most sacred ground of the Civil War. He instinctively understood some of the similarities and differences about these two most transforming moments of United States history that galvanized the American people into unforgettable action. His early musings can now give way to the reflections of historians.

What excites me about this book is its perspective—looking forward from the Civil War to World War II, the unflinching willingness to measure one against the other, to make difficult but illuminating comparisons about these defining American experiences. Pulitzer laureate Robert V. Bruce looks at the road that the United States took to the two most terrifying moments of its history: Fort Sumter and Pearl Harbor. A prolific Steven Ambrose compares two of the giants of these two giant wars, Grant and Eisenhower. Peter Maslowski focuses on the crucial role of military intelligence. Gerald Linderman considers the raw realities of combat for common soldiers. D'Ann Campbell and Richard Jensen shed light on the two wars as points of departure for women. Ira Berlin does the same for African-Americans. Another Pulitzer laureate, Arthur Schlesinger, Jr., compares Lincoln and Franklin Delano Roosevelt as wielders of the Constitution during war time, and Howard Jones looks at them as diplomatists. They thus confront a supreme question—What does the United States stand for; how do we define the nation? Our often false memories of the two great wars are dissected by Michael C. C. Adams. Finally, the dean of American military historians, Russell Weigley, brings sharp light on how we now see the Civil War and World War II and the danger our vision poses for our future. In the Epilogue, a third Pulitzer-winning historian, Don E. Fehrenbacher, a World War II veteran like the other Pulitzer laureates of this book, Bruce and Schlesinger, provides the personal thoughts of a participant of one war who became a leading student of another war.

As we look back to the past, we must also look to the future. I was quite struck by something President Bill Clinton said at the Normandy commemoration at the cemetery over Omaha Beach. He described the beautiful setting as representing the "quiet sounds of democracy." It was the threat to that quiet democracy that brought on the great conflict of the Civil War and, three generations later, World War II. It is conceivable, perhaps certain, that the underlying challenges that brought on those great wars will come again in some form. What we will then do will largely depend on what we will have learned from our past.

After the 50th Anniversary of Normandy   David Eisenhower
and on the Eve of the 131st Anniversary
of the Battle of Gettysburg, 1994

Acknowledgments

"My heart kept getting higher and higher until it felt to me as though it was in my throat," Ulysses Grant recalled his first encounter with the Rebels in the Civil War. He was leading his ill-trained and -equipped Illinois volunteers up a hill in Missouri. The enemy, he knew, waited on the other side. "I would have given anything then to have been back in Illinois, but I had not the moral courage to halt and consider what to do; I kept right on." Then he reached the top. The Rebels were gone. "My heart resumed its place," Grant later wrote, and "it occurred to me at once that [the enemy commander] had been as much afraid of me as I had been of him. . . . I never forgot. . . ."[1]

So Grant began to learn something about the nature of leadership, the importance of optimism under adversity; and in his first real battle at Fort Donelson, he learned more of the same. Stephen Ambrose traces thus Grant's learning in Chapter Two and moves on to Dwight D. Eisenhower's similar road in the following century—from Gibraltar to the 1943 Battle of Kasserine Pass in North Africa. "There is a rough parallel" between the two men, he affirms.[2] Even as the reader is carried enthusiastically along by the sharp insights and sprightly prose that put Ambrose's work on the bestseller list, one is reminded of Lord Bryce's caution cited by Robert Bruce at the start of Chapter One: "The chief practical use of history is to deliver us from plausible historical analogies."[3] The warning fits, as Ambrose and the other contributors understand, Chapter One, Chapter Two, and every chapter in this book.

"The difficulties, obstacles, and ambiguities that confront anyone who tries to compare historical events or processes" are many, Carl Degler wrote in 1991. "Yet," he added, "comparison is truly valuable, we must not be cowards and shrink from our obligations."[4] As one of the finest among those who have dared write comparative history, Degler has earned the right to speak. He provided some of the inspiration for this book.

More enticement came from Arthur Schlesinger, Jr., who delivered a sparkling lecture at Gettysburg College on the 125th anniversary of Lincoln's Gettysburg Address on November 19, 1988. With as many as 1000 people in the audience, some of whom came from long distances for the occasion, he compared Lincoln's and Franklin Roosevelt's use of the Constitution in wartime. In his lecture, reprinted in this volume (the only essay in the book to have been published previously), Schlesinger boldly declared that the American republic "has gone through two awful times of testing since the achievement of independence—two times when the life of the nation was critically at stake. . . ."[5] Though some would want to debate the proposition, as the world got ready to celebrate the landings in Normandy and the coming end of the Second World War, it seemed logical for the Civil War Institute at Gettysburg to turn onto the comparative road.

We have been fortunate to attract historians nearly all of whom have done substantial prior work on both the Civil War and the World War II periods. I enjoyed working with them. I am grateful to them all. Many of the historians read and commented on each other's essays, making them better. In addition, John Y. Simon provided useful criticisms for Chapter Two, Don Markle for Chapter Three, Reid Mitchell for Chapter Five, Joseph Reidy for Chapater Six, and earlier, Mark Neely for Chapter Seven.

Tina Fair, Linda Marshall, and Marti Shaw, who oversee the CWI activities, once again deserve to be recognized for their hard work and high spirits. Our lively student assistants also merit thanks: Melissa

Becker, Dan Boritt, Jake Boritt, Susan Fiedler, Dana Ledger, Howard Lewis, Chris Patterson, Steve Petrus, Tracy Schaal, Dieter Schmidt, and Peter Vermilyea. Dan De Palma volunteers so much work as to earn the title of honorary staff member.

Chris Patterson and Missy Becker also worked on numerous problems associated with any book, checking footnotes and quotations, finding rare sources, and sharing their enthusiasm. Deborah Huso ably helped with Chapter Two.

Michael Vice, Curator at the Gettysburg National Military Park, was kind enough to provide the kepi and helmet for my photograph on the dust jacket of this book. The photo is the work of Melinda Hutton.

I am grateful above all to my family for putting up with the strain that at times rides along with my creative lurches: Liz, my wife, Norse, who created the Pennsylvania Dutch dedication design, Jake, who talked history with me, and our youngest, the unsinkable Daniel Adam Wilson Boritt.

My secretary, Marti Shaw, not only got the manuscript ready for publication, but rode herd on the contributors, corrected my errors, and generally made herself indispensable.

Sheldon Meyer and Leona Capeless, my editors at Oxford, created a supportive, happy working relationship with me. Leona is retiring after many years—and four of my books—and I wish her Godspeed.

The book is dedicated to the American soldiers of World War II with a deep sense of gratitude. I especially wish to single out those who have attended the Civil War Institute and three who contributed chapters to this book: Robert V. Bruce, Don E. Fehrenbacher, and Arthur M. Schlesinger, Jr.

My final word of thanks goes to the Reverend John W. Schildt, who in a little ceremony at the 1994 CWI session presented me with the pin and badge of the Stonewall Brigade. With a lineage that goes back to 1742, the Brigade had fought at Gettysburg and Normandy. I can think of no better way to close than with its motto: "Ever Forward."

Contents

WAR COMES AGAIN

1

Toward Sumter and Pearl: Comparing the Origins of the Civil War and World War II

ROBERT V. BRUCE

1. TWO COMMUNITIES

"WHAT has occurred in this case," said Abraham Lincoln in 1864, "must ever recur in similar cases. Human nature will not change. In any future great national trial, compared with the men of this, we shall have as weak, and as strong; as silly and as wise; as bad and good. Let us, therefore, study the incidents of this, as philosophy to learn wisdom from. . . ."[1] A generation later, however, the English historian and political scientist James Bryce attached a reservation: "The chief practical use of history is to deliver us from plausible historical analogies."[2] Both were right. While comparing our two greatest national trials, we must weigh similarities against singularities.

In the comparison assigned to me, that of origins and outbreaks, the most obvious singularity arises from the very nature of the two wars, one a civil war between North and South, the other a war of foreign powers against the reunited North and South. Nevertheless, the two cases are not altogether incommensurable. This was implied by Charles Sumner in 1845 when he remarked that war between nations "in truth constitutes civil war."[3] Civil war and international war are not diametrical opposites but points on the same spectrum. Civil war can be defined as war within a community. International war can be defined as war between communities. But there are degrees of community. The so-called United States of 1861 were not fully united. The nations of the 1930s were not completely separate and independent. The wars we compare here could even be described conversely to the usual view, the first as a war between Northern and Southern alliances of quasi-nations and the second as a war of secession from the international community by Germany, Italy, and Japan.

Regardless of labels, what we have in each of these cases is the tragedy of a group of states or nations achieving a measure of unity in a common cause, but then, as some sought to expand at the expense of others, coming to blows in a great war. There are major episodes in each story for which there are no equivalents in the other. One of these is the outbreak of hostilities at Fort Sumter and Pearl Harbor. Each occurred in a harbor and touched off a war. Beyond that they are not comparable. I shall discuss the theories that the respective presidents rigged them, but I shall say little about the actions themselves. Instead, I shall draw parallels between the long chains of events leading up to them, reviewing familiar history in an unfamiliar context.

In comparing the American and European experiences, it is helpful to analyze the reasons why smaller communities may coalesce into larger ones. From the days of Egypt and Assyria to those of the Nazis and Soviets, empires have subjugated, consolidated, and exploited diverse ethnic, cultural, and religious groups. But consolidation may be voluntary in the common interest. In such cases three motives operate, singly or together. One is to advance the material interests of the partners by pooling resources to build up the economy. Another motive is defensive, to keep the peace among themselves. And the third is also defensive, to resist or cast off subjection to an alien power. In short, the chief goals of union are growth, peace, and freedom from alien rule.

In the American case, it was the last motive that created the Union in 1776. We owe something to George III as well as to George Washington. Had the British colonies not faced a common danger, they would not have united when they did, if ever. Indeed, not even the menace of the French and Indians had persuaded them to take up Benjamin Franklin's 1754 proposal for a rudimentary union. They differed, more or less, in religious beliefs, in ethnic heritage, in economic pursuits, in social institutions. They were separated by geography. They had closer ties with England than with each other, and it was to England they looked in time of danger. But when the French menace was eliminated in 1763 and England itself threatened to become the despoiler, their only alternatives were to join or die. And so they seceded in a body from the British Empire, declaring their unity and independence to the world.

Even after independence was won, there were motives enough to cement American union. Shays's Rebellion threatened internal conflict; Spain and England still prowled the new nation's borders; and the West lay open to development. So the remarkable document called "The Constitution of the United States of America" was proclaimed the "supreme law of the land." Its preamble explicitly stated the three aforementioned motives for union: "domestic tranquility," "common defence," and "the general welfare."

In Europe the process by which a degree of community arose from the ashes of war was longer, more painful, and far less effective. The Protestant Reformation and the rise of national states had led to a series of national wars for territory and in the name of religion. Still, wars ended with treaties, and in the intervals between wars, ambassadors were exchanged and diplomatic relations carried on. In 1625 the Dutchman Hugo Grotius published his famous treatise entitled "On the Right of War and Peace," which sought at least to limit war by codifying such practices. In it was born the science of international law. It appeared during the long horror of the Thirty Years' War, ended at last by an international congress that drew up the Peace of Westphalia in 1648. The agreement not only put a stop to religious wars, but also laid the foundation for a fragile community of states to shore up the peace through a balance of power. In the nineteenth century that modus vivendi came to be known as the Concert of Europe. In the century from 1815 to 1914 it managed to confine European warfare to a few relatively brief outbreaks of butchery involving only one or two powers on each side.

2. TESTING

But the Concert of Europe rested on narrower and weaker foundations than did the American Union. Enforced unity under Hapsburgs, Bourbons, and Napoleon had been only partial and temporary. As for the three motives for voluntary union, the need for a united defense against outside aggressors had ended centuries before with the repulse of the Moors, Mongols, and Turks. The goal of economic growth was met by the several nations individually through the Industrial Revolution and economic and territorial imperialism in Asia and Africa. That left the single goal of keeping peace among themselves. In our own time, a potential Armageddon would be kept on ice for half a century under penalty of mutual assured destruction. Mankind would become a nuclear family. But before the atom bomb blossomed over Hiroshima, that fear was less compelling. Differences in languages and cultures limited fellowship. Unchecked by an American-style "supreme law of the land," rivalries in trade and empire fed mutual suspicions and in 1914 exploded into what was then called the Great War or the World War, though John Maynard Keynes referred to it as "the European Civil War," and later generations have had sad occasion to rename it World War I.[4]

The American Union, even with its powerful Constitution, also experienced unsettling strains in its early years. In the language of that time, it was not a consolidated government but a federal union. This is not surprising. Americans were used to such an arrangement. It was akin to the relationship between the colonies and the British Empire, in which the central power attended to some matters while the colonial governments, by virtue of charters or the slowness of transatlantic communication, were left to deal with others. Such a structure made political union among bickering allies more palatable in the first instance. It reduced the rancor of policy disagreements by allowing local experiments in such matters as electoral qualifications, lotteries, and prohibition of liquor or slavery—at least so long as they did not deeply offend states that were otherwise minded.

But the principle of states' rights has been merely a useful device, not a philosophical imperative. It is not essential to democracy or public virtue. There are no divine rights of states. And states' rights had their dangers, as the British Empire found out in 1775 and the United States in 1861. The rub comes when some states exercise their local option in ways that others consider morally or materially intolerable. If the federal government cannot compose or smother the quarrel nonviolently and the states come to blows, it turns out that the federal system itself has armed the combatants with ready-made governmental machinery and territorial turf. State lines may be likened to geological fault lines or to perforated lines marked "detach here." In contrast to mob uprisings or military coups in a consolidated government, a federal system invites organized secession. And that is likely to mean organized war.

The danger weighed on the minds of some Americans almost as early as the Declaration of Independence; and even after the adoption of the Constitution, fears persisted that disunion from whatever cause would spell civil war. The whole history of civilization demonstrated that. But the danger would become clear and present only when some concrete issue arose. In 1794 the Whiskey Rebellion tested the bonds of union. But it did not invoke states' rights. Directed against the federal whiskey tax, the uprising spread into four states but did not enlist any of them as states. Without the structure and apparatus of established state government, that rebellion was swept aside by federal power with only scattered violence. Four years later came a threat to the Union that did involve states as such. But instead of seceding, those states, Kentucky and Virginia, attacked the object of their anger, the federal Alien and Sedition Acts, by proposing to nullify them unilaterally. When no other state offered support, the two dissidents drew back from the prospect of a decidedly one-sided civil war, and the offending laws were allowed to expire peaceably soon afterward.

Meanwhile a more ominous threat, that of state secession, had been explicitly raised in New England. There the dominant Federalist party was dismayed by the Jeffersonian capture of the presidency in 1801 and despondent over the likelihood that their section would be dwarfed as new states were born from Jefferson's vast Louisiana Purchase. A few of them talked privately of secession, and one of those warned the House of Representatives in 1811 that if Louisiana were admitted to statehood, "it will be the duty of some [states] to prepare definitely for a separation; amicably if they can, violently if they must."⁵ The War of 1812 threatened New England's maritime enterprises and incited a Hartford Convention of the discontented. But they rejected state secession unless the conflict were "radical and permanent" and then only with the consent of all the other states.⁶ By then the war's end had reopened the seas to the Yankees, and they reflected that membership in a great Union would be better for business than going it alone; they contemplated the menace of federal military coercion; and they presently raised their stature in the Union anyway by taking the lead in its booming industrial development.

3. ERA OF GOOD FEELINGS

To the cynical eye, the War of 1812 does not look very glorious. Because of the slowness of transatlantic communication, it was declared after the British had given in to American demands, and its greatest military victory was won after peace had been concluded in Belgium. Humiliations, including the capture of Washington and the burning of the White House, outweighed triumphs. But what Americans remembered was Perry at Lake Erie, Jackson at New Orleans, and Francis Scott Key checking out the star-spangled banner at Fort McHenry. The banner yet waved, and though none of the original issues were settled by the treaty, we the people declared victory.

Details aside, the people were not far wrong after all, nor was Henry Clay when he called it the Second War for American Independence. The war had effectively ended the danger of foreign attack. While in progress it had been unpopular and divisive, but its final flourish at New Orleans, however irrelevant, aroused a lasting spirit of national pride that fortified American unity as common danger had once done. The inauguration of James Monroe in 1817 was also the inauguration of what came to be called the Era of Good Feelings.

Some were to see World War I as the war to end wars or to make the world safe for democracy. Those who clutched at such hopes found some straws in the Treaty of Versailles, which formally concluded the war in 1919. In redrawing the map of Europe, the Treaty made some progress toward fitting boundaries to ethnic divisions. It defanged Germany by imposing on it a sweeping unilateral disarmament, including the seizure or destruction of all major military weapons. Germany's army was to be limited to a hundred thousand men and its navy to a specific number of small warships, not including submarines. German territory west of the Rhine was to be demilitarized. Still more hopefully, the Treaty provided for a League of Nations not only to reduce armaments generally but also to prevent war. The League did successfully adjudicate clashes between certain smaller nations. And it was also useful in repatriating prisoners of war, fighting the international drug trade, and discouraging traffic in women and children.

Apart from the Treaty and the League, the 1920s brought other hopeful signs of unity. After some turbulence, the German Republic, as it had now become, seemed to settle down under a pleasingly democratic constitution, and in 1926 it was admitted to the League. In 1922 the Washington Naval Conference, to which the United States played host, had taken an encouraging step toward restraining the arms race by agreeing to a specific ratio of battleships among the United States, Great Britain, Japan, France, and Italy. A further earnest of peace seemed to be several treaties signed in 1926 at Locarno, Switzerland, by Germany, France, and other nations, pledging arbitration in lieu of war. And in 1928 came the Kellogg-Briand Pact, signed by the United States and most other nations, renouncing war except in self-defense—each nation, however, to be the sole judge of what it considered to be its self-defense. Given all this it seemed possible to hope, as President Woodrow Wilson had of his cherished project the League of Nations, that a start had been made toward the grand dream of a just and lasting peace and that any flaws or deficiencies could be remedied along the way.

4. FIREBELL IN THE NIGHT, 1819-1821

But in the America of James Monroe and the Europe of Versailles forces were at work that would reveal their Eras of Good Feelings to be Eras of False Hopes. And in both cases the forces were those of territorial expansionism, in the interest not only of material gain but also of philosophies and ideologies deeply repugnant to those being pressed upon.

In what later came to be known as the ante-bellum South, the offensive doctrine was that of racial slavery. Blacks had been profitably enslaved there since the seventeenth century, and despite some soul-searching induced by the Declaration of Independence, most who profited—like the Declaration's author Thomas Jefferson himself—did not give up their investments voluntarily. In the Northern states, however, the great majority of voters did not own slaves and so, exercising states' rights, they came to terms with the ideals of the Revolution and, state by state, emancipated all the slaves within their borders. By the end of the 1820s, the national motto might better have been "E pluribus duo," out of many, two: a solid block of contiguous free states, fretfully bundled under the Constitution with a solid block of contiguous slave states. The federal system had made strange bedfellows. And the mounting fervor of antislavery feelings in the North as in the outside world was making the incompatibility, in the ominous words of the Hartford Convention, both "radical and permanent."

Until then, the federal system had compartmentalized the incompatible philosophies. State lines were serving as fire walls. But the federal system had also created a perilous dilemma. If the North and South had each, like European nations, been legally separate and sovereign, neither could have changed the other's social system by law. They might have turned up their noses at each other and followed their separate ways. Or if, as in Europe, they had come to blows it would probably have been over something more material than philosophical—trade, perhaps, or territory. On the other hand, if the two sections had been part of a consolidated government, the majority in it would have authorized slave-holding either everywhere or nowhere, and any aggrieved group would have had no alternatives but submission or an unstructured uprising, a less promising course than state secession.

Under the Constitution, however, states' rights prevented either section from imposing its mores on the other by a simple majority vote of the whole. Yet neither section could feel entirely safe, since the Constitution could be circumvented to some degree by indirection or judicial interpretation, or changed to any degree through amendment by three-fourths of the states. In theory the amendment process is one of awesome power. It could impose on the minority any command whatever, limited only by a sense of justice or by the minority's threat of armed resistance. So in a conflict that was "radical and permanent," one side would be prey to perennial frustration and the other to perennial apprehension. The Gordian knot could be cut by disunion, but as Daniel Webster and many others firmly believed, the separation would not be amicable. Blood would run.

Paradoxically, the War of 1812 while strengthening national pride had also weakened one of the pillars of unity by diminishing the threat of external attack. The efficacy of that factor is assumed by science fiction plots, which sometimes rest on the unity of the human race in the face of extraterrestrial invasion. The concept was embraced in William Seward's equally fantastic suggestion to Lincoln on All Fools' Day 1861 that the United States be reunited by declaring war on France and Spain. But practically speaking, the penalties for disunity were now narrowed to economic crippling and that which had driven Europe to its fragile modus vivendi, namely, fear of war between its members. That was no trivial fear. Even in the United States it had been a force since independence. The sobering example of Europe's clashing nations had been expressly invoked in support of union by Alexander Hamilton and others. But it would not save Europe itself in 1914.

After the patriotic euphoria of 1815, the Southern empire of cotton and slaves pushed westward. So did the Northern empire of factories and farms. Maintaining a neat balance of power and territory, the two regimes coexisted peacefully for a time. But as their differences deepened, push was about to come to shove. The quivering balance of Congressional voting power suggested an unstable equilibrium, in which the slightest nudge might topple the weight irreversibly to one side or the other of the knife edge. Firm control of Congress could be used to control the admission of states and thus ultimately to wield the superweapon of Constitutional amendment. The Union could thereby be made either all free or all slave, a prospect intolerable to whichever side lost.

By 1819 the imminent admission of Missouri as a slave state threatened to tip the balance in the South's favor. In Congress both factions made predictions, not far removed from threats, of bloody civil war. Enough Northern Congressmen flinched to pass a compromise, balancing the admission of Missouri as a slave state with that of Maine as a free state, while reserving unorganized territory north of 36°30' for free states and opening territory below that line to either.

Meanwhile, preoccupied with a short but painful economic depression, the general public had been far less exercised over the controversy than was Congress. Moreover, the eventual settlement, like Versailles and subsequent treaties, seemed to promise a peaceful future. But old Thomas Jefferson in his Virginia retirement took a different view. To his mind, the fact of confrontation overshadowed the compromise. From Monticello he wrote:

> This momentous question, like a firebell in the night, awakened and filled me with terror. I considered it at once the knell of the Union. . . . A geographical line, coinciding with a marked principle, moral and political, once conceived and held up to the angry passions of men, will never be obliterated; and every new irritation will mark it deeper and deeper.[7]

Jefferson knew something about "angry passions," not only those of the Revolution but also those of the Southern mentality and culture in which he had been raised, which he had studied like everything else he encountered. In one of his passing fits of revulsion against slavery, he wrote:

> The whole commerce between master and slave is a perpetual exercise of the most boisterous passions, the most unremitting despotism on the one part, and degrading submissions on the other. Our children see this, and learn to imitate it . . . and thus nursed, educated, and daily exercised in tyranny, cannot but be stamped by it with odious peculiarities.[8]

Slavery was a taproot of violence, not only in its daily routine and domestic setting but also in its dependence in the field on the use of the whip—and of the pistol if that failed. More formidable resistance was violently dealt with by armed night patrols, vigilantes, or if necessary, militia. But there were other roots of violence in the ante-bellum South's recent frontier past and its rural present. Hunting for food or sport was widespread. Guns were everywhere. White Southerners sprang to arms enthusiastically in 1812 and when the Mexican War broke out in 1846. Between wars, military exercises were favorite diversions. In addition to the numerous Southern military academies, many colleges offered military training, and West Point cadets were disproportionately Southern.

Most significant was the South's concept of honor. It depended on public acknowledgment of one's standing more than on inner convictions of worth. Nothing was so intolerable to the Southern man, gentleman or plebeian, as humiliation in the eyes of the community. Honor then could be regained only by quick and violent reprisal against anyone who had in any way called it into question. In 1847 the *Southern Literary Messenger* proudly declared that "Southerners exercise much forbearance, till the question of honor is raised, and then they rush to the sword."[9] It was a code that today survives in its purest form among the armed youth of our urban ghettos. In that day, too, it often led to savage street brawls among the poorer sort, as well as to the more high-toned gunplay of duels.

Such was the social nitroglycerin on which Northerners trod in stigmatizing slavery and in trying to block its spread to Missouri in 1819. And as slavery withered away in the civilized world outside America, the South's sense of rejection, of honor traduced, goaded it to hostility toward outsiders and to systematic suppression of free speech, thus further alienating the North.

5. FIREBELL IN THE NIGHT, 1919–1933

A century later another firebell like the one that had terrified Jefferson shattered the postwar world's Era of Good Feelings. Even while the hopeful applauded the League of Nations, the Locarno Treaties, and the Kellogg-Briand Pact, an explosive charge was being laid in certain aggrieved and sullen nations. Its components were like those in the antebellum South: violent resentment of past or prospective humiliations, a compensating inflation of ethnic pride to the point of arrogance and racism, the brutal suppression of individual rights, glorification of war and of violence generally, and a corresponding inclination toward aggressive territorial expansion.

Each of the restive nations drew inspiration from a romanticized or mythical past. As the ante-bellum white South had found ethnic and historical self-satisfaction in Sir Walter Scott's rousing tales of medieval Scottish clans, so Germans wallowed in Wagner's somber settings for the operatic warring of Teutonic gods. Italians cheered the jut-jawed bombast of Benito Mussolini in the role of a pouter-pigeon Caesar. And the Japanese fancied themselves as sword-wielding samurai. There were even counterparts of the Southern precept of death before dishonor. Not long before, saber cuts had been displayed like badges of courage by duelling German students. Japanese who revered the code of Bushido, the warrior's way, sometimes disembowelled themselves in response to humiliation. And even in Italy the ancient Roman tradition of falling on one's sword in defeat was remembered, though seldom emulated. Such mindsets colored the outlooks and reactions of decision-makers in the expansionist nations.

Many of the grievances and tribulations of those malcontents were real enough. The achievements of the 1920s seemed increasingly hollow. The most disheartening failure was that of the League of Nations. President Woodrow Wilson had been its leading sponsor, accepting gross betrayals of his other ideals in the Treaty in the desperate hope that the League would put things right in due course. Yet Wilson's own nation committed the ultimate betrayal, as he saw it, by rejecting both the Treaty and the League, fearing impairment of its own sovereign freedom of action. American retreat into isolationism may or may not have made the fatal difference. At any rate, the League proved totally impotent in any dispute involving a major power. Even Poland successfully defied it in seizing Vilna from Lithuania. France had no faith in it and sought to provide her own security by reviving the old system of direct military alliances.

Disillusionment with the League during the 1920s deepened a general spirit of postwar disillusionment already pervading Europe not only in foreign affairs but also in literature, art, and domestic politics. Carving up the map to fit oppressed ethnic minorities merely allowed those former minorities to oppress ethnic subgroups within their own new borders even more ruthlessly, and violent clashes ensued, a process depressingly familiar at the present day. Rival ideologies also made domestic politics fanatical and disruptive, often violent. Postwar tariff barriers blighted international trade. The German economy, formerly the main engine of European prosperity, was greedily plundered and vindictively disabled by the Allies, expecially France. Germany's overseas colonies and some of its most productive home territories were stripped from it. Weakened as it was by the drain of war, the newly democratic nation was saddled with an immense burden of indemnities, including most of its merchant marine, great quantities of livestock, coal, and other goods, and in installments, billions of gold marks, the total amount actually paid still being uncertain.

By 1923 the burden had totally destroyed the value of German currency, including the life savings of millions, leaving them permanently and deeply embittered against France and England. They also unfairly blamed that ordeal on the democratic republic that had signed the Versailles Treaty under pain of renewed war after having been disarmed. Since Germany was now in default anyway, France in 1924 grudgingly eased the terms of reparation. Economic recovery began in Germany and the rest of Europe. But then came the Wall Street crash of 1929 and on its heels the worldwide Great Depression.

It was not the Depression, however, that began the spread of dictatorship among European governments, the counterpart to the spread of slavery in ante-bellum America. That plague had infected Spain, Poland, Greece, Yugoslavia, and Portugal even before the stock market crash. The first major victim was Italy, left all but prostrate by the long strain of the war, its people squeezed between unemployment and inflation. Aggressive socialist and Communist groups fomented strikes and general unrest. They were countered by middle-class groups who called themselves Fascists, from the Roman *fasces*, an ax in a bundle of rods, signifying authority, unity, and order. A disorganized civil war sputtered throughout Italy. Into this inviting turmoil stepped a born agitator with a lust for power, Benito Mussolini, who organized the Fascist bands and by the fall of 1922 controlled the nation. Appealing to the people's hunger for order, unity, and glory, and freely using murder and torture against his opponents, Mussolini created a totalitarian regime, the first major Fascist dictatorship. He solidified his hold on his nation's mind with measured brutality and showy public works. The trains now ran on time, the Fascists boasted. Authority and order prevailed.

The Italian Fascists were good at packaging their brutal doctrine, considering what was in it. This gave the movement pseudo-intellectual respectability and made it more exportable. In contrast, the ante-bellum Southern cause had been handicapped by ideological disjointedness. It marched into battle under reversible banners, on one side "Down with Political Slavery"; on the other, "Up with Human Slavery." Or on one side "States' Rights," on the other "Solidarity Against the Foe." It rested its logic on the proposition that in the sense of "we the people," some people are people, but other people are not people. It did not even have an accepted label. It had its theorists, notably John Calhoun and George Fitzhugh, but somehow "Calhounism" or "Fitzhughism" did not pass into the language. The Fascist philosophy not only had a name but was also more straightforward: all the people must be bound and gagged for their own good, except those doing the binding and gagging. To this the Nazis added the authority of pseudoscience: blonds are superior; brunets, except for Hitler, are inferior.

When the twentieth century's fire alarm bell sounded, however, the alarm came not from Fascist Italy, but from the faraway and increasingly authoritarian Japanese Empire. The bell tolled for the League of Nations, but also in the long run for Hiroshima.

Japan already had a worldwide reputation for skillful copying, industrial, military, even political, though not yet electronic. In its shift toward totalitarianism and expansionism, however, it was not copying Italy. As early as the eighteenth century the amorphous and benign Shinto religion, long dominated by Buddhism but at least a native growth, was recycled into a nationalistic cult exalting the Japanese as superior to all other peoples and destined to rule them. By the 1920s it was established and supported as the official state religion and enhanced by Bushido, deliberately perverted to militarism and pitiless contempt for human life. Mussolini's example had no part in that. It was the Japanese military establishment that capitalized ruthlessly on it. During the 1920s, control of Japan's foreign policy swung back and forth between that establishment and more moderate civilian politicians. But the military's increasing resort to assassination of its political opponents had put it in the saddle by the end of the decade. When the Great Depression hit Japan, the military seized the occasion for conquest in the name of markets.

The ripest prize was Manchuria, a province of China, where Japan had won special privileges in 1905. Those were only appetizers. On September 18, 1931, Japanese troops at Mukden in Manchuria erupted from their allotted zone, alleging a Chinese bandit attack on the railroad, and took over the whole province.

In the rest of the world, as had been true in the Missouri controversy, the current Depression absorbed the mind of the public at large, and in this case the attention of their leaders as well. The nearest equivalent to

Thomas Jefferson in expressing alarm was President Herbert Hoover's Secretary of State, Henry L. Stimson. "The situation," Stimson wrote privately, "is in the hands of virtually mad dogs."[10] But he was guarded in his public and official comments. Nevertheless, Japan had clearly violated the Kellogg-Briand Pact and other treaties to which the United States was a party. Stimson's polite but persistent efforts to negotiate a Japanese withdrawal got nowhere. In the exchange, words seemed to have lost their meanings. The League of Nations could not carry out the threats. The Japanese would not carry out promises. Stimson was outraged by the Japanese bombing of Chinchow, which killed thousands of civilians. Yet President Hoover would not hear of imposing sanctions or even hinting at them. He and the American people were gripped and absorbed by the terrible Depression, getting worse with no end in sight. The people would not stand for any action that might embroil them in war. Stimson could only hope that world opinion, American non-recognition of Japan's conquest, and a League commission of inquiry would bring Japan to its senses. They did not. On the contrary, when the League commission condemned Japan on all points, Japan in March 1933 angrily seceded from the League. The break-up had fairly begun.

Four days earlier, the German Reichstag had formally given Chancellor Adolf Hitler absolute power. All of us, I am sure, have often heard the grim tale of Hitler's rise. I shall only say briefly that Hitler was a twisted product of anti-Semitic Austria, of the front lines in World War I, and of a ruinous and vindictive imposed peace. He was also a consummate demagogue, a hypnotic speaker, who recognized and brilliantly exploited popular rage, despair, and hatred of the scapegoat Jews, for whom Hitler himself had a psychotic hatred. He had a ferocious lust for power, not only national but also global. He was utterly false in his promises. He was insatiably murderous. And by early 1933 he was in absolute control of the great German nation.

6. EXPANSION AND APPEASEMENT

By 1933, then, the line-up for Armageddon was complete. Europe and Asia had reached the point that America had in 1819. In Jefferson's words, "a geographical line, coinciding with a marked principle, moral and political," had been "conceived and held up to the angry passions of men." But in Europe there was no Missouri Compromise to postpone the collapse of peace. Instead there was what the poet William Butler Yeats had envisioned in the disillusionment of 1921:

> Things fall apart; the center cannot hold;
> Mere anarchy is loosed upon the world. . . .
> The best lack all conviction, while the worst
> Are full of passionate intensity.[11]

Mere anarchy was indeed loosed upon the world. The frail bonds of the League fell away, and so did those even frailer bonds of international law identified by Grotius. Treaties became dead letters. Trust and good faith became dreams of the past.

The League Covenant had called for reduction of armaments, but the jealousy and suspicion of the great powers blocked it. In 1932 a deadlock between France and Germany paralyzed a World Disarmament Conference, and when Hitler came to power the next year, he withdrew Germany from both the Conference and the League. Japan followed France and Italy in quitting the naval limitation agreement. After beginning a scarcely concealed rearmament program in violation of the Versailles Treaty, Hitler defiantly announced it in 1935 and formally rejected the treaty. France and Great Britain could have checked him, but they were at odds with each other and so acquiesced. Probing further, Hitler remilitarized the Rhineland. France could have evicted his weak force, but lost its nerve. In 1938 Hitler seized his native Austria without resistance or penalty. Mussolini had conquered Ethiopia in 1935, scornful of the League's ineffectual embargo, and in 1937 he followed Japan and Germany in seceding from the League. Encouraged by all this, the Japanese attacked China in 1937, though they soon realized that they had a tiger by the tail. Despite slaughter of Chinese civilians by the hundreds of thousands, Japan would still be mired in that conflict when it surrendered in World War II. But in 1938 the rogue nations were running their prey like mad dogs, as Henry Stimson might have put it.

This was what secession had brought Europe to. The road toward that point in ante-bellum America had not been so precipitant, and there were hopeful pauses along the way. Thanks to the Constitution, catastrophe could be postponed by the give and take of legislative compromises rather than the one-sided concessions made to appease the twentieth-century dictators. The Constitution largely eliminated the incentive for any state to wrest territory from another. It provided for the free flow of interstate commerce and the same privileges and immunities for all citizens. If any person or group craved what Hitler called *Lebensraum* or living space, they could simply move to where it was.

Unfortunately for intersectional peace, though fortunately for humanity, citizens of slave states were not guaranteed the right to hold slaves in any free state. So they did have reason to crave *Lebensraum*, especially as they began to fear what Abraham Lincoln and other Northerners hoped, that without room to spread, slavery would suffocate. To forestall that, unorganized territories would have to be opened to slavery by Congress or by judicial reinterpretation of the Constitution. So the South pressed for annexation of more such territories.

With the connivance of slaveholding Presidents Jackson, Tyler, and Polk, American migrants to Mexico declared the independence of its Texas province and subsequently joined the Union as a slave state. This led to war with Mexico and the annexation of a huge Southwestern territory. In the North the abolitionist crusade had, meanwhile, been overshadowed by a broader based political movement against slavery expansion. In a long, intense Congressional debate, threats of Southern secession were headed off by the Compromise of 1850, which gave the net advantage to the North but organized New Mexico and Utah Territories without restrictions on slavery. The Vermont-born Senator Stephen A. Douglas of Illinois, who had done more than anyone else to put the Compromise through, proudly proclaimed it the "final settlement" of the quarrel.[12] But as with the acquiescence of Britain and France in Hitler's encroachments, the Compromise of 1850 did little more than postpone the final showdown.

The "final settlement" was finally unsettled by Douglas himself, in cahoots with President Franklin Pierce, a New Hampshire man. In our conspiracy-conscious generation, which makes a pastime of paranoia, we might smell in this a devilish Yankee plot to bring on a civil war that would destroy slavery. That, after all, was what did come of it. But plot-sniffers overlook one of the prime factors in history, that of misinformation, misjudgment, and plain stupidity. Obsessed by his dream of developing the West, Douglas set his heart on organizing Kansas and Nebraska Territories from land north of the Missouri Compromise Line. In return for letting the Kansas-Nebraska bill through, Southern Senators extorted Douglas's consent to include an outright repeal of the Compromise Line. Pierce, a malleable lightweight, had been cultivated by Southerners while in Congress and had cottoned to them and their section. Neither he nor Douglas was sensitive to the moral aspect of the slavery controversy, which they now considered to be outworn. Despite a hurricane of abuse from his own section, Douglas forced the bill through with administration backing. It would turn out to be a disaster for Douglas and a costly triumph for the South.

Adolf Hitler's overweening expansionism achieved its last bloodless triumphs in 1938 and 1939. In order to conquer, depopulate, and resettle Russia with Germans, Hitler set out to eliminate the intervening obstacles of Czechoslovakia and Poland. The inertia of France and Britain in the face of his bold moves convinced him that they would not risk war to save small nations inaccessible to their direct military aid. Prime Minister Neville Chamberlain would now play the part of Franklin Pierce and Stephen Douglas. Though able, intelligent, and well-meaning, Chamberlain felt that no sane human being would risk detonating another world war, and he made the blunder of including Hitler in that category.

Hitler set about dismantling Czechoslovakia by using ethnic Germans already settled in the Sudeten range, Czechoslovakia's main barrier against German invasion. During the spring and summer of 1938, Hitler's agents stirred up violent Sudeten German protests against Czech rule. Chamberlain's resolve was weakened by his feeling that the outbreaks had some moral justification and did not concern Britain directly. By tossing Czechoslovakia to the wolves, he hoped to appease Hitler and buy time. As Hitler's new army crouched to spring, Mussolini, who had nothing to gain from war, prevailed on Hitler to meet Chamberlain and French Premier Daladier at Munich. There Hitler condescended to let Chamberlain and Daladier arm-twist the Czechs into surrendering the Sudetenland. The world has imprinted on its memory the newsreel scene of Chamberlain deplaning in England, gray-faced and shaken, yet happily waving a fluttering piece of paper, proclaiming in the words of the Anglican Book of Common Prayer that it brought "peace in our time," and conveying Hitler's solemn promise that he would make no more territorial demands in Europe.

The stage is now set for a classic dramatic turn, the downfall of hubris, of reckless pride, a familiar plot line in Biblical tales, ancient Greek drama, and the plays of Shakespeare. The pattern was much the same in both the ante-bellum contest and that of fascism against democracy in the 1930s.

7. THE DOWNFALL OF HUBRIS

The British people at first cheered the Munich Pact, but almost immediately began to have doubts. Within six months Hitler browbeat the helpless Czechs into submitting to total partition, Germany devouring the choicest cuts, Bohemia and Moravia. Since England was not ready for war and could not reach Czechoslovakia anyway, Chamberlain took refuge in the excuse that the Czechs had volunteered to be eaten. But he had finally grasped the fact that Hitler was, to use an old-fashioned word, evil, that in Jefferson's words the principle was not only political, it was also moral. Chamberlain had been frantically building up British military strength, and now he prevailed on France to join in pledging military support to Hitler's obvious next victim, Poland, in the event of German attack. Hitler, riding high, nevertheless began a war of nerves by demanding that Poland yield the Baltic port of Danzig and the strip of former German territory connecting it with the rest of Poland. He counted on a Polish capitulation like Czechoslovakia's. Failing that, Hitler was sure that Britain and France would not declare war, but if they did that it would be a mere gesture, sure to be abandoned after a quick German conquest of Poland.

His hubris betrayed Hitler. The Poles stood firm. Nevertheless Hitler startled the world by striking hands with Stalin's Soviet Union, the unwitting main object of his grandiose expansionism. Then, with Poland isolated and the Russians neutralized, Hitler opened a brutal attack on Poland. Two days later, on September 3, 1939, Great Britain and France astonished Hitler by actually keeping their word and declaring war on Germany. World War II had begun.

Germany's descent from hubris to Hell has a parallel in ante-bellum American history. The North's revulsion against the Kansas-Nebraska Act was as swift and emphatic as that of Chamberlain and the British people against the final sacrifice of Czechoslovakia. It took the lasting form of the new Republican party, dedicated to the confinement of slavery and almost exclusively Northern. Douglas tried to salvage his moral standing in the North by appealing to "popular sovereignty" with a vote by Kansas for or against legalizing slavery. But the voting was corrupted by fraud and violence. The skirmishing in "Bleeding Kansas" in the mid-1850s previewed the coming war as did the fighting between German and Soviet "volunteer" units in the Spanish Civil War of 1936–39. And when President James Buchanan, a Pennsylvanian who like his predecessor Franklin Pierce was in the South's pocket, tried to push a rigged pro-slavery Kansas constitution through Congress, he only split the Democratic party.

In 1857 the pro-slavery Supreme Court, in its infamous Dred Scott decision, ruled that Congress had no power to bar slavery in a territory, that the defunct Missouri Compromise Line had been illegal all along. The Republicans, including Abraham Lincoln, their rising star in Douglas's own Illinois, not only denied the validity of the ruling but also raised the possibility that it could logically be extended to the free states. In Lincoln's contest with Douglas for the Senate in 1858, he warned: "A house divided against itself cannot stand. . . . Either the *opponents* of slavery, will arrest the further spread of it . . . or its *advocates* will push it forward, till it shall become alike lawful in all the States, *old* as well as *new*—*North* as well as *South*."[13] The South also felt that sense of high stakes. What the Supreme Court had given, the Supreme Court could take away, if the Republicans held the White House and its appointment power long enough to restock the Court with antislavery justices. Meanwhile, a Republican Congress could hobble the domestic slave trade through its authority over interstate commerce. So when Lincoln became the Republican candidate for president in 1860, the South drew its line. If Lincoln were elected, the South would secede. Its bluff when called by the voters turned out to be no bluff.

After Lincoln's election, the seceding states had four months during which they faced only the lame-duck President Buchanan. In his annual message of December 3, 1860, the agonized Buchanan stoutly denied the right of secession but, unwilling to tie his successor's hands, he also disclaimed authority to suppress secession. While blaming the crisis entirely on the North, he surprisingly rose to the occasion with an eloquent anticipation of what Lincoln would say even more memorably in the coming years, that with the destruction of the Union

> the hopes of the friends of freedom throughout the world would be destroyed, and a long night of leaden despotism would enshroud the nations. Our example for more than eighty years would not only be lost, but it would be quoted as a conclusive proof that man is unfit for self-government.[14]

And after South Carolina seceded on December 20, Buchanan did his beloved United States a crucial service by refusing to give up Fort Sumter in Charleston Harbor to the recusant state. Like Chamberlain after Hitler's dismemberment of Czechoslovakia, Buchanan had belatedly awakened to the moral principle at stake and, bucked up by a reconstituted cabinet, found the courage to live up to it.

While Buchanan played for time, frantic efforts at a peaceful settlement were made in Congress, though a Southern bloc there had already declared that the "honor" of the Southern people could be sustained only by a Southern Confederacy.[15] Virginia sponsored a Peace Convention of twenty-two states in Washington. From these efforts came compromise plans to revive and extend the Missouri Line and in several ways to safeguard slavery where it stood, including an unamendable amendment prohibiting Congress from interfering with it in the states. Through his spokesmen, President-elect Lincoln accepted some of these provisions, even including the unamendable amendment. But he was immovable on the point of slavery expansion in the territories.

So Inauguration Day arrived on March 4, 1861, with an organized Confederate government in place, but with a federal garrison still holding Fort Sumter. Lincoln's address pleaded for reconciliation, promised non-interference with established slavery, and assured the Confederates that while the forts would be held, "you can have no conflict without being yourselves the aggressors."[16] But the Confederates made no move toward reunion.

Lincoln could not accept disunion. As Gabor Boritt has demonstrated in his book *Lincoln and the Economics of the American Dream* (1978), he was possessed by his lifelong vision of a nation in which every human being would have the right to rise to whatever economic and social level his abilities might carry him, or as Jefferson had put it, the right to life, liberty, and the pursuit of happiness. Slavery was therefore anathema to Lincoln, who, unlike Jefferson, owned no slaves. Lincoln could tolerate the existence of slavery in America only if it were confined to its present extent and, as he believed, thereby doomed to ultimate extinction. Furthermore, to give full meaning and scope to the right to rise required a nation of broad and growing opportunities. So Lincoln was especially influenced by the first of the three motives for unity enumerated heretofore, the motive of economic growth.

As provisions ran low at Fort Sumter, Lincoln hesitated. His cabinet was divided. But Northern opinion was hardening in favor of action. At last Lincoln notified Confederate authorities that provisions but no arms or troops would be sent. Confederate President Jefferson Davis ordered bombardment of the fort if its garrison did not agree to surrender by some definite date. Its commander did agree, provided that supplies did not arrive. The supply vessels being already outside the harbor, his reply was rejected, and at 4:30 a.m. on April 12, 1861, shore batteries opened on the fort. The Civil War had begun.

Lincoln had been determined that if war began, the first shot would come from the Confederates. That, he knew, would unite and galvanize the people of the North. During his term in Congress thirteen years earlier, he was best known for his charge that President Polk had cynically provoked the Mexicans to fire first on American troops. Some in 1861 and a few historians later brought the same charge against Lincoln. But Polk had deliberately sent troops into disputed territory not previously held by the United States, whereas the Sumter garrison was peacefully occupying a post that had never been out of federal hands. It was Jefferson Davis who ordered it to be shelled and seized. To say that Lincoln started the war by holding the fort is like saying the Poles started World War II by refusing to surrender Danzig. Lincoln's policy was precisely that of Captain John Parker, who on an earlier April morning reportedly told his company of minutemen on Lexington Green, "Stand your ground. Don't fire unless fired upon, but if they mean to have a war, let it begin here!"[17]

8. SECONDARY EXPLOSION

For the European democracies, Hitler's attack on Poland was the equivalent of Fort Sumter. But not for their less closely engaged associate the United States, which continued along the road to war at its own pace for another two years.

The summons that held Americans on that course had been first sounded by Thomas Jefferson in 1776. The torch of liberty his words lit then had enlightened and transformed the world in his own time, and neither the westward stampede nor the shame of slavery had snuffed it out. Whatever their other preoccupations, Americans felt in their bones the responsibility for keeping the flame alive for themselves, their posterity, and the whole world. Buchanan in the secession crisis, Lincoln at Gettysburg, Wilson in his war message of 1917, all had proclaimed that mission. Americans could not abandon it. And the nations that confronted Hitler in 1939, with all their frailties and blunders, seemed to be closest to supporting it.

The fateful month of March 1933 brought not only Hitler's dictatorship in Germany and Japan's withdrawal from the League of Nations but also Franklin D. Roosevelt's first inauguration. Roosevelt shared Stimson's anger at Japanese aggression against China, and his second cabinet meeting discussed the possibility of war with Japan. But he took office in the midst of the worst national crisis since 1861, and it took precedence over foreign affairs.

Roosevelt demonstrated his priorities in June 1933 by pulling the rug out from under the World Economic Conference in London, for fear its proposals would impede American economic recovery. By then Hitler's savage persecution of Jews was already under way and well reported. Roosevelt remonstrated, then turned to other matters. He could do little else. America had shared in and contributed to the cynicism and disillusionment of the 1920s, which in the thirties fed isolationism. Those who grasped the menace of Nazism were counterbalanced by those who saw a greater menace in the bankers and industrialists painted as the "merchants of death" by Senator Gerald Nye's investigating committee in 1934–35. There were other noninterventionists who, like Douglas, Pierce, and Buchanan in the 1850s and Chamberlain before 1939, were slow to comprehend the moral issue at stake.

Like Lincoln, Roosevelt was acutely mindful of public opinion. In tacking back and forth between the isolationists and interventionists, he laid himself open to charges of vacillation and irresolution as had Lincoln in the Civil War. During Roosevelt's first term, the isolationists held the lead, knocking down his half-hearted efforts to discourage aggressions by Japan and Italy. He gave up entirely on the Rhineland and the Spanish Civil War.

Japan's all-out assault on China in 1937 jolted Roosevelt into proposing a vaguely defined "quarantine" against the aggressor. But he dropped the notion when the public turned against it. Soon afterward he accepted a Japanese apology and indemnity for the deliberate bombing and sinking of the U.S. gunboat *Panay* in the Yangtze River. He played no significant role in the Austrian and Czechoslovakian crises of 1938. The Nazis' murderous rampage against Jews on the infamous *Kristallnacht* of November 1938 raised American hostility toward Hitler to a new pitch, but isolationism continued strong. When World War II began in 1939, more than two-thirds of Americans polled wanted the Allies to win, expected America to be drawn in, and yet opposed involvement.

It was the Nazis' stunning victories over Norway, Denmark, the Low Countries, and France in 1940 that shocked the United States into feverish preparation for war. The public cheered Britain's heroic resistance to Nazi bombing and were stirred by Prime Minister Winston Churchill's oratory. Roosevelt was now able to make a stand against totalitarian expansionism as firm as that of Lincoln against slavery expansion during the secession winter and of Chamberlain against Nazi aggression in September 1939.

In the election of 1940, both Roosevelt and his unsuccessful opponent Wendell Willkie championed all possible aid to the British short of war. That December, Roosevelt called on the nation to become the great arsenal of democracy. He quoted Hitler's recent statement that "there are two worlds that stand opposed to each other."[18] Roosevelt instead saw what Willkie would later label "One World." Lincoln's "House Divided" was the Union; Roosevelt's was the world. In his annual address to Congress a few days later, Roosevelt, like Lincoln at Gettysburg, summed up the goals of the war he saw coming: for all the people of the world, freedom of speech and religion, freedom from want and fear.

The massive Lend-Lease program of supplies to Britain began in the spring of 1941. By June 80 percent of Americans polled considered the United States to be already in the war "for all practical purposes."[19] Roosevelt now felt that the time had come for America to go in all the way. But he also believed, as Lincoln had during the Sumter crisis, that the American people would best be aroused and unified if the enemy fired first. Through the summer and fall of 1941, Roosevelt gradually escalated American naval protection for the shipment of supplies to Britain, hoping to goad Nazi submarines into attacking. Hitler did not oblige, since he wanted to knock the Russians out of the war before taking on the Americans. The first shot thus came from an unexpected quarter, the same one that had sounded the firebell of 1931.

The Japanese were bogged down in China and running low on war material, especially oil. The fall of France and the Netherlands in 1940 tempted them to turn south into French Indochina, the Dutch East Indies, and British Malaya for the necessary raw materials. But like most Americans, they considered the United States now to be in the war "for all practical purposes" and therefore bound to come to the aid of the British. Furthermore, the Americans were pressing Japan to withdraw from China and renounce its designs on Southeast Asia, demands incompatible with Japanese pride and military needs. Like Lincoln in the secession crisis and Chamberlain in the Polish crisis, Roosevelt was drawing the line against further expansion by the adversary, Japanese as well as Nazi.

The Japanese military thereupon began planning a grand simultaneous strike against the British, Dutch, and Americans. Civilian leaders were fearful of the consequences, and even the military agreed that outright military conquest of the United States was impossible. But like the Confederacy in 1861 and Hitler in 1939, they counted on war weariness to bring their enemy to a negotiated settlement. In July 1941, Roosevelt embargoed oil shipments to Japan. Like Lincoln's refusal to give up Fort

Sumter, the oil embargo threw down the gauntlet. With oil stocks low, desperation now impelled the Japanese to execute their daring and brilliantly prepared strike against Pearl Harbor on December 7, 1941.

The strike succeeded beyond all expectations, except that American carriers happened to be at sea. Four days later Adolf Hitler, for one of the few times in his career, kept a promise and joined his Japanese ally in declaring war on the United States, probably driven by bottled-up rage and the recognition that war was inevitable. It was an ill-judged move. Each of America's adversaries had now clearly been the aggressor, and so, as in the case of Fort Sumter, the American people came out fighting mad. There would be no war-weary parleying.

As in the case of Lincoln and Fort Sumter, some of those who like to believe that nothing important is accidental have theorized that Roosevelt knowingly rigged the debacle at Pearl, that he somehow lured the Japanese into striking. There are fatal flaws in that theory. From intercepting and breaking the Japanese diplomatic code, it was known only that the Japanese were going to attack somewhere at about the time they did. The rational target would have been the Dutch and British territories. If the Americans had known it was to be Pearl Harbor, they could have ensured minimum damage at Pearl and maximum damage to the attackers. The public would have been just as much outraged. At Sumter not a man was lost to Confederate fire, yet the North rose up in fury. Unless Roosevelt had an inexplicable grudge against the nation that had elected him President three times, he would not knowingly have permitted such pointless losses. Furthermore, if he could have prevented the attack entirely he would have done so, because he wanted to concentrate American power against Hitler and was hopeful of drawing the first shot from him. But Admiral Yamamoto, the planner of the Pearl Harbor attack, did not consult Roosevelt in advance. In any case, Roosevelt could not have assumed that Hitler would leap to the defense of Japan. Hitler was technically not bound under the Axis treaty, since Japan had not been attacked (not that Hitler would have respected a treaty anyway). He would rationally have rejoiced that Japan had diverted the United States from the European theater and would have left Japan to fend for itelf while he finished off the Russians. And the infuriated American public would have been loath to take the heat off Japan by challenging Hitler.

9. CONCLUSIONS

What is there to compare between Sumter and Pearl, those curtain raisers for the wars to come? Very little in their details. One began in early morning darkness, the other in broad daylight. One was an attack by land artillery, the other by carrier-based bombers. One was a clash between small forces, the other a confrontation of armadas. In one the attackers were Americans; in the other they were as alien as the planet holds. In one, no defender died; in the other, the death toll was in the thousands. In one case the place was determined long in advance, but the time was uncertain. In the other the precise time was known shortly in advance, but the place was unexpected.

The congruence of Sumter and Pearl was in the long course of their coming and in their impact. Each was the culmination of painfully achieved community, short-lived hope, growing divergence in philosophy and morals, bitter hostility, reckless pride, and the fatal challenge. The immediate effect of each was a rush of national adrenalin, a fusion of rage, energy, and principle into unparalleled unity. The long-range effect in each case was the overthrow of brutal oppression and the clearing of ground for a more just and lasting peace. The ultimate result is not within the purview of historians, who speak only for the past.

What "wisdom," as Lincoln put it, can we learn from these parallel tragedies? Nothing very precise, I fear, nothing to generate a computer program. Similar cases are not necessarily identical. Human nature comes in many varieties and guises. History in general can do little more to keep us out of trouble other than alerting us to the forms it can take. When trouble does come, the long view of history helps to damp down our swings between hubris and despair and thereby steadies our judgment.

Comparative history can give us a little more by suggesting the odds-on success for a particular response to that trouble. Those who consider this a sure thing in the short run I would advise to stay away from the racetrack. The odds-on favorite may stumble. In history, too, unforeseen trivialities may radically alter the pace and course of great events, trivialities like the shape of Cleopatra's nose, the want of a horseshoe nail, the discarded paper that betrayed Lee's campaign plan before Antietam, the crazed assassin at Ford's Theater. Nevertheless, we improve our chances by playing the odds. And in the long run, the basic direction prevails. We cannot be sure which of the horses will win the race, but we can be pretty sure they will not run backward. Neither will history.

2

Grant and Eisenhower

STEPHEN E. AMBROSE

GENERAL/PRESIDENT George Washington stood first in war, first in peace, first in the hearts of his countrymen. In the nineteenth century, only General/President Ulysses S. Grant came close to such a pinnacle. In the twentieth century, it was General/President Dwight D. Eisenhower who came closest. Washington, Grant, and Eisenhower commanded the largest armies their country had ever put into the field in the biggest wars their country had ever fought.

Washington, Grant, and Eisenhower served two terms as President of the United States, and they accomplished their major political objectives. Washington built a nation, established precedents, and healed wounds; his task was to bring together a country that had just fought what was as much a civil war as a war for independence. Grant had to bind up a nations' wounds and bring Southerners back into the body politic after a terrible civil war. Eisenhower also had to bind up wounds after the upheavals of World War II and the Korean War, and bring the Germans back into the community of Western Civilization.

For Grant and for Eisenhower, a terrible price had to be paid for reconciliation—in Grants' case, the South was brought back into the Union at the expense of black Americans; in Eisenhower's case, the West Germans were brought back into the alliance of freedom-loving nations at the expense of the East Germans.

No comparisons are exact. As President, Washington, Grant, and Eisenhower faced different problems in different times and necessarily adopted different policies that had different results. So too as generals; the size of the armies, the technology and weaponry of war, the requirements of leadership were vastly different in the late eighteenth, mid-nineteenth, and mid-twentieth centuries. Yet there are comparisons that are valid, parallels that are striking, about the three men, especially between Grant and Eisenhower. Some of these comparisons and parallels are of the "is that so?" type, of only passing interest; others provoke serious thought or teach lessons that resonate today.

The first comparison immediately separates Grant and Eisenhower from Washington. The first President was a major figure on the national stage before his war began; indeed, he was selected to command the first American army because he was the leading military figure in the country. He was also a landed aristocrat. Had he died on the eve of the Revolutionary War, he would still be a man worthy of notice in the nation's history.

Grant and Eisenhower were men from the great American middle class. On the eve of their wars, they were obscure figures. Had they died in 1861 and 1941 respectively, they would be completely unknown today. Their remarkable rise to world fame is central to the American dream. They proved in their persons that anyone could climb to the top in the United States. What made them even more appealing as folk heroes to their countrymen was that they embodied the essence of America. Theodore Lyman, a young Harvard graduate on General George Meade's staff, said of Grant, "He is the concentration of all that is American."[1] At the victory celebration at London's Guildhall in June 1945, in his first formal public address, General Eisenhower said of himself, "I come from the heart of America."[2]

Their fathers were men who worked with their hands. Grant's father was a tanner, Eisenhower's father was a mechanic. The two boys, Ulysses and Dwight, grew up in small Midwestern houses, hardly traveled out of their home counties, knew no luxuries and had to scrape for necessities, went to public schools where they were indifferent students and showed little in the way of leadership traits except in athletic endeavors. Grant was a superb horseman; Eisenhower a good baseball and football player.

As high school students, neither Grant nor Eisenhower had any consuming ambition or goal. They wanted to get ahead in the world but had no specific ideas about how to do it. Their motives for going to West Point were more or less casual; certainly they had no dreams of becoming soldiers. In Grant's case, he went because his father made him; in Eisenhower's case, he had nothing better to do and liked the idea of playing big-time college football. The more basic reason each boy went to the Academy was that it was free—only at West Point could they get a college education.

Neither cadet did anything of note at West Point. They were popular enough, and managed to pass their courses—although in some cases just barely—but they developed no passion for the soldier's life. Grant hated the Academy, although perhaps not quite so vehemently as Edgar Allan Poe, who in 1830 judged it a "God-forsaken place" and just walked away after one year. Nine years later, when Grant was a plebe, Congress considered abolishing the Academy. "I favored the bill," Grant wrote in his memoirs, because "I saw in this an honorable way to obtain a discharge." The bill did not pass and Grant stuck it out, even though a "military life had no charms for me, and I had not the faintest idea of staying in the army."[3] His goal was to get his degree, perhaps obtain a detail teaching mathematics at the Academy for a few years, then become a college professor.

Eisenhower rather enjoyed his first year and a half at West Point. Like Grant, he detested the grind and the hazing, but he had football to play and it was a consuming passion with him. He was good at the game; by the middle of the season of his second year he was a starting halfback and called by the *New York Times* "one of the most promising backs in Eastern football."[4] But in a game against Tufts College he twisted his knee so badly that his football career was permanently over. He grew despondent; his roommate had to talk him out of resigning. When he graduated in 1915, an army doctor told him his knee might prevent his getting a commission. He shrugged, made no protest, and instead sent off for literature on Argentina. He had a vague notion he might try life on the frontier in South America. When the doctor relented, Eisenhower accepted his commission, primarily on the same grounds that Ulysses Grant had taken his commission in 1843—he could think of nothing better to do.

The most important thing Grant and Eisenhower did as junior offcers was to get married, in each case to young women who had strong army ties and came from families whose fortunes were considerably above theirs. Julia Dent's father was a colonel, a land-owner, and a slave-owner. Her brother was a West Point classmate of Grant. Mamie Doud's father was a wealthy land-owner in Denver who brought his family to San Antonio for the winters, where they lived on the edge of Fort Sam Houston and socialized with the officers. In each case the father acquiesced in rather than encouraged his daughter's choice; in each case it proved to be a happy one. For Grant and for Eisenhower, their marriages were a source of strength as well as of happiness. Julia and Mamie endured much as wives of underpaid junior officers whose careers were getting nowhere for the first twenty years of marriage. They surely got their reward as wives of world-figures—a role both relished and played to the hilt. Through it all they were at their husbands' side, fiercely loyal, always faithful—as were their husbands to them.*

Devotion to family was a trait Grant and Eisenhower shared, and one the American people appreciated and admired. Washington had Martha with him at Valley Forge; Julia Grant and Mamie Eisenhower were with their husbands whenever it was possible. Grant had his son, Ulysses, Jr., serve as his secretary while President; Eisenhower had his only son, John, with him right after D-Day, during the occupation of Germany, and during his Presidency.

Grant saw battle at first-hand, heard the whistle of rifle bullets past his ear, led a charge against the enemy. Still his role was basically a modest one—he served as a quartermaster. That experience, however, was in-

---

*The rumors about Eisenhower's supposed affair with Kay Summersby are false. There was a flirtation, especially by Kay, but it never went beyond that point. For fifty years, except when he was away at war, Ike and Mamie slept in the same bed. That is what I would call a solid marriage.

valuable. When one thinks about Grant as a general in the Civil War, a trait that stands out is his mastery of logistics. He was in command of armies in the field that were larger than any ever seen before (or since) on the North American continent. Most of the time, he kept the men well supplied, surely the first requirement of generalship.

Grant also learned some valuable lessons about cutting loose from the supply line and living off the land. He wrote in his memoirs of General Winfield Scott's campaign against Mexico City, "both the strategy and tactics displayed were faultless." That strategy and those tactics must have been in his mind when he undertook his 1863 campaign against Vicksburg.

Grant also noted that Scott's dispositions were so "perfect that the chief was able to give his order to his various subordinates with all the precision he could use on an ordinary march." He added, "I mean, up to the points from which the attack was to commence. After that point is reached the enemy often induces a change of orders not before contemplated."[5]

One of Eisenhower's favorite sayings parallels Grant's comment. According to Eisenhower, "In war, plans are everything—before the battle is joined. Once it begins, plans are worthless."

Eisenhower's WWI experience was much different in its externals from Grant's in Mexico—Eisenhower never got out of the country, never saw a battle, never heard a shot fired in anger. Yet he too learned valuable lessons. He spent the war at training camps—eventually, in command at Camp Colt in Gettysburg, Pennsylvania, of the Tank Corps. This put him in direct contact with tanks, which were still experimental in WWI but would be the critical weapon in the land battles of WWII. It also gave him firsthand experience at setting up and running a camp of thousands of men, for creating and supervising their training schedule, for preparing them for combat. And in 1928–29 he finally got to go to Europe, where he wrote a guidebook on the American battlefields of WWI. That doesn't sound like much of an assignment for a professional soldier, but it gave Eisenhower a chance to walk across the battlefields, to get to know the lay of the land over which his armies would be fighting in 1944, to study General John J. Pershing's methods and style. It was almost as if he were being groomed for high command in the next war.

In many ways, he was—and here Eisenhower's career diverges sharply from Grant's. After the Mexican War, Grant went from lack of distinction in the army to failure in private life—a dreary story, well known, too painful to dwell on. For our purposes, the main point is that he made no study of war, or leadership, or command. His preparation for the Civil War essentially ended when the Mexican War ended.

Eisenhower's experience was totally different, a reflection not so much of personality differences—although they were surely there—as of the professionalization of the U.S. Army in the twentieth century, and its expanded size and responsibilities. Grant had been stuck on a frontier post in California with no prospect of promotion and almost nothing to do—and a commanding officer whom he hated and who did nothing to encourage Grant. Eisenhower had a variety of choice assignments— Panama, the Command and General Staff College in Leavenworth, Kansas, the Army War College in Washington, D.C., Paris, Washington again, where he served on Pershing's staff. In Panama, his commanding officer was General Fox Connor, who had been operations officer for Pershing and who was a superb teacher, who put Eisenhower through what amounted to an advanced course in strategy and coalition warfare. At C&GS, and at the War College, Eisenhower continued to study his profession. As an aide to Pershing, he saw problems from the point of view of the high command. Then he became an aide to Chief of Staff Douglas MacArthur, and later served MacArthur in the Philippines. Mainly he learned from MacArthur what not to do—but he continued learning.

Still, in 1939, he was only a lieutenant-colonel. He hardly considered himself a failure, but he could hardly be called a success. He had an excellent reputation in the army—every C.O. wanted him on his staff— but the army, as constituted, had no place for a forty-nine-year-old light colonel. He anticipated a forced retirement. If he was not quite Ulysses Grant in Galena, living off the old man, he may have thought of himself as not much better off.

And the war came—for Grant in 1861, for Eisenhower in 1941. Within a year each man entered a wholly new world. They had gone from obscurity to public figures who were recognizable anywhere; they had gone from no command at all to the command of vast armies. It was this incredible rise, as much as what they did in command, that made them into legends. Eisenhower's parents had said to him, "In America, opportunity is all about you. Reach out and seize it." Grant and Eisenhower proved the truth of David and Ida Eisenhower's observation, in the process proving the American dream.

Fame and success did not come without a struggle or without setbacks. What stands out about the early wartime experiences of the two generals is how quickly they learned from what they saw around them. In Grant's case, he described in one of the most powerful paragraphs in his memoirs his first encounter with the enemy. He was leading a regiment of poorly equipped, ill-trained Illinois volunteers into Missouri. The enemy was presumed to be on the other side of the hill.

"My heart kept getting higher and higher until it felt to me as though it was in my throat," Grant recalled. "I would have given anything then to have been back in Illinois, but I had not the moral courage to halt and consider what to do; I kept right on." When he reached the top of the hill, he discovered that the enemy had skee-daddled. "My heart resumed its place. It occurred to me at once that [the enemy commander] had been as much afraid of me as I had been of him. This was a view of the question I had never taken before; but it was one I never forgot afterwards. From that event to the close of the war, I never experienced trepidation upon confronting an enemy. . . . I never forgot that he had as much reason to fear my forces as I had his."[6]

In his first real battle, at Fort Donelson in early 1862, Grant made some questionable dispositions of his divisions and had been too far from the field when the fighting began. His division commanders—chosen not by him but by higher authority—were making a botch of things. When he got to the field, the Union troops were dispirited and essentially leaderless. They had run out of ammunition, and no staff existed at that stage of the war to see to it that they were resupplied. Grant rallied the men by exuding optimism. To a member of his staff, he said, "Some of our men are pretty badly demoralized, but the enemy must be more so. . . . The one who attacks first now will be victorious and the enemy will have to be in a hurry if he gets ahead of me." To the men, he called out, "Fill your cartridge-boxes, quick, and get into line; the enemy is trying to escape and he must not be permitted to do so."

"This worked like a charm," Grant noted with well-earned satisfaction. "The men only wanted some one to give them a command."[7]

Eisenhower's first battle came in November 1942, when he had a command post at Gibraltar for the invasion of North Africa. Although, as noted, he had made a much more thorough study of war than Grant, he had no more experience in directing large armies than Grant, and no sense of the anxieties of a battle joined. But like Grant, he was an instant learner. What he learned at Gibraltar was as central to his later success as what Grant learned in Missouri and at Fort Donelson. Eisenhower described it in one of the most powerful parts of his memoirs (although he choose not to publish it in the final version).

It was at Gibraltar, he wrote, "that I first realized how inexorably and inescapably strain and tension wear away at the leader's endurance, his judgment and his confidence." In such a situation, he quickly realized, the commander had to "preserve optimism in himself and in his command. Optimism and pessimism are infections and they spread more rapidly from the head downward than in any other direction." Maintaining a positive attitude in uncertain circumstances had manifold benefits, beginning with this: "The habit tends to minimize potentialities within the individual himself to become demoralized." In addition, "it has a most extraordinary effect upon all with whom the commander comes in contact. With this clear realization, I firmly determined that my mannerisms and speech in public would always reflect the cheerful certainty of victory— that any pessimism and discouragement I might ever feel would be reserved for my pillow."[8]

The words Eisenhower wrote about his lesson learned on the Rock, words that he was too modest to put into the published version of his memoirs, are a classic expression of one of the most critical aspects of leadership, perfectly said by a man who knew more about the subject than almost anyone else. They might have been written by Grant—who had learned in Missouri and at Fort Donelson to save all his doubts for his pillow.

There is a rough parallel between Eisenhower's experiences at the Battle of Kasserine Pass (February 1943) and Grant's at Fort Donelson. When the contest began, Eisenhower was too far from the battlefield. His division and corps commanders on the site had not been chosen by him. They reacted badly to the initial attack. So did the troops. Eisenhower did not ride to the battlefield, as Grant had done at Fort Donelson. Napoleon and Wellington had been in sight of each other all day at Waterloo; Grant was often within rifle range, and nearly always in artillery range, of the rebel guns. But twentieth-century generals controlled such large forces— and had radio for communications—that they were seldom eye-witnesses to battles. Still, Eisenhower rushed reinforcements to the battle and gave clear orders and exhortations to his generals, who managed to hold the line and then drive the Germans back to their start point.

Kasserine was a major learning experience for Eisenhower and the American army. One lesson, as Eisenhower put it in a private letter to a West Point classmate, was that "Officers who fail must be ruthlessly weeded out. Considerations of friendship, family, kindliness and nice personality have nothing whatsoever to do with the problem. You must be tough and get rid of the lazy, the slothful, the indifferent or the complacent."[9]

Eisenhower followed his own advice—with American officers. Chief of Staff George Marshall had selected the general who failed at Kasserine; after the battle, Eisenhower relieved him, and thereafter Marshall gave Eisenhower a free hand in picking his corps and division commanders. Abraham Lincoln and his chief of staff, Henry Halleck, never gave Grant so much authority, although Grant did finally manage to fire General John McClernand. But Grant recognized that he had to put up with politically powerful generals, even after he became General in Chief. He was keenly sensitive to the pressures on Lincoln, and he did the best he could to work with such men as General Nathaniel Banks and General Benjamin Butler, despite his serious reservations about their abilities. But he also made sure that the commanders in the critical campaigns were his personal choice, most notably General William T. Sherman in Georgia in 1864 and General Phil Sheridan in the Shenandoah Valley in 1864.

Eisenhower also had a keen sensitivity to political necessity. Despite his serious reservations about General Bernard Law Montgomery's abilities, he did his best to work effectively with Monty. He ignored pleas from his own staff—including many British senior officers—that he dismiss the man. Eisenhower recognized that sacking Monty would put a serious strain on the alliance with Britain.*

Over all, it is remarkable how good Grant and Eisenhower were at bringing out the best in their subordinates. It was done through a combination of sensitivity, prodding, pushing, listening, explaining, creating a sense of team. Most of their corps and division commanders had big egos and short tempers, festering jealousies and raging ambitions. And most of them thought that they, not Grant or Eisenhower, should be in the top command. Nevertheless, Grant managed to work well with George Meade, and Eisenhower with Montgomery. Indeed it is one of the miracles of Eisenhower's leadership that he managed to keep Monty and George S. Patton fighting the Germans rather than each other.

The American army had gone into the Kasserine Pass battle thinking its men were tough and well trained. Eisenhower, and his subordinates, and the men discovered that they were neither. "All our people," Eisenhower wrote to Chief of Staff George Marshall, "from the very highest [meaning himself] to the very lowest have learned that this is not a child's game and are ready and eager to get down to business." Specifically, he promised that thereafter no unit under his command "will ever stop training," including units on the front line.[10]

From then on, Eisenhower put a much greater emphasis on realistic, tough training than Grant had done. This reflected the difference between fighting in the Civil War and in World War II. The weapons were much more complicated in the twentieth century, and there were many more of them. Essentially, Civil War soldiers had to master loading, aiming, and firing their muskets if they were in the infantry, and close order drill. Artillery pieces were relatively simple. Cavalry drill, while intricate, could be mastered in a relatively short time. Offensive tactics were not subtle; basically they involved charging the enemy in a line with the main

---

*The British government and press had built Montgomery up to almost a Wellington-like status after the El Alamein battle (the only British victory on the battlefield in the first three years of the war). It rankled enough with the British that Eisenhower, not Montgomery, was the Supreme Commander; Eisenhower was wise enough to realize that he did not have the option of dumping Montgomery.

requirement being to keep in rank. Defensive tactics were little more than holding a line from behind breastworks.

In World War II, infantry had to master tactics of advancing in short dashes, one man firing while another moved forward; how to work with tanks; how to handle mortars; how to throw grenades or use flame-throwers and hand-held anti-tank weapons; how to use radio; and much more. Artillery was exceedingly complex. So were tanks, half-tracks, and other armored vehicles. Coordination with airplanes was critical. In short, fighting effectively in World War II required constant, realistic, stressful training—and Eisenhower saw to it that his men got it, especially in England in the months leading up to the invasion of France.

D-Day, June 6, 1944, was for Eisenhower what May 3, 1864, was for Grant, the beginning of the critical and climatic campaign of the war. Each general was at the peak of his powers, physically fit, mentally alert, morally confident in himself and in his cause. Each had traits that inspired confidence. They looked like generals, Eisenhower perhaps more so than Grant, as he was taller and his uniform fit better and had a better cut to it—but it would be a mistake to dismiss Grant as an ordinary-looking man. As with Eisenhower, when Grant entered a room all eyes turned to him.

One reason was that the general was who he was; another was his eyes. Like Eisenhower's, Grant's eyes were astonishingly expressive. They moved quickly and inquisitively. Each man locked his eyes on those of anyone to whom he was talking. Their concentration was intense, almost a physical embrace. They bespoke each man's supreme self-confidence, a certainly of belief in himself and his abilities.

Theirs was not a blind or egotistical confidence. As has been seen, each general was a sharp and insightful critic of his own decisions and actions, but the self-criticism was searching and positive, designed to eliminate errors and improve performance. On the eve of their greatest campaigns, each general had already made, and would have yet to make, countless decisions, decisions that involved the lives of tens of thousands of men, and the nation itself. They did so with the certainty that they had taken everything into account, gathered all relevant information, and considered all possible consequences; then they acted. This is the essence of command.

Their self-confidence inspired the confidence of others in them. When associates described Eisenhower, there was one word that almost all of them used. It was trust. People trusted Eisenhower for the most obvious reason—he was trustworthy. Disagree as they might and often did with his decisions, they never doubted his motives. Montgomery did not think much of Eisenhower as a soldier, but he admired him as a man. He said of Eisenhower, "He has the power of drawing the hearts of men towards him as a magnet attracts the bit of metal. He merely has to smile at you, and you trust him at once."[11]

Eisenhower smiled a lot. Grant smiled rarely. Yet Grant, like Eisenhower, inspired trust. Lincoln trusted him; his staff and his generals trusted him; his troops trusted him; the country trusted him. For Eisenhower it was just the same, and for the same reason—he did what he said he was going to do. His reward—Grant's reward—was the trust people placed in him. Because of that trust, and because of the qualities he possessed that brought it about, Eisenhower's appointment as Supreme Commander Allied Expeditionary Force was a brilliant choice, perhaps the best appointment Franklin Roosevelt ever made. Just so with Grant— his appointment as General in Chief was perhaps the best appointment Lincoln ever made.

It is worth noting that one reason for the trust the two Presidents put in the two generals was that they were not challengers for the Presidency. The year each general got his appointment to the top command was also a presidential election year. (It is worth noting also that the United States was the only nation to hold an election in the midst of a Civil War, just as the United States was the only nation to hold an election in the midst of World War II.) There had been some talk of Grant as a candidate in early 1864; there had been some talk of Eisenhower as a candidate in late 1943. There is always such talk about generals—and in 1864 General George McClellan was the Democratic candidate, and in 1944 General Douglas MacArthur yearned to be the Republican candidate. But Grant and Eisenhower scornfully dismissed talk of becoming a candidate or of challenging their political superior in any way, something Lincoln and Roosevelt surely appreciated.

On June 5, 1944, the Allied Expeditionary Force was set to go. In Eisenhower's words, "The mighty host was tense as a coiled spring, ready for the moment when its energy should be released and it would vault the English Channel."[12] Grant might have written the same words about the Army of the Potomac on May 3, 1864.

Instead, the quartermaster in him took over. Grant wrote, "Ten days' rations, with a supply of forage and ammunition were taken in wagons. Beef cattle were driven with the trains, and butchered as wanted. Three days' rations in addition, in haversacks, and fifty rounds of cartridges, were carried on the person of each soldier. . . . There never was a corps better organized than was the quartermaster's corps with the Army of the Potomac in 1864."[13] Eisenhower might have written the same words about the Services of Supply for the Allied Expeditionary Force on June 5.

Obviously they didn't do it alone. Grant and Eisenhower were generals of democracies at war. They were the beneficiaries of what Eisenhower called "the fury of an aroused democracy." Their country had pulled off miracles of production to make certain that its troops would both outnumber and be better fed, better supplied, better equipped, better armed than the enemy's. The United States gave Grant and Eisenhower the tools to do the job. This did not, however, by itself ensure victory.

They were up against world-famous opponents, Robert E. Lee and Erwin Rommel. Lee and Rommel were accustomed to fighting—and winning—with inferior manpower and equipment. It was their special genius to gain victories by out-thinking and out-maneuvering their enemies. Lee absolutely, and Rommel almost so, had managed to inflict an inferiority complex on his enemy, generals and soldiers alike.

Nevertheless, on the eve of battle Grant and Eisenhower exuded confidence. "This campaign is being planned as a victory," Eisenhower told his staff. He told Marshall, "The smell of victory is in the air."[14] On May 2, 1864, Grant wrote Julia, "I know the greatest anxiety is now felt in the North for the success of this move, and that anxiety will increase when it is once known that the Army is in motion. I feel well myself. Do not know that this is any criterion from which to judge results because I have never felt otherwise. I believe it has never been my misfortune to be in a place where I lost my presence of mind."[15]

Grant's great decision came five days later, after the fearful struggle in the Wilderness. Lee had checked his advance, just as Lee had checked the Army of the Potomac at Chancellorsville, only fifteen miles away, the previous spring. After Chancellorsville, General Joseph Hooker had cut his losses and retreated back across the Rapidan River. Grant, instead of retreating made the decision to move south—to continue the campaign—to stay after Lee until he had destroyed the Army of Northern Virginia—in his own words, perhaps the most famous he ever uttered, "to fight it out on this line if it takes all summer."[16]

Eisenhower's great decision came on the eve of D-Day, when he decided to risk the weather and go ahead with what Prime Minister Winston Churchill called "the greatest and most complicated operation ever to take place." Watching Eisenhower pace and think as he made his decision, General Walter B. Smith was struck by the "loneliness and isolation of a commander at a time when such a momentous decision was to be taken by him, with full knowledge that failure or success rests on his individual decision."[17]

Grant, too, knew the loneliness and isolation of high command.

Grant and Eisenhower were generals who hated war. Small wonder, considering the sights they saw. Grant wrote of Shiloh, "I saw an open field . . . so covered with dead that it would have been possible to walk across the clearing, in any direction, stepping on dead bodies, without a foot touching the ground."[18] At the Falaise Gap, Eisenhower wrote that what he saw "could be described only by Dante. It was literally possible to walk for hundreds of yards at a time, stepping on nothing but dead and decaying flesh."[19]

Some generals can ignore such sights. Not all generals hate war. Some revel in it—one thinks of Phil Sheridan and George Custer in Grant's war, or George Patton in Eisenhower's. But for Grant and Eisenhower, it was a sickening business. War is waste, of equipment, buildings, treasure, most of all of men. "How I wish this cruel business of war could be completed quickly," Eisenhower wrote Mamie (like Grant, he revealed his innermost feelings in his letters to his wife). Counting the human costs was "a terribly sad business." It made him heartsick to think about "how many youngsters are gone forever," and although he had developed "a veneer of callousness," he could "never escape a recognition of the fact that back home the news brings anguish and suffering to families all over the country. . . . War demands real toughness of fiber—not only in the soldiers that must endure, but in the homes that must sacrifice their best."[20]

Grant too developed a veneer of callousness, but he too had a toughness of fiber. Eisenhower made explicit what Grant knew instinctively, that in war everything is expendable—including generals—in the quest for victory. Only victory counted. As Eisenhower put it in a letter to his son, "The only unforgivable sin in war is not doing your duty."[21]

There were some marked similarities between Grant's 1864 campaign in Virginia and Eisenhower's 1944 campaign in Northwest Europe. In each case, the opening weeks of the campaign were marked by heavy losses and few gains. Progress was agonizingly slow and terribly expensive. The enemy appeared to have imposed a stalemate on the U.S. Army. Grant and Eisenhower apparently settled on a strategy of attrition, if attrition can be called a stragegy. They were evidently ready to fight until only one man was left, so long as that man was a U.S. soldier. Grant was called a butcher. Eisenhower might have been had his armies not broken out at the beginning of August 1944 and dashed across France—only to be checked again on the German border, where another apparent stalemate ensued.

Critics of Grant's and Eisenhower's campaigns are numerous, well informed, often insightful, always indignant. William McFeely writes: "In May 1864 Ulysses Grant began a vast campaign that was a hideous disaster in every respect. . . . He led his troops into the Wilderness and there produced a nightmare of inhumanity and inept military strategy that ranks with the worst such episodes in the history of warfare."* Montgomery, and others, said that Eisenhower's strategy in France had "failed."

After the Allied armies liberated France, Montgomery wanted Patton stopped where he was, on the German border, and all Patton's supplies given to him so that he could make a "single thrust" into northern Germany and on to Berlin. He wanted, in other words, to out-maneuver the

---

*McFeely has the good sense to add to his "hideous disaster" judgment, "in every respect save one—it worked."

Germans, to out-think them more than out-fight them. He believed that German morale was on the verge of collapse and one blow would cause it to disappear. But Eisenhower insisted on attacking all along his broad front, with his armies more or less abreast and all engaged in the offensive. Alan Brooke complained that this business of attack everywhere "must be" a strange "American doctrine."[22]

Actually, it was Eisenhower's version of Grant's Wilderness campaign. Like Grant, Eisenhower was ready to fight it out on this line if it took all winter. And for the same reason. It was Eisenhower's insight that the Germans were never going to collapse, not so long as the Nazi Party held its grip on the German people. The Germans would not quit until they had been beaten into the ground. They would fight to the last bullet. They could not be out-thought, out-maneuvered; they would have to be out-fought. Grant realized the same about Lee and the Confederacy.

Eisenhower's worst and best moment in his war came on December 16–17, 1944, when the Germans surprised the Allies with a massive counter-offensive in what came to be called the Battle of the Bulge. Grant's worst and best moment in his war came on April 6–7, 1862, at Shiloh. In each case, the commanding general was badly, inexcusably, surprised by the initial attack; in each case, as the men around him were going into something close to panic, the commanding general stayed calm, rallied his troops, started a counter-attack, and won the battle.

Although the enemy was making preparations for attack that should have been spotted, neither Grant nor Eisenhower managed to make the leap into his opposite number's mind that the situation required. Both commanding generals were guilty of over-confidence, of thinking too much about what they were going to do to the enemy and not enough about what the enemy might do to them.

In Grant's case, on the eve of the battle he reported to his superior, General Halleck, "I have scarcely the faintest idea of an attack being made upon us," even though he was in enemy territory and about to penetrate further south, into Mississippi.[23] In Eisenhower's case, on the eve of the battle he attended a party to celebrate his promotion to five-star general, then played some bridge. His concerns were with his own offensive. He had not the slightest idea that he was about to be attacked.

The achievement of surprise gave the Confederates and the Germans great initial advantage. The early stages of the battles went exceedingly badly for the U.S. troops. In Grant's case, he mounted his horse, rode to the front, and ordered his retreating men to advance upon the enemy. His intervention was decisive. His self-control and stubbornness carried the day. He did not panic. His men held the ground and the next day drove the Confederates from the field.

In Eisenhower's case, he met with his subordinates on the second day of the battle. They were downcast, depressed, embarrassed. Eisenhower's first words to them were, "The present situation is to be regarded as one of opportunity for us and not of disaster. There will be only cheerful faces at this conference table."[24] He picked Bastogne as the place that had to be held and rushed the 101st Airborne Division to it. He set in motion counter-attacks north and south of the Bulge. He took control of the battle and made it his. He held the line, then drove the Germans from the field. It was his greatest moment.

During the crisis of the Bulge, Eisenhower ran out of reinforcements. He turned to an untapped asset of the American army, its black troops. They were segregated into the Services of Supply, unloading ships, driving trucks, not allowed into combat. Eisenhower told the black troops that if they volunteered for infantry duty they would be placed in existing units on an integrated basis. Thousands did volunteer, including sergeants who had to give up their stripes for the privilege of fighting for their country.

In late July 1864, Grant was running out of reinforcements during the siege of Petersburg. He turned to black troops and put them in the line.

Neither Grant nor Eisenhower was a social reformer. As President, Grant did not do enough for black Americans; indeed in many ways he was rightly charged with abandoning blacks to their former masters. As President, Eisenhower could hardly be described as a crusader for civil rights—although he did appoint Earl Warren to the Supreme Court, and he did uphold *Brown v. Topeka* at a critical moment in Little Rock in 1957. But when they had to, Grant and Eisenhower used black troops, because they believed that in war everything is expendable in the pursuit of victory—including a so-called way of life that was based on slavery or segregation.

In April 1865, Grant won a total victory. In May 1945, Eisenhower won a total victory. There is a remarkable similarity between their final reports to their superiors.

Grant's, addressed to Secretary of War Edwin Stanton, read: "Headquarters Appomattox C.H., Va. April 9th, 1865, 4:30 P.M.: General Lee surrendered the Army of Northern Virginia this afternoon on terms proposed by myself. The accompanying additional correspondence will show the conditions fully. U. S. Grant, Lieut.-General."[25]

Eisenhower's, addressed to the Combined Chiefs of Staff, read: "SHAEF Main, Reims, France: The mission of this Allied force was fulfilled at 0241 local time, May 7, 1945."[26]

Eisenhower had accepted the unconditional surrender of the German armed forces. The words provided a direct link to Grant, who was the first to use them, at Fort Donelson in 1862.

As everyone knows, Grant's surrender terms to Lee were exceedingly generous. Over the next decade, Grant continued to reach out his hand to the defeated enemy, to help the former Confederates get back on their feet, to bring them back into the Union. "Let us have peace," he said, and he played a leading role in bringing about the reconciliation.

As head of the American occupation of Germany, and later as the first NATO commander and then as President, Eisenhower reached out his hand to the defeated enemy (although not to the leaders of the Nazi Party), to help the Germans get back on their feet, to bring them back into the community of democratic nations. When he arrived in Germany in January 1951 as the NATO commander, he said that when he had last been in the country, "I bore in my heart a very definite antagonism toward Germany and certainly a hatred for all that the Nazis stood for, and I fought as hard as I knew how to destroy it. But, for my part, by-gones are by-gones. I hope that some day the great German people are lined up with the rest of the free world, because I believe in the essential freedom-loving quality of the German people."[27]

Final judgments on Grant and Eisenhower as generals and as Presidents will never be possible. Historians and arm-chair strategists will continue to argue over their actions, decisions, roles, and impact. For them, however, there was one judgment that mattered—that of the soldiers who fought under their command. No exact figures are possible, but surely a large majority of the boys in blue and a large majority of the GIs who fought in the European Theater of Operations cast their votes— proudly—for Grant and Eisenhower.

Of all their honors, I rather think that was the one they were proudest of.

Of course, Washington got all the votes of his veterans, an honor that will never be equaled. Another difference: Washington was said to have been one of the richest men in America, while Grant and Eisenhower at the end of their wars were world-figures who were broke. In 1948, when he retired from the army, Eisenhower bought Mamie her first fur coat and a new car. After he paid for them, he showed her his checkbook; he had $35. No stocks, no bonds, no property, just a G.I. insurance policy and his pension. "Darling," he said to Mamie as he pointed to the car, "there's the entire result of thirty-seven years' work since I caught the train out of Abilene [for West Point]."[28]

Of course he had his reputation, which got him a good job as president of Columbia University, at a salary of $25,000 per year. And he had his memories, for which publishers were eager to pay him big money if he turned them into a memoir.

Grant had no fortune when his war ended. He acquired a modest one after his reirement as President, then lost it. As he approached his death, he was broke. Humiliated. About to leave Julia and his children in poverty. But he too had his memories, for which there was a tremendous market, if he could turn them into a memoir.

As everyone knows, Eisenhower produced a classic memoir. As everyone knows, Grant managed to complete his work days before his death and produced a classic memoir. *Crusade in Europe* made Eisenhower a rich man; the *Personal Memoirs of U. S. Grant* made a substantial fortune for the Grant family. Far more important than the financial return, the memoirs added immeasurably to the luster and the reputations of Grant and Eisenhower. They are the best ever produced by American soldiers, among the best ever produced by any soldier anywhere—comparable, really, to Caesar's histories.

Both memoirs are marked by their author's modesty, candor, fairness, tact, and general humanity. They are free of any hint of pretension. The prose marches like a well-ordered army. No long convoluted sentences for these generals—just a straight-forward telling of the story, with insights, drama, and information on virtually every page.

In the field of memoir writing, Grant and Eisenhower managed to accomplish something Washington never tried. And so long as there is a United States of America, there will be avid new readers of their books, meaning that every succeeding generation of Americans will get to know these great men from their own words. The memoirs are a marvelous legacy.

3

Military Intelligence: Unmasking Those Fearsome Apparitions

PETER MASLOWSKI

F RANK Rowlett did not know what the word meant. A country boy
from Rose Hill, Virginia, Rowlett had shown an aptitude for science
and mathematics almost as soon as he began making the mile-and-a-half
trek to the local one-room schoolhouse. After graduating from high school
he attended a small college nearby, where he tutored students in algebra
and geometry. By the time he was a junior, he was teaching a regular
college math class, as well as serving as a laboratory assistant in physics
and chemistry. Rowlett intended to do graduate work in math, but during
his senior year he saw an announcement for a U.S. Civil Service examination for a mathematician. Shortly after taking the exam a telegram arrived
offering Rowlett a job: $2000 a year as a "cryptanalyst."

What in the world was a cryptanalyst? Rowlett consulted a dictionary, but it did not contain the word. However, "crypt" was in there and he knew what that meant. Probably, thought Rowlett, the job dealt with statistical problems relating to Americans buried in French cemeteries as a result of World War I. Working for the Graves Registration Service was not his ideal in life, but the prospect of a permanent salary overrode his qualms. On April 1, 1930, Rowlett reported to the Munitions Building in Washington, D.C., ready to commence life as a cryptanalyst, whatever it might be.

As it turned out, Rowlett's new position had nothing to do with Graves Registration. Instead, he was the first junior member of the army's recently created Signal Intelligence Service (SIS), headed by William F. Friedman. Rowlett did not know what a cryptanalyst was because Signal Intelligence Service's employment of the word was its first official use anywhere. Friedman's outfit specialized in the study of secret communications, or cryptology, which included both cryptography and cryptanalysis; the former deals with code- and cipher-making, the latter with code- and cipher-breaking.[1] Thus a cryptanalyst was a code-breaker.

The establishment of SIS and the institutionalization of cryptology symbolized profound developments in military intelligence. Between the Civil War and World War II, military intelligence, like warfare itself, shifted from one paradigm to another—from being human-centered, personalized, and qualitative, to being increasingly machine-centered, bureaucratized, quantitative, technical, and technological. A leader in the "scientific" trend in military intelligence, Friedman had not hired a mathematician by accident.

The military theorist Carl von Clausewitz warned that "War has a way of masking the stage with scenery crudely daubed with fearsome apparitions,"[2] and the function of military intelligence is to illuminate the stage so brightly that the apparitions—the ghosts and demons lurking in a commander's mind—disappear. Whether dealing with the Napoleonic Wars, the American Civil War, or World War II, the purpose of military intelligence remained unchanged.

Another constant aspect of intelligence was that it remained ancillary to the combat forces. "Intelligence itself," wrote a World War II intelligence officer, "makes no decisions."[3] The best it could do was assist a commander in making decisions, though it could not guarantee that they were wise ones. Commanders were sometimes so intent upon following an operational concept or held such strong preconceived notions of the enemy's situation that they ignored intelligence warnings contradicting their plans or their mental image of the enemy. And no matter how accurate and complete the intelligence and how appropriate the commander's decisions, it still took well-trained, well-equipped, and courageous combatants to capitalize on it in battle. Even exquisite intelligence could not *ensure* battlefield victory; it could only make it easier to achieve.

The intelligence cycle—direction, collection, processing, and dissemination—also had not changed. A commander directed the information collection effort in certain directions, and then operatives acquired the information. Raw information, however, was of scant value until it had been processed into intelligence by evaluating and interpreting the data to assess its veracity and significance. As one Allied study stressed, "even a small number of facts concerning the enemy could, if properly evaluated, lead to a correct understanding and knowledge of the enemy," while even "a great number of facts, if not correctly evaluated, could never provide a correct picture."[4] Since each intelligence source was susceptible to falsehood and deception—Clausewitz had warned that intelligence reports were invariably uncertain, contradictory, or false—one crucial aspect of the evaluation process was to collate information from multiple sources. Intelligence officers sought confirmation for each piece of information, always preferring cumulative corroboration to having to rely upon a single source, no matter how reliable it seemed. Finally, intelligence must be dispatched to the appropriate commanders in a timely manner, creating tension between the necessity to disseminate intelligence to make it useful and the desire to maintain security by limiting the number of recipients.

What had changed from the 1860s to 1940s, and dramatically so, were the methods of collecting information, especially information that could be processed into operational intelligence for battlefield use. The most fundamental aspect of operational intelligence concerned the enemy's order of battle: its strength, organization, armaments, experience, morale, leadership, disposition, and possible actions. In short, order of battle intelligence helped a commander understand what the enemy *could* do and therefore *might* do.

During the Civil War most operational military intelligence was human intelligence (or humint). It came from human-centered activities—spying, reconnaissance, observation, captured enemy documents, and interrogations. Although festooned with exaggerations and legends regarding the alleged exploits of Rose O'Neal Greenhow, Belle Boyd, Lafayette C. Baker, and Allan Pinkerton, spying was not without some importance in the Civil War. Late in the war the Union was especially well served by two loosely connected spy rings, one headed by Elizabeth L. Van Lew and the other by Samuel Ruth, operating in Richmond. When Union armies besieged Richmond and Petersburg, Van Lew and Ruth established communications with Ulysses S. Grant's headquarters and provided the Union high command with plentiful information. Another successful Union spy was actually a double agent. Richard Montgomery, alias James Thompson, served as a courier between the Confederate government and Southern agents in Canada, but on each journey he stopped in Washington to allow Union authorities to read the messages he carried.

Reconnaissance missions conducted by scouts and cavalry patrols were more important than spying as an intelligence source. To gain knowledge of the terrain that lay ahead or for the active probing of the enemy's position, some commanders used aides and staff officers as scouts. Jedediah Hotchkiss, General Thomas J. ("Stonewall") Jackson's renowned mapmaker, frequently went on scouting missions, and on the second day at Gettysburg General Robert E. Lee sent three small parties under trusted staff officers to scout out the Union left flank. Other generals created specialized scout units. Much of General Philip Sheridan's Shenandoah Valley success resulted from his scout battalion commanded by Major Henry H. Young and composed primarily of local men familiar with the region. The cavalry's primary role was intelligence gathering rather than fighting. Indeed, one initial Confederate advantage was that Jeb Stuart's cavalry excelled on reconnaissance missions. As Lee once told Stuart, he "received no positive information of the movements of the enemy, except through you."[5] By mid-war, however, the North's horsemen were approaching parity with the South's in reconnaissance capabilities. Although excellent mounted reconnaissance never guaranteed success, its absence frequently contributed to defeat, as exemplified by

Joseph Hooker's misuse of his cavalry during the Chancellorsville campaign and Lee's cavalry troubles at Gettysburg.

Closely related to reconnaissance was simple visual observation, which implied the on-going surveillance of a particular place or small area, usually from within one's own lines. Picket lines and sentinels routinely surveyed the ground in front of their armies. And no one can stand on the hallowed ground at Gettysburg without recognizing observation's profound significance. As Confederate forces maneuvered into attack positions on the battle's second day, the officer commanding General James Longstreet's artillery "was particularly cautioned, in moving the artillery, to keep it out of sight of the signal-station upon [Little] Round Top." That "wretched little signal-station" also compelled some of Longstreet's infantry to countermarch to avoid being spotted, delaying the assault for several hours, during which time a Union corps arrived on the battlefield.[6] Throughout the war the belligerents established signal stations wherever the armies went, always seeking some high point from which to scan the greatest distance, whether it be a hill, tree top, church steeple, courthouse cupola, ship mast, or special tower.

Both sides resorted to balloons for aerial observation. As with most technological innovations, the resource-poor South could not compete on equal terms with the North and produced only a handful of balloons compared with the Yankees. Although providing a modest amount of information for Union forces from the Peninsula campaign through Chancellorsville, like any new wartime technology, ballooning suffered teething troubles. With favorable weather conditions and competent observers overhead, an army was relatively secure from enemy surprises, but neither of these conditions prevailed very often. Wind, fog, rain, and battlefield dust and smoke hindered vision, as did enemy artillery fire, which kept balloonists ducking and sometimes forced them into a premature groundward retreat. Most balloonists were civilians who were unable to estimate enemy forces accurately, and even when army personnel went aloft, oblique distortion and the enemy's use of camouflage and terrain features for concealment impaired their observations. Nonetheless, lamented a Confederate officer, Union balloons "forced upon us constant troublesome precautions in efforts to conceal our marches."[7]

Enemy documents, including newspapers, were a Civil War intelligence cornucopia. On August 22, 1862, Stuart raided General John Pope's headquarters, capturing his official papers, which alerted Lee that Pope had only 45,000 men and did not intend to attack until he had been reinforced. Consequently, Lee launched a pre-emptive attack and routed Pope at Second Bull Run. Perhaps the war's most famous captured document was Lee's Special Orders No. 191, found by a Union corporal on September 13, 1862, near Frederick, Maryland. The document, which revealed Lee's detailed and explicit operational plan for the capture of Harpers Ferry, gave Union commander George B. McClellan priceless intelligence: Lee had fragmented his army into four widely dispersed elements. Although the captured orders gave McClellan an unprecedented opportunity to crush the Army of Northern Virginia, he failed to exploit it at the inconclusive Battle of Antietam. If Second Bull Run demonstrated a superb commander's shrewd use of intelligence, Antietam proved that in the hands of an inept commander even the most excellent intelligence was of limited utility.

Northern newspapers, thought General William T. Sherman, published so much reliable information that correspondents "should be treated as spies." "Napoleon himself," he complained, "would have been defeated with a free press."[8] The French emperor was eventually defeated without a free press, but Sherman had a point. Since neither the North nor South systematically censored the press, newspapers contained so much military information that both sides regularly acquired each other's papers. It may not be coincidental that two of the most avid readers of enemy newspapers were also two of the war's most successful generals, Grant and Lee. When Confederate papers disclosed that Wilmington's defenses had been reduced so that reinforcements could be sent to oppose Sherman's March, Grant hastened the departure of a Union expedition against the North Carolina seaport. And Grant was so dependent on Confederate news reports for information about Sherman's campaigns that his adjutant believed "it would be well not to take official notice of this summary of news from the Richmond papers lest the rebel authorities prohibit the publication of news from [sic: about] Sherman altogether."[9] After scrutinizing Northern papers, Lee often forwarded them to Confederate President Jefferson Davis along with a note directing his attention to relevant items. And Lee advised a corps commanders to "get the Northern papers as they will keep you advised of their preparations to oppose you."[10]

The interrogation of prisoners of war, deserters, fugitive slaves, and refugees was the fifth human-centered military intelligence source. General McClellan issued special circulars and orders to ensure that such persons were thoroughly examined, and high-ranking officers such as Sheridan and General George G. Meade often became personally involved in interrogations. Recognizing that captured soldiers represented a dangerous information hemorrhage, Lee urged his men that if taken prisoner they should "preserve entire silence with regard to everything connected with the army, the positions, movements, organizations, or probable strength of any portion of it."[11] Maintaining silence may have been difficult since some interrogations were less than polite. When forwarding George McKay, who claimed to be a Confederate deserter, to Grant's headquarters, an interrogation expert advised the recipient that "I think it useless to abuse the man McKay as Dunkle had him tortured here and it made a perfect lunatic of him for twenty-four hours."[12]

Although these familiar humint activities predominated, a new, though feeble, intelligence source arose during the Civil War: signal intelligence (or sigint). Like steam and steel warships, submarines, railroads, and rifled firepower, the emergence of sigint presaged twentieth-century developments. Sigint developed out of the necessity to communicate rapidly over long distances by sending signals. Naturally the enemy tried to intercept the signals, which in turn impelled those sending a message to encode it. Inevitably, signaling in code led to code-breaking.

Almost all Civil War cryptological activity revolved around messages that Signal Corps troops sent from atop their observation stations by wagging flags or flares to imitate telegraphic dots and dashes. Especially when the armies were in static positions rather than on the move, Signal Corps personnel on both sides watched each other's observation stations, jotting down the signals and almost routinely decoding the communications. As one Signal Corps officer noted, "the enemy can read our signals when the regular code is used, and it is equally evident to the minds of all who have had anythng to do with interpreting ciphers that our cipher is unsafe and cannot be trusted."[13] The ease with which each side read the other's wig-wag flag traffic inhibited either side from sending important messages this way.

Although far less plentiful than sigint from Signal Corps observation posts, sigint based on a machine-centered system, the telegraph, more clearly portended the future. The Union, which had a denser telegraphic communications network than the Confederacy, initially established a two-tiered system. The Signal Corps developed a field telegraph system for tactical use, first employing it during the Peninsula campaign. Meanwhile, for strategic communications the North created the United States Military Telegraph, an essentially civilian organization under the direct control of Secretary of War Edwin M. Stanton, which utilized the telegraphic system devised by Samuel F. B. Morse. Since the distinction between the Signal Corps' tactical telegraphy and the Military Telegraph's strategic message service was artificial, each organization soon claimed responsibility for all telegraphic communications. The conflict ended in late 1863 with the Military Telegraph winning, which brought the Morse system into universal use throughout the North.

At both the strategic and tactical levels, authorities depended on the telegraph, with the Union military and government averaging 4500 telegrams a day during the war. Long before the war ended, the Military Telegraph operated a network that linked the War Department to various army headquarters. From there, field lines reached down to corps and division headquarters, and then snaked outward to front-line breastworks, Signal Corps observation posts, and picket lines; on rare occasions, telegraphers even strung wire into enemy lines during a battle. The orchestration of advances or retreats, the steady flow of logistical support, the dispatch of timely reinforcements, the relaying of the latest information about the enemy—all depended on electrical impulses flashing along strands of wire. To a lesser extent the same could be said about the Confederacy, where private commercial companies handled wartime telegraphic communications.

With important military data humming along the wires, wiretapping became a potentially lucrative intelligence source. If the enemy was sending unenciphered messages, an interloper could gain vital information simply by listening, or he could confuse the enemy by sending false messages. In 1863 two Military Telegraph employees tapped into the Confederate line connecting Knoxville and Chattanooga and gathered information for a week before hearing a message ordering the area searched for two Union spies, which sent them scooting back toward Union lines. Another federal operator gained valuable intelligence through wiretapping during Sherman's March to the Sea, and General George Stoneman conducted a successful raid into southwestern Virginia partly because he captured the Bristol telegraph office, where his operator not only listened to enemy communications but also forced the Southern operator to send bogus messages.

To prevent the enemy from acquiring sigint through wiretaps, the belligerents resorted to encryption. The Union's first telegraphic cryptographic system was so simple that it fit on a single card, but the original system steadily expanded, eventually filling forty-eight pages. By 1864 Union armies never moved without being accompanied by cipher operators sworn to secrecy. Grant's cipher clerk, Samuel H. Beckwith, was constantly at the general's side, and Sherman took nine cipher operators with him through Georgia. While no definitive judgment is possible, since the fires that swept Richmond in April 1865 destroyed the papers of the so-called Confederate Signal & Secret Service Bureau, it appears that the Confederates never broke Military Telegraph ciphers. Thus, in 1864 a Confederate telegrapher spent many frustrating weeks tapped into a line connecting the War Department with Grant's headquarters near Richmond, copying down messages and sending the intercepts to Lee's headquarters. But aside from a few administrative telegrams the Yankees sent in the clear, all the messages were in cipher and Confederate cryptanalysts were unable to decipher them. On the other hand, Union cipher operators did read some enciphered enemy communications, though all of these messages were delivered by spies or captured in the field rather than resulting from wiretaps.

Because neither the North nor the South developed national centralized intelligence organizations, each commanding officer devised his own "secret service" operations. Consequently, intelligence organizations ranged from the virtually non-existent, such as at Lee's headquarters, to the Army of the Potomac's sophisticated Bureau of Military Information. Headed by Colonel George H. Sharpe, the bureau became the war's most professional intelligence unit, one that collected and processed information from all the available humint and sigint sources and disseminated unusually reliable reports regarding Lee's order of battle. Although created by General Hooker in early 1863, the bureau reached its apogee under Grant's supervision. Beginning in late summer 1864, it ably served the headquarters of both the Commanding General and the Army of the Potomac.

Grant's relationship with the Bureau of Military Information began with a near catastrophe, when it failed to discover General Jubal Early's raid down the Shenandoah Valley in the summer of 1864. For more than three weeks after Early's corps departed the Richmond area early on June 13, Grant remained unaware of its location and thus misunderstood the strategic situation. Since he did not want anything to disrupt his operations at Richmond and Petersburg, the image of the Valley being devoid of Confederates nicely fit his preconceptions—and his wishful thinking. Only at the last moment did he dispatch reinforcements to Washington, which arrived there just in time to dissuade Early from launching a major attack against the Union capital.

Impelled by this intelligence failure and by the realization that timely intelligence would allow him to coordinate his own movements so as to render Lee's army and Early's corps incapable of supporting each other, Grant refined the intelligence structure he had inherited. He did this by enhancing his control over the Bureau of Military Information and expanding its operations. Although most bureau personnel remained at Meade's headquarters, Grant transferred Colonel Sharpe to his headquarters as his personal intelligence officer. Sharpe soon focused bureau resources to detect any Confederate movement between Richmond and the Valley. Under his direction, the bureau recruited as spies three Virginia Unionists who lived near depots on the rail lines entering the Valley. These railroad monitors relayed their observations to bureau scouts who visited them several times a week. The scouts forwarded the spies' reports to Washington, and from there the War Department telegraphed the information to Sharpe. Meanwhile, to keep watch on the Richmond nexus, Sharpe conducted interrogations, read Confederate newspapers, and established closer connections with the Van Lew and Ruth spy rings. The spies became so proficient that, as a Confederate War Department clerk recognized, the Union was "fully informed of everything transpiring here" and the Southern cause was hopeless "unless communication with the enemy's country were checked. . . ."[14] Completing the revamped intelligence network was Sheridan's spy battalion under Major Young, which coordinated its operations with Sharpe's bureau.

An excellent example of how Grant's new intelligence structure functioned was the fate of General Joseph B. Kershaw's division in August and September 1864. When Lee dispatched reinforcements, including Kershaw's division, to the Shenandoah on August 6, it took the bureau only five days to confirm it; from then on, intelligence operatives kept such close tabs on the division that the Union rendered it ineffective. On August 11, Grant informed Chief of Staff Henry W. Halleck of the movement and asked him to alert Sheridan, who received the message before Kershaw reached Early. While Sheridan prudently fell back on the defensive in light of Early's imminent increase in strength, Grant struck at Lee's depleted lines on August 13 and then again four days later in an assault that severed the critical Weldon Railroad. With Lee's situation desperate and with Sheridan so wary that Early believed he was an excessively timid commander, Confederate authorities decided to return Kershaw to Richmond. Sheridan's intelligence antennae soon discerned the movement, and in short order his army crushed Early at the battles of Winchester and Fisher's Hill. These Union victories compelled Lee to stop Kershaw on September 23, before he reached Richmond, and send him back to Early's mangled corps. Thus Kershaw was unavailable to Lee when Grant launched a major offensive on September 29 that captured Fort Harrison, one of the redoubts anchoring the Confederate lines, and extended the siege works another three miles. The foremost scholar on this subject has written, "Utilizing quality intelligence, Grant and Sheridan had effectively isolated Kershaw while in transit between the two theaters, denying both Early and Lee the services of a veteran division at crucial times."[15]

All the humint sources collectively so vital to Civil War military intelligence were also present in the Second World War. When General Dwight D. Eisenhower's intelligence officer throughout most of World War II, Major General Sir Kenneth Strong, published his memoirs, he was apologetic "that so little of the 'spy' element appears in these pages. But it would be quite misleading to ascribe a dominant role to the agent in

Military Intelligence in time of war."[16] Yet, as in the Civil War, in some cases spies or agents did provide crucial information. Fritz Kolbe, an employee in the German Foreign Office who handled worldwide diplomatic cable traffic, smuggled more than 1500 documents to officials of the Office of Strategic Services (OSS) in Switzerland. The OSS also sent agents into occupied France. Under the Sussex plan, that organization's Secret Intelligence Branch in London infiltrated twenty-six two-man teams into France to assist the Normandy invasion. Most arrived by parachute, floating down to a pre-arranged landing zone where members of the Resistance awaited them. They radioed in intelligence items ranging from data on V-1 sites to the location of Luftwaffe ordnance dumps. Supplementing the Sussex missions was the Proust project, designed to dispatch individual agents behind enemy lines to acquire post-D-Day intelligence as unexpected emergencies arose. Of the forty-three Proust agents, one, code-named "Grenier," was "a super agent who never broke security. Every time he sent in a message [an enemy] convoy was blown sky high. . . . His messages resulted in convoys being bombed within two hours."[17]

Getting spies into occupied France was easy compared with inserting them into Germany, where no organized Resistance provided a welcoming party, few safe addresses were available, and communicating with friendly forces was difficult. By the end of 1944 only the Labor Division of the London Special Intelligence Branch had any agents—four of them—in Germany. But none of them had established communications with the Allies, much less supplied any information. Undaunted, in November 1944 the OSS created the Division of Intelligence Procurement—resulting in that wonderful acronym, DIP—to nurture the German venture. DIP eventually inserted almost two hundred agents into the Reich. Many were killed, captured, or missing and others were unable to communicate with their spymasters. However, using a novel radio system called "Joan-Eleanor," which allowed agents to send messages to an airplane circling overhead, some of the spies relayed important information concerning the German order of battle, bombing targets, and military movements.

Perhaps the Pacific Theater's most effective spies were the "coast-watchers" operating under the direction of General Douglas MacArthur's

Allied Intelligence Bureau (AIB). Having refused to allow the OSS into his theater, MacArthur established the AIB as an equivalent organization and gave it the task of getting spies into the vast area conquered by Japan. To fulfill this mission, at least in part, AIB took over the Royal Australian Navy's Coastwatcher Service. Operating behind enemy lines in remote areas of the Bismarcks, the Solomons, and New Guinea, these rugged (some might say crazy) individualists repeatedly radioed timely intelligence reports. For example, during the Battle of Guadalcanal, Japanese bombers routinely passed over the Coastwatcher stations of Paul E. Mason and W. J. "Jack" Read on Bougainville, allowing them to radio advance warnings to the hard-pressed Americans on Guadalcanal.

Reconnaissance remained a vital intelligence tool in World War II, with infantry foot patrols and specialized scouting used as standard methods. Typically consisting of a non-commissioned officer and three or four men, an infantry patrol would try to avoid contact and slither through and around the enemy's lines to locate terrain features, command posts, minefields, and barbed wire entanglements. Patrols had the advantage of being able to move at night and in bad weather, but they moved slowly and had limited range. Scouting organizations akin to Major Young's Shenandoah Valley unit proliferated during the Second World War. In MacArthur's Southwest Pacific Area the Sixth Army's Alamo Scouts and the AIB teams conducted hundreds of long-range reconnaissance missions. As a result of the North African and Sicily invasions, in Europe the Allies formed Combined Operations Pilotage Parties to conduct night-time beach reconnaissances. Carried close to shore in midget submarines and then going the rest of the way in a rubber dinghy or by swimming, these parties surveyed the Normandy beaches months before D-Day, collecting data on beach gradients, the soil's consistency and load-bearing capacity, and the location of beach obstacles.

Civil War cavalry reconnaissance had been replaced by machine-based methods, with jeeps and airplanes superseding horseflesh. As just one example of the use of jeeps, during the Battle of the Bulge the First Battalion, 333rd Infantry Regiment, 84th Division, probed more than a dozen miles west of its position at Marche by sending out jeep-mounted patrols to locate the enemy's line of advance. As for aerial recon, it could be visual or photographic, but the latter, with the camera substituting for the human eye, was exceptionally valuable. Attesting to the significance of aerial recon, an Allied study of enemy intelligence concluded that a "major contributory cause of the weakness of German intelligence was their loss toward the end of the war of an important source of intelligence: air reconnaissance. The failure of the German air force to stay in the air during the last two years of the war meant an almost paralyzing loss of eyesight to the German army."[18] Fortunately for the Allies, they suffered no such permanent blindness, though enemy defensive measures, bad weather, and the time lag between a request for aerial coverage and the delivery of the photos sometimes adversely affected their air recon. Photo interpretation was also far from perfect. Analyzing aerial photos involved viewing the world in an unusual way (vertically or obliquely instead of horizontally); required a patient attention to detail that entailed recognizing subtle differences in shapes, shadows, tones, and textures; and necessitated working under intense pressure that often literally involved life and death issues. Over all, however, the Allies achieved a decided advantage over their foes in this intelligence category.

Skillful photo reconnaissance and interpretation could produce an amazing amount of intelligence. Just one example will have to suffice. According to the Chief of Photo Intelligence for the Okinawa campaign, Rear Admiral Robert N. Colwell, photo recon was the decisive factor in selecting the invasion beaches. Before deciding where to invade, the Americans needed to know "offshore water depths; coral conditions; wave heights; surf behavior; beach dimensions, slope and trafficability; height and sturdiness of seawalls; and the location and usability of beach exits. Besides, we will need to know about such enemy installations as coast defense guns, antiaircraft weapons, underwater obstacles, barbed wire entanglements, and machine-gun emplacements."[19] Based on the initial high altitude vertical aerial photography, which revealed a great deal about these matters, Colwell decided the Hagushi beaches represented the most promising invasion area. After the invasion commander agreed on the Hagushi beaches, Colwell ordered two special series of photographs for that area, one of low-altitude offshore oblique photos and the other of low-altitude vertical photos. The former provided a "coxswain's eye" view of the beaches; during the invasion, each coxswain had an annotated oblique photo showing exactly where he should land. The latter allowed

Colwell to measure water depths to ascertain where landing craft might run aground; after the invasion, he found his photo-based estimates for depths up to thirty feet were usually off by less than a foot. The low-altitude verticals also revealed seawall heights to within two inches, and showed that the levees surrounding nearby rice paddies were unusually high and steep. Tests demonstrated that some vehicles scheduled for the invasion could not surmount these levees, but that a tracked vehicle called a Weasel could. Consequently, the commanding general canceled orders for the vehicles that had flunked the tests and increased the number of Weasels.

Along with intrusive reconnaissance missions, mere observation remained important, as attested by the ubiquity of Observations Posts (OPs) in soldiers' letters, diaries, and memoirs. During their attack against Peleliu's infamous Bloody Nose Ridge, the Marines gained a respite from a Japanese mortar crew because, wrote one Marine, it "was afraid to fire too much for fear of being seen by our observers."[20] In the fighting near Lindern, Germany, a rifle company used a barn tower and the top of a wrecked house as OPs. Since darkness and terrain features limited ground-bound observation, listening posts and visual aerial observation supplemented the OPs. Because large machines such as tanks and trucks made distinctive sounds, soldiers learned to identify them by listening, much as an ornithologist can distinguish a titmouse from a chickadee without ever seeing the bird. For aerial observation nothing surpassed the slow-moving Piper Cub, loitering on its air observation post near enemy lines while the pilot and observer scanned beyond hills and forests into the enemy's positions.

Although built as a sub rescue ship, the *Chanticleer* took on a novel duty in the spring of 1945: for almost a month it hovered over the Japanese heavy cruiser *Nachi*, sunk in Manila Bay in November 1944, while its divers scoured the hulk for documents. The Office of Naval Intelligence ordered the divers to salvage every scrap of paper on the *Nachi*, which ultimately yielded an underwater intelligence treasure trove—twenty mailbags stuffed with official charts, manuals, and reports, standing orders, operations orders, diaries, official and private correspondence. So successful was this operation that underwater documentary "research" became a standard procedure called "Mother Alpha."

"Mother Alpha" procedures came to the war late, but legions of other examples attest to a war-long quest for enemy documents. In 1942, the British established No. 30 Commando (later renamed No. 30 Assault Unit), a specially trained force that landed with the first invasion waves to seize documents and equipment. In 1944 Eisenhower's headquarters issued a directive on "Intelligence from Enemy Service Documents," which identified documents that deserved special attention, beginning with "All Operations Orders, operational messages or marked maps which deal with enemy current or future operational plans,"[21] and including such other categories as signal documents, engineering plans, and espionage and counter-espionage activity. Half a globe away the Translation Section of the Joint Intelligence Center, Pacific Ocean Area (JICPOA), contained fifteen subsections to analyze captured documents relating to specific enemy activity, such as aviation, radar and sonar, and ordnance. Although employing more than 200 translators by 1944, JICPOA could not keep pace with the tidal wave of documents flowing in from the battlefronts— fifty *tons* from Saipan alone.

Because of both voluntary and imposed censorship, newspapers were less productive intelligence sources than they had been during the Civil War. Still, careful gleaning could produce vital information. Provincial newspapers often contained news about local soldiers, including their unit and whereabouts, and an advertisement for a specialist engineer alerted Allied intelligence to a new synthetic oil complex in the Sudetenland. After the Battle of Midway, had the Japanese acquired the *Chicago Tribune*, listened to radio news analyst Walter Winchell, or kept tabs on Congressional debates, they could have saved themselves much subsequent grief. "NAVY HAD WORD OF JAP PLAN TO STRIKE AT SEA" blared the headline over a story describing how the navy had advance knowledge of the enemy's plans and dispositions. Winchell relayed the same information to his listeners, not just once but twice, and Congressman Elmer J. Holland, while excoriating the *Tribune* on the House floor, noted, "Somehow our Navy had secured and broken the secret code of the Japanese Navy."[22]

As in the American fratricidal conflict, interrogations remained a febrile intelligence source. Prisoners of war and deserters were often scarce and ill-informed about their own armed forces—"One can hardly underestimate the depth of an average prisoner's ignorance," wrote an intelligence officer.[23] Yet despite these limitations, considerable information could be obtained from captives by skilled interrogators or by informants and bugging devices in holding cells. Sometimes one prisoner could make a substantial difference. When the American 2nd Division prepared to attack Brest, maps showed only one heavily defended road into its sector of the city. But the night before the assault, a prisoner of war revealed a second road, little used and lightly defended. Attacking along this route, the 2nd Division easily broke into the city.

Despite the stereotype of Japanese soldiers fighting to the death and of American soldiers firing first and never asking questions, thousands of Japanese did surrender. True, the Japanese had a deep-seated aversion to the concept of surrender. And to the dismay of intelligence officers who found themselves deprived of an intelligence source of immense tactical value, Americans often did kill those trying to surrender. To convince GIs they should welcome surrendering enemy troops, authorities undertook an educational campaign. One pamphlet entitled "A Short-Cut to Victory" urged soldiers not to believe the adage that "the only good Jap was a dead one." "We haven't the troops, the resources, or the time to kill them all," the leaflet explained, "our short-cut to victory is through Japanese surrender." Japanese prisoners were often surprisingly cooperative since they had never been instructed on proper behavior if captured, and because they viewed themselves as having begun life anew after surrendering. Said one captive, "We must fulfill our loyalty to America the same as we did to the Emperor before."[24]

Just as the Union army could depend on the interrogation of Southern Unionists and slaves for information concerning Confederate forces, so Allied armies could rely on civilians in Axis-occupied regions for valuable intelligence. One pleasant surprise intelligence officers received in France and Belgium and throughout the Southwest Pacific Area was the superb information provided by local citizens, who were especially reliable in reporting on terrain features, fortified strongpoints, and the direction in which enemy forces were moving. As an authority on Eisenhower's use of intelligence concluded, one reason the Allied advance came to a sudden halt in September 1944 "was precisely that when Allied armies reached the German frontier, local sources of information disappeared."[25]

Although the humint sources that had dominated Civil War intelligence thus continued in World War II, they had declined in over-all importance. By contrast, sigint, which had been comparatively insignificant in the 1860s, had evolved so dramatically and become so robust that its World War II role constituted an intelligence revolution.

Sigint no longer concerned wig-wag flags and telegraph lines but centered on radios, which had become essential for efficient military operations in World War II at both the tactical and strategic levels. Wise signalers enciphered their messages since radio waves were free to the taker, friend or foe, and each side relentlessly intercepted its adversaries' wireless communications.

Vital information could be gleaned from eavesdropping on plain-language communications and by breaking low-grade codes, and even by subjecting enciphered, but unbroken, messages to careful scrutiny. Direction finding could locate and identify enemy radio transmitters, allowing skilled analysts to make informed judgments about the enemy's disposition and strength. Traffic analysis involved monitoring such features as the call signs, addresses, and number and strength of radio signals. The number of messages, for instance, usually followed set patterns. The quantity for a corps headquarters was greater than that of a smaller unit such as a division. And traffic swelled preceding an offensive as commanders arranged for logistical support and issued orders; declined just before the attack since arrangements had been completed; and then became a torrent as the battle unfolded. By monitoring Japanese picket boat and tactical air radio networks, a shipboard Radio Intelligence Unit could alert a commander if the enemy had spotted his carrier task force and, based on signal strength, forecast the attack force's arrival time.

It may be that neither the Axis nor the Allies established clear superiority in direction-finding and traffic analysis, but the British and Americans achieved a stunning advantage over the Germans and Japanese in breaking high-grade cryptosystems. The Axis broke a few high-level Allied codes early in the war, but read none of them consistently after mid-war. On the other hand, the Western Allies broke many of their adversaries' most important codes and read them regularly for much of the war. Although Allied code-breakers occasionally succeeded solely through pen-and-paper cryptanalysis, they generally prevailed only with the help of captured cryptography equipment and documents, with the aid of numerous careless errors by enemy radio operators and code clerks, and with the assistance of complex electromechanical machines and sophisticated mathematical theories. As an example of the latter, here is how one code-breaker described a critical breakthrough: "Because of the reciprocal property of [the German Enigma enciphering machine], the number of possible alphabets is not $26! = 4.0 \times 10$ to the 26th power but 'only' $25.23.21.19 \ldots 3 = 26!/(13!2$ to the thirteenth power$) = 7.9 \times 10$ to the 12th power. It was, therefore, necessary to find about 129 db (decibans) from somewhere."[26] This is why mathematicians such as Frank Rowlett dominated code-breaking.

Well before Pearl Harbor, William Friedman's SIS team of cryptanalysts penetrated Japan's foremost diplomatic code, which the United States read until V-J Day. As with all high-level codes, Japan's diplomatic traffic relied on an electromechanical machine, called Purple by the Americans, that enciphered the message on the sending end and deciphered it at the receiving end. Since an enciphering machine could generate more combinations of letters and numbers than the human brain could process, virtually the only way to solve a cipher was by using an analogous machine. In a testimony to brilliant mathematical and scientific labor, and to painstaking trial-and-error persistence, Friedman's team built a successful counterpart machine in the fall of 1940. Even after solving a cipher and converting the message into plain text, the Japanese language itself was almost another cryptographic system involving excruciating translation problems. One difficulty was the large number of homonyms. "Kaisen" could mean decisive engagement, sea battle, opening of hostilities, ghost ship, barge, rotation, reelection, or itch. Thus Japanese communications were hidden "behind the double veils of sophisticated ciphers and complex language."[27]

Ironically, the intelligence resulting from breaking the Purple machine, code-named MAGIC, was probably more vital in the war against Germany than against Japan. Messages to Tokyo from the Japanese ambassador in Berlin, General Oshima Hiroshi, reporting his interviews with Hitler and other leading Nazis and describing his investigations of German defenses in France, were an invaluable information source. Oshima was an energetic and inquisitive ambassador; between Pearl Harbor and V-E Day he sent nearly 1500 messages, some of them as long as thirty single-spaced typed pages. As Army Chief of Staff George C. Marshall wrote in September 1944, "our main basis of information regarding Hitler's intentions in Europe is obtained from Baron Oshima's messages from Berlin. . . ."[28]

In the Pacific Theater the Americans also generated ULTRA, which was intelligence gleaned from breaking enemy military (as opposed to diplomatic) codes. Navy code-breakers partially solved the Japanese navy's primary code, JN25b, just before the Battle of Coral Sea. Intelligence from this source, after being subjected to careful evaluation, allowed the U.S. and Australian navies to deflect the Japanese invasion of Port Moresby. The following month, revelations from JN25b enabled Admiral Chester W. Nimitz to station the Pacific Fleet in such a favorable position that it surprised and defeated the Japanese Imperial Fleet during the decisive carrier engagement at Midway. Although Japan continually introduced modifications to the code, American code-breakers, despite some blackouts, never completely lost the ability to read it. Another naval cryptographic triumph was solving the Japanese Navy's Water Transport Code, which became possible in early 1942 when divers salvaged a set of codebooks from a sunken enemy sub.

General MacArthur's code-breaking agency, Central Bureau, attacked enemy army codes, which proved more difficult to crack than the naval codes. Working closely with the SIS and employing IBM tabulators, Central Bureau achieved its first triumph in April 1943 when, operating on purely cryptographic principles, it solved the Japanese army's Water Transport Code, which revealed such essential data as the locations, routes, and cargoes of merchants ships and troop transports. Five months after solving the Water Transport Code, SIS code-breakers scored another coup by solving the Japanese military attaché enciphering system, which became such a prized source of high quality strategic intelligence that War Department officials quipped about the Japanese attachés being the most efficient spies the U.S. had in some regions of the world.

Meanwhile, Central Bureau's work on the Japanese army's two main codes had yielded nothing but frustration. The Imperial army's highest echelons used 4-digit systems, while regimental-level units and below used 3-digit systems. On the assumption that the 3-digit systems would be easier to break than the 4-digit, Central Bureau was still unsuccessfully working on them in January 1944 when good fortune intervened. Australian infantrymen on New Guinea found a complete 4-digit cryptographic library that a retreating enemy division had failed to destroy. Almost overnight code-breakers began solving several tens of thousands of the enemy army's communications *every month*. In addition to these feats, Central Bureau routinely read several Japanese army air force ciphers. Even though they never broke the 3-digit systems, by early 1944 army cryptanalysts rivaled their naval counterparts in the ease with which they read Japan's military mail.

Allied code-breakers, primarily British rather than American, enjoyed equally spectacular success in the European Theater and Mediterranean Theater. Like the Americans in the Pacific Theater, the British Government Code and Cipher School at Bletchley Park also produced ULTRA intelligence, which in this case referred to information obtained from messages enciphered on German machines known as Enigma and Fish; the major Fish species were "Tunny" (used by the German army) and "Sturgeon" (used by the German air force). Enigma was used for tactical and operational messages, while Fish carried strategic-level traffic.

Enigma was the standard German enciphering machine used by the armed forces, the secret services, and a few civilian agencies. The Germans assumed that the enemy might capture an Enigma machine, or at least eventually understand how it worked, and so they put their faith not in the machine, but in the keying procedure. Setting a key was a complicated process but easy to do, so the Germans often changed keys—some as frequently as once a day. Keeping in mind that tremendous variations existed, in generic terms setting a key involved selecting three out of the five different code wheels (or rotors); inserting them into the Enigma in a particular order, such as IV–I–III; setting each of these rotors to one of its twenty-six alphabetic positions; cross-plugging ten of the thirteen pairings on the machine's twenty-six-letter "steckerboard" (for mathematical reasons the maximum number of permutations resulted from ten rather than thirteen pairings); and inserting a preambular key into each message by having the operator type in three letters at random. Those who worked at

Bletchley Park differ as to how many keys were theoretically possible. One says 150 quintillion (150 million million million), another 200 quintillion. But what are a few tens of quintillions among friends? Suffice it to say that the Enigma machine produced such an astronomically large number of keys that it would take *billions of years* for a team of 1000 cryptanalysts, each testing 240 keys an hour, all day, every day, to test them all.

The keying procedure made the Enigma machine unbreakable—provided the Germans used it properly. But radio operators and communications security personnel repeatedly made mistakes that gave code-breakers a "crib," which was anything in a message that suggested it contained a certain phrase, such as a stereotyped address or message—the Allies broke more than one key because an Enigma operator at an isolated outpost signaled "Nothing to report" almost daily. A good crib reduced the number of potential keys from quintillions to "only" a few hundred thousand, a number still so large that code-breakers could not succeed on brainpower alone. Their gray matter needed assistance from a massive electromechanical machine called a "Bombe," which was a precursor to the computer, to sort through the possible keys. By mid-1942 Bletchley Park was breaking perhaps twenty of the fifty keys in use at any one time.

Since each of the German armed forces used the Enigma differently, introduced different versions of the machine, and oversaw its own security measures, some Enigma traffic was easier to read than others. In 1940 Bletchley Park made its initial breakthrough against Luftwaffe Enigma communications, which remained relatively easy to read for the duration. German navy messages were more difficult to break, and could be done only with assistance from captured enciphering equipment and documents. Army Enigma messages were so hard to solve that code-breakers read comparatively few of them.

Fortunately for the Allies, the German army did not use Enigma for communications between the highest authorities in Berlin and the headquarters of theater and army group commanders. Those messages went over Tunny links. Because Bletchley Park easily read Luftwaffe Enigma traffic, it concentrated on Tunny rather than Sturgeon, but breaking Tunny was theoretically even more difficult than cracking Enigma. The latter used an alphabet of twenty-six symbols, Fish used a thirty-two-symbol alphabet; Enigma used only three or four rotors, Fish a dozen.

The British broke Enigma with the aid of Bombes, but needed "Colossus," the first true programmable electronic digital computer, to filet Fish. However, since Bletchley Park read so few army Enigma messages the strenuous efforts to break Tunny were richly rewarding; not only did it carry supremely important army information, but for technical reasons an Enigma message could be no more than several hundred letters long while a Fish message could contain thousands of letters. By producing army information, Fish nicely complemented Enigma traffic, which primarily provided information on the air force and navy.

Three caveats are in order. First, ULTRA was not omniscient and could not produce information on demand. The enemy sometimes imposed radio silence as a security measure, or sent messages over telephone or teleprinter land-lines rather than radios. When the Germans or Japanese did use radios, atmospheric conditions, wavering frequencies, or sheer distance often prevented the Allies from intercepting the signals. Even when they intercepted a signal, long delays sometimes occurred in cracking a particular key, and some could never be broken. The Allies read some keys some of the time, not all the keys all of the time.

Second, because ULTRA was imperfect the Allies rarely relied on it alone, almost always integrating sigint with humint as they sought to confirm information from multiple sources. ULTRA intelligence officers warned against relying solely on sigint and thereby allowing it "to become a substitute for analysis and evaluation of other intelligence." They stressed that ULTRA "must be looked on as one of a number of sources; it must not be taken as a neatly packaged replacement for tedious work with other evidence." General Strong, Eisenhower's G-2, "had at one time a staff of well over a thousand, shifting, analyzing, cross-checking, and collating information received and reducing it to manageable proportions." Indeed, one of ULTRA's most important roles was to serve as "the guide and the censor to conclusions arrived at by means of other intelligence."[29]

Finally, although ULTRA provided occasional dramatic revelations of enemy grand designs, much of the intercepted material consisted of details, odd bits and pieces of information that were not of immediate, evident value. But when painstakingly stitched together and carefully inte-

grated with humint over months or even years, sigint provided a remarkably well-focused picture of the enemy's order of battle.

Despite these caveats, compared with any previous intelligence
source, high-level sigint was more voluminous, more currently available,
more nearly continuous over a long period of time, and more reliable since
it came from the enemy's high command. The SIS, Central Bureau,
Bletchley Park, and other code-breaking centers became factories employing thousands of workers, frequently operating in round-the-clock
shifts, and producing intelligence with assembly-line efficiency. By the
autumn of 1943, ULTRA was averaging 84,000 Enigma messages *per
month;* code-breakers also caught about 320 Fish per month during that
year, and the number of Fish added to the string increased thereafter.
Bletchley Park signaled urgent intercepts to commanders in the field, with
many of the signals carrying near real-time information. Aided by the
Bombe, the Allies decrypted much Enigma traffic within three or four
hours after intercepting a message. However, it took at best several days to
crack a Tunny message, even with help from Colossus.

The prompt and relatively comprehensive manner in which the Allies
read their enemies' secret communications meant that military intelligence exerted an unprecedented influence during World War II. By
putting an Allied commander in the position of a poker player who was
allowed to peek at three or four cards in his opponents' hands before
having to bet, MAGIC and ULTRA eliminated some of the uncertainty
that normally pervaded warfare. Sigint partially negated Clausewitz's
warnings about the "general unreliability of all information" that compelled commanders to operate "in a kind of twilight, which, like fog or
moonlight, often tends to make things seem grotesque and larger than
they really are."[30] With their unparalleled insight into the enemy's intentions, order of battle, and problems, British and American commanders
could avoid potential pitfalls while marshalling their forces in the most
efficient way to hammer their foes.

Examples of sigint's impact abound. In the Pacific, ULTRA permitted air and sea power to interdict the sea lanes linking Japan's far-flung
empire. Because of ULTRA, General George C. Kenney, MacArthur's
chief air officer, executed a number of aerial ambushes. One dramatic
example occurred in early March 1943, when the Japanese tried to rein-

force Lae in eastern New Guinea with the 51st Division, then stationed at Rabaul. With ULTRA providing advance notice of the convoy's departure and likely destination, Kenney's airmen were waiting as the eight transports and eight destroyers neared their destination. When the fliers were finished, all eight transports and four of the destroyers had been sunk. Out of 6900 soldiers on the transports, only 1000 ultimately reached their original destination. After this failure to reinforce Lae, the initiative in eastern New Guinea passed to the Allies.

Sigint allowed submarines to launch devastating attacks that complemented the aerial campaign. In the war's early stages Japanese freighters, tankers, and transports safely carried reinforcements and logistical support to and from outlying garrisons and returned to the home islands with raw materials from the conquered territories. But ULTRA began revealing the merchant ships' cargoes, sailing dates, routes, and daily noon positions. It also detailed enemy naval mine-laying activity so completely that, according to the Commander Submarines Pacific Fleet, enemy minefields "served our purpose rather than his. Not only were our submarines able to avoid the areas of danger, but Japanese ships, being required to avoid them as well, were forced into relatively narrow traffic lanes, making it easier for the submarines to locate and attack them."[31]

Sometimes every U.S. sub on patrol was working on the basis of sigint, being routed into the vicinity of lucrative targets and thus avoiding long, fuel-consuming, and potentially futile searches in the vast Pacific. The fate of the so-called TAKE Convoy was illustrative. Consisting of nine merchant ships and seven escorts, the convoy departed China in April 1944, carrying the 32nd Division and most of the 35th Division as reinforcements for the Netherlands East Indies and western New Guinea. ULTRA revealed the convoy's route, destination, speed, and noon positions. Acting on this knowledge, subs sent four transports to the bottom, killing 4000 troops and destroying much equipment. Leaving Japanese defenses in western New Guinea without a strategic reserve, this disaster allowed MacArthur to accelerate his campaign.

Although the relationship between ULTRA and the air and sea blockade of the Japanese empire is clear-cut, MacArthur's record in using sigint is mixed—a superb example of how intelligence by itself makes no decisions but was often only one of several elements influencing a commander. Gripped by a sense of destiny, the SWPA commander never allowed military intelligence to interfere with his strategic vision of recapturing the Philippines. When ULTRA accorded with this strategy, he used it magnificently, as illustrated by the Hollandia invasion. But when sigint contravened his vision, MacArthur discounted it, as demonstrated by the decision to invade Luzon.

It may have seemed like a reckless gamble, but the long leapfrog from eastern New Guinea to Hollandia was close to a sure bet. ULTRA not only revealed that the Japanese expected an invasion in the Hansa Bay region and had prepared a trap there, but also guided Allied forces as they severed enemy supply lines and devastated Japanese aircraft in the Hollandia area. Sigint also allowed intelligence officers to surmise that most of the Japanese at Hollandia were construction and service personnel, not combat troops. With American forces controlling Hollandia, Japan's New Guinea defenses had been split atwain. Contrasting with Hollandia was MacArthur's misuse of intelligence at Luzon. Based on all sources, including lavish doses of ULTRA, MacArthur's G-2 estimated enemy strength on Luzon at 137,000. Using the same data the Sixth Army's G-2 concluded that 234,500 troops held the island. When the Sixth Army's Chief of Staff tried to explain the basis for the higher figure, MacArthur exclaimed, "Bunk!" and simply ignored the 100,000 troop discrepancy. "There aren't that many Japanese there," he insisted.[32] As those Americans who endured the cadaver-creating combat on Luzon discovered, even the Sixth Army's estimate was too low by more than 30,000 soldiers.

If ULTRA was in large part responsible for the strangulation of Japan through submarine warfare, ULTRA was also instrumental in saving Britain from the same fate, for the Allies could not have prevailed in the Battle of the Atlantiç without it. The commander of the German submarine effort, Admiral Karl Doenitz, coordinated U-boat wolf-pack attacks through enciphered radio communications. With assistance provided by the capture of enciphering equipment and documents from two weather ships, a whaling trawler, and two U-boats, Bletchley Park periodically cracked the Enigma until February 1942, when the German navy introduced a fourth rotor to the machine, resulting in a nearly complete ULTRA blackout. Since the Allies could no longer route their convoys around the wolf packs, sinkings soared. Fortunately for the Allied cause the British captured from the U-559 documents that permitted Bletchley Park to break the four-rotor Engima in December 1942. The results were dramatic: losses in January and February 1943 were only half what they had been the previous two months. Because of this sudden shift in fortune Doenitz became concerned about Enigma's security. But an investigation concluded—erroneously—that Allied success resulted from superb direction-finding, French Resistance reports on the time and direction of U-boat departures, and especially the development of "centimetric radar," which allowed Allied aerial recon to locate the U-boats from so far away that the subs did not know they had been spotted. After a momentary scare in March occasioned by another Enigma modification, Bletchley Park mastered the naval Enigma for the rest of the war. Thanks primarily to ULTRA, the Allies won the Battle of the Atlantic.

While ULTRA was vital in permitting the Allies' build-up in England, it also played a significant role in getting them ashore on D-Day and helped them defeat the German armies in France. Allied forces conducting the Normandy landings operated on such narrow margins that they might have failed without precise, comprehensive, and reliable intelligence about the German order of battle, and without knowing that the most complex deception plan in history had befuddled the enemy. On June 6, 1944, Germany had fifty-eight divisions in the West. Thanks primarily to ULTRA, the Allies had identified all fifty-eight and precisely located all but two of them. The British and Americans also knew a great deal about these divisions, in large part because Fish decrypts provided detailed personnel and equipment returns and status reports. One Tunny decrypt explained that the 363rd Infantry Division had grave deficiencies in its motor transport and non-commissioned officers, that its horses were suffering from a serious infection that curtailed artillery training, and that the division was classified as Category IV (suitable only for the static defensive). Another decrypt showed that the 12th SS Panzer Division had an authorized strength of 25,170 but was understrength by 182 officers and 2500 non-commissioned officers, and suffered serious tractor and truck shortages. Meanwhile, Enigma messages provided extensive order of battle details about the German air force and navy.

All the order of battle knowledge would have been of questionable value had it not been for Operation Bodyguard, the strategic deception plan to conceal Allied intentions regarding the location, timing, and size of the invasion that would open a "second front" in 1944. The operation's purpose was to "tie down as many German divisions as possible as far as possible from Normandy for as long as possible."[33] Consisting of three major parts—Plan Zeppelin directed toward the Balkans, Fortitude North aimed at Scandinavia, and Fortitude South pointed at the Pas de Calais—Operation Bodyguard depended upon ULTRA and the Double Cross System.

Since Bletchley Park read the Abwehr's Enigma codes, the British captured every German spy in England. MI5, the British internal security agency, converted some of the captives into double agents. To build up the agents' veracity in the eyes of their spymasters, MI5 realized that the "spies" had to provide at least some accurate information. Thus it established the Twenty Committee to concoct a carefully prepared brew of reliable information and misinformation for the agents to send their controllers. In Roman numerals, twenty is XX, or a double cross—hence the Double Cross System. At the committee's first meeting its chairperson prophetically proposed that the credibility of a few agents should be enhanced so they could be available "for a large-scale deception which could at the critical moment be of paramount operational importance."[34] Of the agents participating in the Double Cross System, the star was Garbo (Juan Pujol), who "recruited" twenty-seven sub-agents, all of them figments of the rich imaginations of Garbo and his case officer. Garbo sent more than 500 radio messages, judiciously mixing fact and fiction, in the six months before D-Day and seemed so reliable that Hitler awarded him the Iron Cross.

ULTRA interacted with the Double Cross System in three crucial ways. It guaranteed that no uncontrolled German spies, who might expose the double agents, were in England. By unveiling German fears, hopes, and expectations regarding the Allied threat, ULTRA allowed the Twenty Committee to craft the agents' reports so that they accorded with enemy perceptions, thus adhering to the foremost rule of deception operations: they work best when they reinforce preconceptions. Finally, by monitoring enemy reactions to the agents' reports the Allies could refine subsequent data, playing the Germans like a finely tuned violin.

ULTRA and the Double Cross System manipulated the Germans

into overestimating Allied strength, which distorted their perceptions of Allied capabilities. Through the double agents the Allies created bogus formations in the minds and file folders of German intelligence personnel. By late May 1944, Fremde Heere West (FHW), the organization responsible for evaluating intelligence about the British and Americans, estimated they had seventy-nine divisions in England, which inflated the number of troops by about 50 percent. Many of the bogus troops belonged to two major notional organizations, the 4th British Army in Scotland and the First United States Army Group (FUSAG) in southeastern England. The fake units in the fictional FUSAG did have a genuine commander, General George Patton, Jr. Patton's army group was allegedly poised to leap across the Channel to the Pas de Calais. To reinforce the reports from Garbo and other double agents about FUSAG, radio operators working from prepared scripts sent out a stream of communications that mimicked an army group, knowing that German intercept stations would monitor them. Meanwhile, for the benefit of enemy aerial recon, engineers constructed dummy landing craft in the Thames River and established supply depots bulging with dummy trucks, tanks, and artillery pieces.

The British 4th Army and FUSAG were the central elements in Fortitude North and South, the cover plans for Operation Overlord. According to the initial phase of the Fortitude plans, Allied operations would begin with the 4th Army assaulting Norway. The hope was that this threat would keep German divisions pinned in Scandinavia and perhaps entice reinforcements there. Pending a 4th Army victory, probably sometime in July, FUSAG would invade the Pas de Calais area, defended by the German 15th Army. After the real invasion occurred at Normandy, Fortitude's second phase would insinuate that Normandy was a feint to lure reserves from the 15th Army, and that when the Germans committed themselves to Normandy, FUSAG would strike. Planning documents estimated the second phase might buy as much as two weeks for the Allies.

The Fortitude deception exceeded expectations. By early June the Germans had no clearer insight into Allied plans than they had six months earlier. Fewer than twenty-four hours before Normandy, the German supreme commander in western Europe issued a situation report stating that "As yet there is no immediate prospect for the invasion."[35] Even after General Montgomery's 21st Army Group went ashore on D-Day, worries about FUSAG, reinforced by the double agents, muted the German reaction for two *months*, not two weeks. On the evening of June 6, FHW concluded that the Normandy invaders represented "a comparatively small part of the total available," that "the American First Army Group, comprising about 25 divisions north and south of the Thames, has not yet been employed," and that the enemy "plans a further large-scale undertaking in the Channel area. . . ."[36] Three weeks later the Germans still feared "the American Army Group assembled in Southeast England which is ready to jump off. It is stronger than Montgomery's Army Group."[37] Not until late July did the Germans conclude that no second invasion was coming. In the interim approximately twenty German divisions remained idle at the Pas de Calais.

One close call had occurred but ULTRA and Garbo rescued the Allies. Despite their FUSAG anxieties, the Germans had quickly ordered two 15th Army armored divisions to Normandy, hoping to win a rapid victory there before the second, larger invasion commenced. Learning of this decision through ULTRA, on the evening of June 8–9, when the Allies had barely cleaved out a toenail-hold in Normandy, Garbo sent an urgent warning that Normandy was a diversion intended to draw off the 15th Army's reserves so that the Allies could make a decisive attack elsewhere, probably the Pas de Calais. Received in Berlin late on June 9th, the message went to the Chief of Intelligence, then to the chief of the OKW operations office, and finally to Hitler. Fortuitously reinforced by a similar report from an Abwehr officer in Stockholm who was not a double agent, Garbo's warning resulted in the cancellation of the two divisions' movement orders.

ULTRA blossomed in the post-invasion period as air attacks and Resistance sabotage destroyed telephone lines, compelling the Germans to resort increasingly to radio communication. On June 10, ULTRA located the headquarters of Panzer Gruppe West, an armored striking force, and the resulting bombing strike killed and wounded so many officers that the organization did not become operational for two weeks. Prior to Operation Cobra, the late July breakout from the beachhead at Saint-Lô, ULTRA reassured the Allies they would achieve surprise because the Germans were not expecting an attack there. When the Germans launched the Mortain counterattack in August, ULTRA betrayed it.

General Elwood R. Quesada, commander of the 9th Tactical Air Command, recalled meeting with American 1st Army commander General Omar Bradley after learning about the enemy's intentions: "I can still see that moment when we stood with those signals in our hands, and grinned, and said 'We've got them.'"[38] It took hard fighting against the tough German army, but the Mortain attack was smashed. Other examples of the direct relationship between sigint and operations could be piled up, but Patton's 3rd Army summed up the battle for France when he said that "Ultra was invaluable every mile of the way."[39]

As always, however, excellent intelligence did not guarantee success, as the Germans' Ardennes counterattack demonstrated. To conceal the forthcoming offensive, Hitler relied on extensive security precautions and deception measures. Nonetheless, ULTRA decrypts unmistakably indicated the Germans were organizing a major assault in the area. But Allied authorities ignored these warnings because they had strong preconceptions about the enemy's capabilities, believing that after their catastrophic defeat in France the Germans could no longer mount a large offensive. On December 16, 1944, Montgomery's 21st Army Group issued an intelligence appreciation declaring that "The enemy is at present fighting a defensive campaign on all fronts; his situation is such that he cannot stage major offensive operations."[40] At 5:30 that morning a German artillery bombardment had begun preparing the battlefield for an assault by three entire armies.

Thankfully for the Allies, ULTRA insured that nasty strategic surprises like the Ardennes attack were, by far, the exception rather than the rule.

Without military intelligence, humint or sigint, the Civil War might well have lasted about four years, resulted in more than 600,000 deaths, and ended in a Union victory. That is, military intelligence made no fundamental difference in that war; however, so little sophisticated, detailed work has been done on the subject that this cannot be stated with certainty. The same cannot be said about World War II, when military intelligence clearly had a profound impact. Without the Allies' sigint superiority, the war would have been longer, American and British casualties would have been far greater, and the postwar world would undoubtedly have been different. The Western Allies might have met the Soviets on the Rhine instead of the Elbe. And perhaps after a joint occupation of Japan with Soviet armies, that prostrated nation would have been fragmented into a North and South Japan akin to a North and South Korea or an East and West Germany. In such ruminations lies the revolutionary impact that military intelligence had during the Second World War.

4

Battle in Two Wars: The Combat Soldier's Perspective

GERALD F. LINDERMAN

A T first glance, dissimilarities between the Civil War and World War II so leap forward as to seem to preclude even a modest comparison of the combat experience of the two wars. Theirs were different social settings—in the 1860s a small-town America at its zenith; in the 1940s an urban-industrial America moving to its own apogee—and thus nineteenth- and twentieth-century recruits brought to their wars divergent sets of social assumptions. One conflict was entirely internecine, with heavy destruction sustained internally; the other was wholly foreign, with the homeland left untouched. In the eighty years separating the wars, moreover, military technology altered momentously. The Civil War began—and concluded—with the soldier and his musket still the basic unit of warfare. In World War II the GI and his M-1 were subordinated to complex orchestrations of infantry, armor, aircraft, artillery, and other team-served weapons. The scale of conflict, too, varied dramatically. The lament of writer and Pacific Theater soldier James Jones—that World War II was a case of "massed, managerial, industrial-production techno-logical warfare [in which] a single infantryman . . . was about as . . . important as a single mosquito in an airplane-launched DDT spray campaign"—found few forerunners in the American Civil War.[1]

Anyone undertaking to set the experience of battle in 1861–65 against that of 1941–45 must also contend with an omission in the literature of war. Comparison requires the ability to establish for each war a represen-tative combat-soldier experience and then to devise a framework within which those two experiences might be weighed against one another, but here the sources are seldom directly helpful. Battle histories, a principal component of the literature, are narratives in which individual soldiers and their reactions figure only infrequently. Soldier letters, whose con-tents were grounded in the resolve not to alarm the homefolk, often eschewed reality for reassurance. Postwar soldier accounts, though nu-merous, were often intent on establishing their authors' individuality, even to the point of denying the existence of representative patterns of combat experience. "Make no mistake about it," warned a World War II line officer of the 29th Infantry Division, ". . . each man's war is separate and personal unto himself and not exactly like that of any other." "Each [American in uniform] had a unique personal experience," insisted a junior naval officer in the Pacific. "There was enormous variation, and no two experiences were identical even within the same Military Unit."[2]

Still, to read among those several thousand Civil War and World War II soldier narratives and to ponder their content is to become convinced that it is possible to identify both the lineaments of a common experience within each war and elements within each experience common to both wars. The latter congruency, particularly, came as a surprise—similarities in Civil War and World War II soldiers' expectations of combat, in the shocks combat administered to them, in their attempts to adapt to the unexpected, in their exertions—largely unsuccessful—to ward off the ef-fects of sustained combat as disintegrative experience. Both wars ulti-mately bore down on participants in ways that constricted severely the range of individual response, and in both conflicts the combat soldier's

pathway led from confidence to dubiousness and abjectness, from san-
guineness to despondency, from ingenuousness to harsh realism. The
approach here, then, must attempt to place the combat soldiers of both
wars within this structure of shared perception and reaction while still
making clear variations in emphasis reflective of important differences
between the wars.

Soldiers in both wars anticipated positively their first experience of battle.
In their impatient expectation, they very early-on thought themselves fully
prepared for combat. In the Civil War, training was minimal—no one
except the career military believed that soldiering required anything bor-
dering on technical qualifications; the best citizens, it was assumed, would
rather easily make the best soldiers—so this confidence was based princi-
pally on who soldiers thought they were: fighters better, righter, and
stronger than their enemies. In World War II assurance flowed from some
of that sense of superior attributes and, since by then some specialized
knowledge was conceded to be a prerequisite of effective performance in
battle, from soldiers' centainty that their training left them wholly ready to
fight. Said Marine Raider Mario Sabetelli on the eve of the invasion of
Tulagi: "I felt cool and confident. My feeling was that it was going to be
tough, but after the training we'd had I felt this was my business and I was
ready for it." Ernie Pyle pointed out that when American troops landing
on Sicily met no enemy resistance, they were disappointed, for they
thought themselves "trained to such a point that instead of being pleased
with no opposition they were thoroughly annoyed."[3]

Such aplomb led soldiers in both wars to expect that their role in the
fighting would invariably be an aggressvie one: they desired to close with
the enemy swiftly, in combat envisioned as very personal and highly indi-
vidualized. As Sabetelli put it, "We wanted to get our hands on Japs."
Another Marine who, aboard his troop transport, had received laborious
instruction in sector maps and units roles for the Guadalcanal landing
insisted on another, private focus: "I just want to kill a Jap, that's all."
Morton Eustis, an army private who rose to first lieutenant, wrote home,
"If I don't kill at least ten [Germans] personally, I shall be most unhappy!"
The first dead enemy was to be dedicated to his mother and the second to
his brother. And implicit in that concentration on the uncomplicated

destruction of the enemy were an impatience to be about it—Carlton McCarthy worried that the war would end before he and his friends in the Richmond Howitzers "had a chance to make a record" for themselves; Eustis feared that Germany would capitulate "before we have a crack at her"—and a tendency, strong at the outset of both wars, to depreciate the capacities of the enemy. Boasts early in the war that one Confederate could lick three, or five or ten Yankees courted disdain no less than early-war recitations of imagined Japanese physiological defects (poor eyesight, faulty balance, bowed legs, etc.).[4]

Beneath the initial heartiness were serious concerns, but seldom did they include what one would have thought the great fear, that the soldier would himself be killed. Soldiers in the early stages of both conflicts understood only in the most distant and abstract sense that any war would, as its requisite condition, be constituted of woundings and dyings. During his first advance under fire, Captain John W. DeForest of the 12th Connecticut was "not scared . . . It seemed perfectly natural that others should be killed and that I should escape." "You hear of casualties, see casualties, and read of casualties," explained a member of an army ordnance unit in North Africa, "but you believe it will never happen to you." In describing his first hour of combat on Guadalcanal, a marine sergeant reported that although Japanese shells "were falling closer and more of our men were being hit . . . there was no panic and very little real fear. Somehow you figured they would never get you." Neither the Civil War nor the World War II soldier was prepared to contemplate the encounter with his own death.[5]

Pre-combat worry was less of death or injury than of the quality of one's performance in battle, and here the Civil War soldier carried a far heavier burden than his World War II counterpart. Traditionally young soldiers viewed combat as a test that would provide answers to such questions as "Am I a man?" and "At my core, what kind of person am I?" In the Civil War, soldiers thought it essential to settle both; eighty years later, only the first question seemed pertinent.

Eighteen-sixties' volunteers were convinced that their conduct in combat would reveal definitively their essential and unalterable natures—courageous or cowardly; strong or weak. A taut Confederate private, John Dooley, asked himself a question many of his comrades nervously pondered: "Was I to run and [thus] prove myself a coward?"[6] By the 1940s, however, there was an altered consciousness, rooted in the experience of the Great War of 1914–18, that the sphere of individual performance in war had diminished. Soldiers could no longer think of battle as a neutral setting, an impartial arena, in which they would act in accordance with their basic natures and, by measuring their comportment against opponents like themselves, make those fundamental discoveries about themselves and either strengthen as their basic virtues were enhanced or decline as their basic defects revealed themselves. World War I soldiers had to do much more than contend, at relatively short range, with enemy soldiers, their muskets and their bayonets. The Great War, with its far more lethal weapons effective at much longer distances, had introduced a complex of destructive processes and had provided so many more ways to die than in close encounter with the enemy. A shrapnel wound inflicted by a shell fired from miles away seemed to say nothing of the soldier, except that he had been hit.

Confederate John O. Casler, a private in the Stonewall Brigade, had been confident of battle's message to him: "I do not consider myself a hero [but] neither do I consider myself a coward, for I have been in positions that tested me thoroughly, and such as a coward could not stand." World War II G.I.s observed that they and their comrades would on some occasions act in ways that seemed courageous and at other time in ways that appeared cowardly and that none of them could predict which or determine why. Marine Russell Davis, who fought on Peleliu and Okinawa, concluded that "Bravery is a fickle thing. . . . One day a man is a lion in the fight; the next day a mouse. . . . I have seen men who were brave when their feet were dry, cowards when they were wet. . . ." G.I. Lester Atwell "never formed moral judgments . . . for different men had different breaking points, and it was not always a matter within their control." "Nobody knows any other human being," decided another veteran of combat in Europe, "well enough to call him a coward." By the 1940s war had lost much of its capability to tell soldiers who they were.[7]

Still, some semblance of the test, pallid by Civil War standards, persisted in World War II. Since fundamental discoveries about one's essence as a human being were no longer at issue, the soldier's question, far less onerous, was "How will I do?" And it was asked in a way that seemed half resolve to do well and half curiosity, as if the G.I. were watching himself to see *how* he would do. The goal, ordinarily, was confirmation that the soldier had moved beyond adolescence. Notwithstanding the experience of World War I and the anti-war climate of the 1930s, both working to narrow the personal expectations that the G.I. brought to battle, youthful soldiers still hoped to find there confirmation of their transition to manfulness.

The World War II soldier's psychic burden was further lightened by the jettisoning of 1860s' convictions that while courage and fearlessness worked to ensure their possessors' survival in battle, the presence of fear revealed a character essentially cowardly. In the Civil War fear had been a formidable personal adversary, one to be expelled or at least stifled, but by 1941 even the army itself had declared fear in battle to be "normal" and had thus opened the way for soldiers to disencumber themselves by talking about it with one another.

Peculiarly, whatever the talk of that warfare of unprecedented destructiveness inaugurated in 1914, World War II soldiers seemed no less convinced of their personal invulnerability in 1941 than had Civil War soldiers in 1861. True, the grounds of confidence had narrowed. The Civil War recruit had seemed to reason: The brave will live and the cowardly will die. I shall be all right because I am a good person, one of courage, probity, and faith. My character, and especially my courage, will protect me. World War II soldiers took more modest, but no less confident, stands. Geddes Mumford wrote to his father, the respected social critic-philosopher-historian Lewis Mumford, that "Worrying about my getting killed . . . is foolish. I have no intention of doing anything but returning. Most men get killed in battle because they forget to take cover or make some such tactical mistake. I'll make no mistake like that."[8] How little transmission there seems to have been of the World War I European soldier's mounting sense of his own powerlessness; the assumption that the soldier's willed behavior would determine what happened to him in combat and that his personal survival was unquestionable remained intact in 1941.

In both the Civil War and World War II, combat soldiers of sanguine spirit encountered in battle a series of severe shocks. (Perhaps the single most easily defensible proposition regarding any war is that the experience of combat will not be as soldiers in training expect it to be.) I have tried to describe elsewhere the jolts administered to Union and Confederate volunteers: prior to battle, the extent and lethality of sickness; in battle, the destruction of bodies, the suffering of the wounded, etc. The World War II soldiers were protected by the advances of military medicine from the ravages of epidemic illness, and that was no minor blessing: in many Civil War narratives daily deaths from measles, mumps, and smallpox in the first months of the war and from pneumonia, dysentery, and malaria throughout were of greater moment than battle deaths. But G.I.s were not spared the shocks of battle. Events challenged and then overthrew confident assumptions of control and invulnerability. The battlefield compelled reconsideration, and somewhere in the escalating severity of its sights, soldiers of both wars met with a decisive episode—whether in the first view of enemy wounded, or of enemy dead, or of friendly wounded and dead, or of dead from one's own unit, or of the body of someone one knew, or of that of a close friend, or in a first wound of one's own. "I shall never forget," wrote Sergeant Leander Stillwell of the 61st Illinois, "how awfully I felt on seeing for the first time a man killed in battle. . . . I stared at his body, perfectly horrified! Only a few seconds ago that man was alive and well, and now he was lying on the ground, done for, forever!" For Henry M. Stanley, it was the dead of Shiloh who became indelible: "I can never forget the impression that those wide-open dead eyes made on me." For Bill Mauldin, it was a wound inflicted by a German mortar in the mountains above Venafro, Italy: "I was hit very lightly, but it was a shock. . . . It can't happen to you. But something *did* happen to me . . . and suddenly the war became very real to me."[9]

It was clear, however, as experience expelled "It can't happen to me" and installed in its place "It *can* happen to me," that whatever the reappraisal of war as soldier experience following 1914–18, it was not of such consequence that it imparted to soldiers approaching combat in the 1940s an anticipation of battle much more realistic than that of their nineteenth-century forebears. G.I.s frequently testified to their surprise at the discovery that someone actually desired to cause their deaths. Paratrooper Robert Houston, enroute to Normandy, watched anti-aircraft fire climbing toward his C-47 and asked, "Were those people on the ground really trying to kill us?" Marine Grady Gallant reported incredulously his experience on Guadalcanal: "My own death had never been considered by me." But now "the very real possibility flooded my mind with crystal clarity. . . . It came to me that a Japanese would no more hesitate to kill me than I would hesitate to slay him. He *would.* I could expect no mercy. There would be no negotiation. It would either be I would kill him or he would kill me. . . . [One] of us would kill the other. . . . Death might come to me, personally."[10]

Once survival could no longer be assumed, doubt and a painful awareness of exposure ousted invulnerability and the assurance of control. For combat soldiers, that transition appears to have been more rapid in World War II than in the Civil War, largely because the destructive power to which combatants were laid bare was more violent and thus more daunting in 1941–45 than in 1861–65.

Artillery quickly came to dominate World War II combat, as it had not during the Civil War. No doubt Yanks and Rebs found artillery bombardment difficult to endure. During a Wilderness battle Massachusetts soldier John D. Billings found himself in a position exposed to Southern artillery fire: it was, he said, "a season of mortal agony." At Antietam, a Virginia lieutenant, William Nathaniel Wood, confronted a semi-circle of Union batteries on the hills above him: "[Of] all mean things, the climax is reached when [the soldier is] compelled to receive the fury of cannonading with no opportunity [oneself] to inflict damage [on the enemy]." Ira Dodd, a New Jersey soldier, described his ordeal in enduring the cannonade: "Death seems even nearer and more horrible than in close battle where you can do as well as suffer." It is clear, however, that the principal source of the Civil War soldier's turmoil was being fired on without being able to fire back rather than the unendurability of the force that artillery brought against him. By contrast, Ernie Pyle's account of a German bombardment of the Anzio beachhead—"One gigantic explosion came after another. The concussion was terrific. It was like a great blast of air in which my body felt as light and as helpless as a leaf tossed in a whirlwind"— resembles many World War II reports depicting the force of artillery barrages as so crushing that the battered soldier-target could not so much as contemplate any counter-action.[11]

Confederate William Blackford, first a cavalryman with J. E. B. Stuart and later a lieutenant-colonel of engineers, revealed the necessity of Civil War soldiers to confront some escalation in firepower—and their ability to accommodate to it. "Is it very curious how soldiers become so familiar with one kind of danger, to which they have been exposed, as to disregard it almost entirely, and yet become demoralized when danger in a new form presents itself. Our men did not mind musketry and field artillery after the first two or three battles, but when they came under fire from the big guns on the gunboats below Richmond in 1862, they became nervous at seeing large trees cut off clean and whirled bottom upwards. To this they became accustomed. Then the mortar shells came, at the siege of Petersburg. . . ." Blackford hated trench life—and the mortar, which he described almost as if it were a personal enemy. "These mortar shells were the most disgusting, low-lived things imaginable; there was not a particle of the sense of honor about them; they would go rolling about and prying into the most private places in a sneaking sort of way. They would be tossed over from the trenches of the other side just as if they were balls thrown by hand, not a bit faster did they come, and then they would roll down the parapet into the trench and if the trench was on a slope, down the trench they would roll, the men standing up flat against the sides or flattening themselves on the ground to one side of the shell's path, each moment expecting the deadly explosion of the nasty, hissing, sputtering thing."[12]

Doubtless the Petersburg trenches constituted the nadir of the Civil War combat experience, but even there Blackford was able to respond to the effect of the enemy's weaponry within such a genteel category as honor—and even privacy. And, he added, even those mortar shells did "in time become familiar" to the men.[13]

The reactions of Civil War soldiers thus seldom reach to the level of trauma evinced in World War II descriptions. The latter reflected technology's evolution—quick firing, reliable fusing, accurate control from the front, more powerful explosives in much stronger steel shells—and signalled physiological and psychological reactions of far greater severity. Often G.I.s caught in shellings could not control their muscles and were wracked sometimes by spasms, sometimes by paralysis, and to establish such invasiveness required an imagery far more dire than that employed in the Civil War. "When I heard the whistle of an approaching [shell]," recounted Marine Eugene Sledge, "every muscle in my body contracted."

"To me, artillery was an invention of hell. The onrushing . . . scream of the big steel package of destruction was the pinnacle of violent fury and the embodiment of pent-up evil. It was the essence of violence and of man's inhumanity to man." Thought army private Lester Atwell: "It was as if an enraged giant were hurling with all his force an entire string of trains, screaming locomotive and all." Infantryman Walter Bernstein was convinced that there was "something about heavy artillery that is inhuman and terribly frightening. . . . It is like the finger of God."[14]

Air attacks, strafings, and particularly bombings also often brought to their human targets sensations of a force more overwhelming than they felt could be borne.

Still another twentieth-century weapon, the anti-personnel mine, exacted a toll rarely imposed on the soldiery of 1861–65. Alfred Bellard of the 5th New Jersey reacted angrily when land-torpedo "infernal machines" left behind by the Confederates in the rows between graves killed three or four Unionists, but Civil War mines were ordinarily of low destructive power, uncertain operation, infrequent and limited use. In World War II, once campaigning had moved to the European mainland, the mine seemed to be everywhere. Army officer William Dreux thought that he could cope with German machine-guns and rifles. "Behind each such weapon was an enemy and I might get him before he could get me." "[At] least I thought . . . I had a chance." It was the mine he "dreaded most." Infantry replacement George Wilson had a similar reaction: "By now I had gone through aerial bombing, artillery and mortar shelling, open combat, direct rifle and machine gun firing, night patrolling, and ambush. Against all this we had some kind of chance; against mines we had none. . . . They churned our guts." Even most artillery shells emitted shrieks warning the soldier that danger was descending; often the only indication of the presence of a mine was the explosion that maimed or killed. "The most frightening weapon of the war," Wilson called it.[15]

Different weapons technologies created very different zones of safety in the two wars. The Civil War soldier was ordinarily able to assume that if enemy forces were not within his range of vision, they could not injure him. In contrast, the World War II soldier, even far removed from the presence of the enemy, remained in jeopardy—from distant artillery, air assault, mines and booby-traps. Given twentieth-century weapons' greater destructive power and reach, and a combat more intense and protracted than that of the Civil War (granting even the acceleration of fighting in 1864 with the opening of Grant's Wilderness campaign), it is no surprise that G.I.s rapidly became aware not only of a profound physical corrosion but of their psychological deterioration, both of an order not often encountered in the Civil War.

World War II soldiers thus lost more rapidly than Civil War counterparts their sense of control in war. Geddes Mumford watched men "cry like babies after they have been under [shelling] too long. I've seen men almost unable to walk just from nervous exhaustion." Sledge reported that in the face of an artillery bombardment, "I braced myself in a puny effort to keep from being swept away." He feared that if, for so much as a moment, he lost control of himself under shellfire, "my mind would be shattered." Often this sense of slippage fully ran its course to a certainty of powerlessness felt by Civil War soldiers only in rare moments. "We were reduced to the size of ants," Atwell was convinced. "I felt cowardly and small," Bernstein reported; "I felt like a fly about to be swatted." Sledge cited comparable feelings—"of utter and absolute helplessness."[16]

A related casualty was the World War II soldier's early-war interest in personalized combat. The weaponry of 1941–45 dictated that soldiers would see the enemy in battle far less than in the Civil War. In the Pacific, where terrain cover and the enemy's resistance to surrender were also contributing factors, Americans glimpsed Japanese more often dead than alive; and even in Europe, soldiers seldom fired aimed shots as they had on the firing range and almost never charged as they had on the bayonet course. Moreover, while in the Civil War, even after the frontal assault had been reduced to minimal resort, combat remained at relatively close quarters, the range and lethality of World War II weapons both separated antagonists and eliminated mass movements. Atwell was stunned at the result: "This wasn't anything as I had imagined actual combat, this lonely little string of men. When I thought of it at all, I saw a battlefield and rows of men advancing shoulder to shoulder, cannons firing, the first ranks being mowed down. I realized I had been thinking of [Civil War soldiers in] scenes from *Birth of a Nation.*" Both the weapons and the consequent tactics of World War II lent themselves to a depersonalization seldom suffered by the Civil War soldier. To Blackford,

Petersburg mortar shells were "disgusting" and "low-lived" and "nasty." To George Wilson, World War II mines were "viciously, deadly . . . inhuman."[17]

In both wars soldiers had to resort to the same range of strategies in their efforts to cope with the unexpected stresses of combat.

The most rational and purposeful was the acquisition of specialized knowledge advancing the likelihood of survival. In the Civil War, soldiers rapidly taught themselves the "tricks"—e.g., ducking when they saw the distant puff of smoke from a sharpshooter's rifle. They learned before their officers that "spades were trumps" and that remaining alive required that they dig; though to do so had been thought dishonorable, they "scratch[ed] gravel on every occasion, with great ardor" and took shelter behind their mounds of earth.[18] G.I.s had to learn shell-sounds (in flight—differentiating incoming and outgoing—and at explosion); familiarity with weapons-sounds taught them to distinguish friendly and hostile machine-guns, etc. The many tricks and signs vital to combat had to be mastered. Did the soldier know that when the Germans fired machine-gun tracer ammunition high to coax Americans to maneuver well beneath it, they often next fired low without tracers? Had he learned that infantrymen not informed of where they were being taken could still judge their danger by the rapidity with which the trucks were driven away from their destination? Did he know how to stifle sneezes and coughs on patrol, how to shape his hole so that a shell landing nearby would not blow out his eardrums, how to identify what many claimed was the distinctive smell of the German soldier? If combat soldiers learned enough and lived long enough, they seemed to develop, in their attempts to counter many of the threats of battle, responses to danger that appeared almost intuitive.

Another approach—the attempt to negotiate exemptions from injury and death—was more recondite. Civil War soldiers were more likely than World War II soldiers to attempt to bargain with God, using prayer or worship to invite the deity's favorable intervention and offering in exchange professions of faith, etc. Most often Civil War soldiers pledged to declare for Christ at a prayer meeting, but the Virginia cavalryman Alexander Hunter told of a soldier who vowed to God that if he were allowed to live he would be moral, control his temper, carry all his comrades' canteens to the spring, give food to others, go to church, give up his pipe, throw away his pack of cards—and become a minister! World War II soldiers were more likely to negotiate with Luck, Fortune, or the odds, using rituals and talismans in their attempts to ensure that fortune remained good fortune. Airman Beirne Lay, Jr., patted the blanket on the foot of his bed prior to departure on every bombing mission. A B-29 crew in the Pacific all wore identical dark-blue baseball caps with their unit's number in yellow on the crowns. When the major forgot his, one of the enlisted men went to retrieve it before the mission began. Wrote John Muirhead, "We did everything we could to please [Luck]: we showed her trinkets, crucifixes, St. Christopher medals, the foot of a rabbit, vials of holy water, small pieces of paper with prayers written on them, lucky coins, sacred photographs in gold lockets, a pair of loaded dice, a pressed flower from a girl, a picture of a child in an embossed leather case, and many other beloved charms." Here both God and Fortune were entreated, in confused and overlying combinations. For his life, "The soldier prays to his God," wrote John B. George of the American Division in the Pacific—or to "his luck," he added. James Jones simply merged the two: the God of the American combat soldier was "the Great Roulette Wheel"—still another signal of a greater doubt than occupied Civil War soldiers that God, or any other agency, controlled what transpired on the battlefield.[19]

As part of this process of negotiating with transhuman forces, many soldiers became willing to accept injurious contingencies beyond any contemplation earlier but subsequently deemed necessary to limit their vulnerability, to hold it short of death—e.g., It is possible that I might suffer injury later, just not now; I might be hit in an arm or a leg but not in the head or the abdomen; I might be wounded, but surely I will not be killed.

Another adaptation, apparently less dependent on the soldier's will than on his nervous system's effort to protect and preserve itself, was a numbing of the emotions, a phenomenon often setting in train a process that led the soldier through hardening to coarsening and beyond to—far more in World War II than in the Civil War—brutalization.

Some soldiers in both wars, unable to find ways to accommodate to the strains of battle, sought some way to remove themselves from combat—briefly, through alcohol; for longer periods or permanently, by exposing a limb to enemy fire in invitation of a debilitating wound; by inflicting a wound on oneself; by maneuvering to be taken prisoner (with the Pacific Theater an exception); by resorting to desertion, etc.

The majority remained with their units at the front, but for most soldiers committed in both wars to prolonged combat, no one or any combination of these mechanisms proved capable of arresting the erosion of their physical and psychological resources. And as soldiers recognized their debilitation, fatalism became the dominant mode of thought and expression. Here those of 1864 and 1944 would have understood one another perfectly. "If you're going to be hit, you're going to be hit . . ." "When I'm going to die, I'm going to die. If the bullet's got my name written on it, there's nothing I can do." "You go when your time comes." "Gradually, one by one and sometimes faster, our numbers grow less and less. Someday, if the war continues long enough, we will all be gone." Robert G. Carter of the 22nd Massachusetts told his family, "Many wrote yesterday and today are dead. I hardly dare to write you of my [own] safety, lest I am a dead man before [this] vain assurance reaches you." World War II's American exemplar-infantryman, Audie Murphy, experienced "no inward emotion when assigned away from combat. A bullet will still find me. I am so much a part of the war now that it doesn't matter."[20]

A kindred phenomenon was the combat soldier's sense of the endlessness of his war. When Stephen M. Weld of Massachusetts, a staff officer and regimental commander in the Army of the Potomac, was chided by his sister for the "want of enthusiasm" with which he received the news of the enemy's capitulation at Appomattox, he explained to her that he was simply unable to comprehend that the war was over; Robert E. Lee and the Army of Northern Virginia, he said, had become to him and his comrades just as were those ghosts to the children they distressed, and he had learned to live with the certain belief that they would fight for the rest of their lives. Eighty years later Audie Murphy shared such a conviction: "The war goes on forever." So did another American soldier who wrote home during the war years: "In 1958 we'll be fighting the battle of Tibet. We will never get out of the Army."[21]

Such forebodings intensified as soldiers in both wars struggled with a sharpening sense of their alienation from others on their own side. Union soldiers felt betrayed by peace advocates ("cowardly skunks"), by draft rioters ("I only wish that I could be in New York to help kill some of the rascals"), by others who evaded military service ("miserable cowardly sneaks at home"), by profit-hungry businessmen whose shoddy goods had become military issue ("those ignoble sons who have . . . reaped the home harvest"). Soldiers were made angry, too, by civilian incomprehension of the combat experience. Some, in the ultimate fantasy, imagined that they would be able to carry the war into their own towns and cities: "We would like to go back and fight Northern cowards and traitors [better] than to fight rebels." World War II European-Theater infantrymen sometimes felt themselves separated from their own tankers, the presence of whose machines brought down enemy fire on nearby foot soldiers; from the artillery and the air force, whose mistakes often cost infantry lives; from their own high command, whose orders too often seemed to ordain attacks that proved bloody and futile; from the rear echelon, whose personnel transgressed by being in a place of safety; and from profiteers, strikers, and 4-Fs at home. Although these grievances were easily exaggerated—few G.I.s, for example, failed to appreciate the effectiveness of the artillery in helping to save infantry lives by breaking up enemy assaults and breaking down enemy defenses—there was at the heart of the matter a deep-seated anger that they were there, in battle, and that others—safe in bivouac, at the rear, or at home—were not. In the last stages of both wars combat soldiers felt acutely their own isolation.[22]

Still, if it is possible to speak of a world within war created by the impairment of efficacy and by fatalism, alienation, and isolation, one must judge that World War II soldiers moved further into that world than did Civil War soldiers. Units in 1861–65 were linked with specific locales in ways that would disappear prior to World War II. The hometown maintained strong connections with "its" company not only via letters but via streams of visitors—family members, hometown newspaper correspondents, relief workers, hospital volunteers, etc. Figures of moral authority—clerics, editors, teachers—maintained contact with the boys in uniform. Civil War soldiers, moreover, were far more likely than World War II combat soldiers to return home, occasionally on furloughs, occasionally, by unit, to vote. The persistence of these ties between hometowns and hometown soldiers in quite homogeneous units, and an experience of combat that, while severe, was less disaffecting than that of 1941–45, meant that Civil War soldiers ordinarily felt less acutely than World War II soldiers estrangement from their prewar existences. World War II combat severed more links with the familiar, made more isolated—and thus more desolate—the G.I.s' world within war.

If, at first, mail helped to keep World War II soldiers feeling closely attached to home, and the radio, films and newspapers were welcome as ways of letting them know what was happening elsewhere, the necessity to accept combat's harsh realities brought a day when a hometown news-paper, a snatch of popular music, a baby's picture, a Betty Grable pin-up became, to those most deeply affected, painful reminders of a world withdrawn from them, one to which they thought they would not return. There is little comparable testimony in the narratives of Civil War sol-diers.

True, there are other categories of observation in which the results of combat appear to vary little between the wars—the loss of volubility, for example. G.I.s sent from training camps to war "in such loquacious quan-tities" were often stilled by their experience of battle, a condition neither transient nor superficial. When the 16th Infantry Regiment was brought to England to prepare for the Normandy invasion, its men were ordered, for purposes of security, to conceal their participation in combat in North Africa and Sicily. "They were to [tell others] that they had [just] come from the United States." The men of the 16th held to their orders, even under the severest of provocations—earlier arrivals shouting at them, "Hey, what took you guys so long in getting over here?" and "Were you afraid to leave your mommas?" But not even stiff will and model discipline could carry the deception. English civilians, grasping the similarity of spirit between the 16th and their own veterans, knew immediately that these Americans had been in battle. They were "too quiet." Similarly, Mary Livermore, on a journey south in which she recorded the "bois-terous enthusiasm" of singing and shouting recruits, passed other groups of Union soldiers who had already been under fire; the latter moved along "in a grim silence that was most oppressive." In both wars soldiers lost their early war ebullience to battle.[23]

In most categories, however, twentieth-century results appear more severe—in the matter of physical aging, for example. All young soldiers expect war to alter them physically, enroute to full maturation. They also expect that physical exertion, exposure to the elements, irregular food and sleep, etc. might effect some physical change. But World War II soldiers were not prepared for effects so severe that many of them would acquire "the look and movements of middle age." George Hunt observed of his marine comrades that "every face seemed older than it should have been, more hard-bitten." Infantryman Grady Arrington barely recognized a college friend who had recently seen combat, but by his friend's reaction when he hailed him, Arrington realized that he would have to introduce himself: his friend entirely failed to recognize him. There was ample Civil War testimony to the physical costs of combat. Confederate Robert Stiles, watching Mahone's division return from the Petersburg trenches, wrote that the soldiers' appearance "made us realize, for the first time, what our comrades . . . were undergoing. We were shocked at the condition, the complexion, the expression of the men . . . [Indeed,] we could scarcely realize that the unwashed, uncombed, unfed and almost unclad creatures we saw were officers of rank and reputation in the army." But here, as in almost all Civil War narratives, the sense conveyed was one of a discrete trial of special severity rather than a profound and enduring physical transformation.[24]

Soldiers of the Civil War and World War II followed similar pathways in moving from their expectations to the actualities of combat. In both conflicts, battle took a heavy toll of their physical and psychological resources. But the World War II soldier confronted a combat whose scale, intensity, and strength of weaponry threatened his constitution in ways that seldom emerged in the Civil War. While, in the latter, the consequences of combat could ordinarily be confined within the category of disillusionment, in the case of the World War II soldier persisting in combat, they more often proceeded to physical and psychological disintegration.

Seldom was there in the Civil War a *cri de coeur* like that of combat pilot John Muirhead—"We fought because [the man beside us] fought; we died because he died."[25]—so exemplary of the World War II soldier's greater absorption in combat, his more profound loss of control and efficacy; his lesser ability to envision activity beyond battle or existence beyond war; his gravitation to the conclusion that for him, there was no alternative but simply going on—and going on.

5

Gendering Two Wars

D'ANN CAMPBELL
RICHARD JENSEN

AMILY, gender, and death were inextricably bound up in what it
meant to be a soldier in the Civil War and World War II. This essay
will look at some aspects of family and gender roles, with special emphasis
on how soldiers were tied to their families, especially their womenfolk, and
how in turn the families and women related to the war, and to the threat of
death. Private versus public was the classic tension in the lives of American women. But the patriotic demands of wartime highlighted the tension
and added new dimensions as well.

Both wars were "total wars"—in the sense that virtually every sector
of society and economy became involved. To call women "civilians" is a
technicality; in total war everyone contributes to the war effort. World War
II is distinctive from the Civil War in that the fighting was much more
remote, and the government apparatus that affected women much more
complex and effective. On the other hand, the emotional and patriotic
identification with the nation-state and the war effort may have been

greater during the Civil War. By comparing two total wars that happened eighty years apart, we can see how changing social structures and changing values affected the responses of Americans to issues of gender and family. We can see if the total war element created psychological pressures and broke down internal barriers to traditional gender roles. By looking at the crises of separation, fear, and death we can probe a little deeper into just which values Americans held most dear, and which values they reluctantly gave up. From the point of view of the nation, we can ask how the morale and support of the civilian population affected national decisions. We have the advantage for World War II of numerous surveys of soldiers and civilians. We also have interviews taken many years later with veterans—with female veterans, that is, for the male veterans of World War II have been strangely ignored by scholars.

The morale of the homefront populace was a critical element for both North and South in the Civil War, and for the entire nation in World War II. As Robert E. Lee explained a month before Appomattox, "Everything in my opinion has depended and still depends upon the disposition and feelings of the people . . . the difficulties and sufferings of their condition."[1] Historians must examine what roles women played in creating and maintaining, or undermining, that morale. The reverse, the impact of the war on women, may be thought of as the other side of the coin. The intrusion of public warfare into the private domain of family and home had critical consequences. We will look at the consequences of withdrawing the young male breadwinners from the family economy, and the psychological consequences of the threat of death of loved ones, and (for the Confederacy) devastation of homes and homelife. The communications between the soldiers and their womenfolk were critical to the morale of the army and the nation. Most of all, we will look at the central emotional theme of both wars, death itself. First let us consider the communication linkages between soldiers and the homefront.

LETTERS

The main mechanism of long-distance communications was the letter. In peacetime, the enlisted men of the army and navy were rarely connected to their families and communities of origin. The army was often an escape; instead of enjoying the esteem of the community, soldiers were reviled. In wartime, on the other hand, soldiers were not alienated but comprised the most committed, the most attached, Americans. Connections between home and field were strong, with the maintenance of the ties largely a female role. During the Civil War, most regiments were geographically based. Indeed, hometown politicians often raised the regiment in the first place, and officers included many aspiring politicians eager to make use of military contacts in their postwar careers. The effect of geographical concentration was to increase greatly the flow of information to soldiers. They often read letters aloud, and if one man's correspondent gave an overly rosy picture of conditions at home, the letters from the next two or three men would set it straight. Conversely, the behavior of any one soldier was public knowledge in his home community because his comrades could and did write to the same community. The Civil War soldiers, both South and North, had a sense of fighting for their homes, their families, and their communities; they stayed in close touch and their communities kept watch over them.

An insight into the domesticity dimension of the correspondence comes from looking at an important ingredient in the letters from Confederate soldiers: food, a topic clearly in the female domain. Men accustomed to rich peacetime diets were sometimes more afraid of starvation than of Yankees. Inadequate nutrition helped bring on depression, lethargy, and night blindness, and made the soldiers more susceptible to infectious disease. The situation steadily worsened in the rebel army, but even more threatening to morale were the letters from home reporting that actual starvation for the women and children was a real threat. As a young Confederate woman explained:

> Two more months of danger, difficulties, perplexities, and starvation will lay [Mother] in her grave. . . . Lilly has been obliged to put her children to bed to make them forget they were supperless, and when she followed their example, could not sleep herself, for very hunger.[2]

In World War II, military units were not tied to localities; National Guard divisions had a state base, but they usually had too large a cachement base to sustain a sense of community identity. The constant flow of letters between home and camp provided the daily tangible evidence not so much of community as of the support of the narrower base of family and friends. (In the peacetime army, letters from home and boxes of cookies and socks played a minor role in maintaining morale.) As a Hoosier stationed in Alaska discovered in 1943, "To me, letters from home or meeting a home town boy, are much more welcome than 'pay call.'"[3]

Communication in the other direction was difficult to maintain in World War II. Townspeople relied upon generalized newsreel footage, canned magazine stories, and standardized publicity stories churned out by the military to keep track of the boys in uniform, but the perfunctory stories provided precious little detail and rarely any human interest. The Civil War practice of hometown boys sending back a stream of letters designed for publication in the local press seems to have been much less common.

Illiteracy—or at least inability to compose a letter—was widespread, but there was usually someone around who could write or read a message, especially if the contents were important enough. Illiterate soldiers were less effective soldiers. The navy discovered in World War II that men unable to read or write letters home developed morale problems. As the navy's Director of Training reported: "A knowledge of reading and writing helped overcome feelings of inferiority, and tended to develop initiative, aggressiveness, and more willing acceptance of the condition of military life."[4] Army psychiatrists felt that there should be a nationwide educational program to educate civilians in how to write effective letters to their soldiers.

INFORMATION & RUMOR

In both wars, information was a weapon, as indeed was misinformation. In World War II the government systematically controlled and monitored the media, censoring news and vetting the scripts of Hollywood movies. The goals were to maintain military and civilian morale, to detect deviations in public opinion from Washington's official policies, and to identify trouble spots that might require federal intervention. The military systematically censored letters, in part to eliminate information that might be useful to the enemy, and in part to monitor exactly what the men were

thinking. Censorship units compiled fat monthly reports of soldiers' attitudes. (Censorship seemed at first a natural job for the WAC, but too
many women were stunned and nauseated by the contents of the mail;
they had to be replaced by men.) The government provided movies and
briefings for the troops, but hard news was at a premium.

The belief that had developed in the late 1930s that the public opinion poll was a powerful democratic instrument for putting the people in
touch with their government—without intermediaries like the media or
the politicians—was now turned on its head. Polls became a device to
ensure that the people stayed in line with the government. The main
survey program was centered in the Department of Agriculture, with
support from the National Opinion Research Center in Denver. In totalitarian Germany and in democratic Britain, the governments likewise
systematically collected reports on public opinion on the homefront. Supplementing the statistical surveys, the Office of War Information systematically clipped and classified newspaper editorials, sent its own reporters
across the country to look for trouble brewing, and enlisted large teams of
volunteer community leaders, labor observers, and plain housewives to
write weekly reports on local conditions. The censorship and monitoring
soon gave way to direct manipulation of public opinion. In early 1943 the
Office of War Information pressed for publication of the available atrocity
stories. They were to serve as an antidote to complacency about the war
and preoccupation with internal controversies; as an incentive to production and the war bond drive; and as a safety valve for pent-up frustration
concerning the Pacific front.

The problem with manipulating the news was that women paid scant
attention. Men and boys closely followed the latest radio, newsreel, and
newspaper reports from the world's battlefronts. Single women, however,
were for the most part uninterested in the war: "A big tank or bomber gets
my boy friend all excited, but it leaves me completely cold."[5] Married
women related war news to their family concerns, and usually were more
troubled about rationing snafus and shortages than military campaigns. A
solution to the lack of interest of women was the government's effort to
present the war as an opportunity to fulfill private goals. Norman Rockwell
translated Roosevelt's Four Freedoms into hometown terms. This was to
be literally a war for apple pie and the girl left behind. One unanticipated

consequence was a shift to the right politically, as the collective liberal goals of the New Deal were forgotten. No matter how much the old New Dealers railed against "fascism at home," the movement was toward a conservative nuclear family safely ensconced in its suburb.

In the Civil War, misinformation was a grave problem, as the newspapers especially were given to gross exaggeration. Soldiers often boasted how they won battles that later historians would agree were victories for the other side. Not until the last year of the war did the Confederate infantry realize how badly it had been defeated. On the homefront, expectations and fears restructured what news was available. In the Confederacy, where economic disruptions largely largely shut down the news media, rumor seized control. Henrietta Barr of Virginia understood the risks as she wrote in July 1862:

> People are in an awful state of excitement. . . . They are just about ready to believe anything they hear provided it is horrible. . . . I am getting so skeptical I am afraid I shall not believe the truth if I ever I should be fortunate enough to hear it again.[6]

Whatever critical sense she steeled herself with, rusted as the war progressed. A year later she told her diary:

> A rumor reaches us of a great battle at Gettysburg. Of course General Lee is victorious although the Yankee papers are not willing to give him full credit for it. . . . A report that "Vicksburg has fallen" I do not credit. I must have better proof than mere hearsay.[7]

The government—and the media—could not really control public opinion. Rumor outran fact; private needs overrode patriotic demands. The people created their own images of the war and fitted them to their own values.

FURLOUGHS

About furloughs little is known, except that the soldiers and their women of course appreciated and demanded them. The Confederacy shifted from a fairly lenient policy to one that made furloughs hard to get—even though armies did little fighting in winter, they had to be kept in camp. Sick men were to be kept in hospitals, not sent home for care, perhaps because of suspicion they would not so quickly return to the ranks. The internal transportation system in the Confederacy was so poor that it would have been difficult indeed for a soldier to travel 200 miles on furlough and return in a month's time. When units were transferred far from home, desertions surged. Often hard-pressed commanders did not honor promises of furloughs; other times the men would forge passes, sell passes, or overstay authorized leaves. The rebels who enlisted for one year's service in the Army of Tennessee were stunned to discover that General Bragg would neither release them nor allow them furloughs to return home after a year. At least one regiment mutinied—Bragg crushed the mutiny—and many subsequently deserted to care for families that were by now behind Union lines. (Bragg shot any deserter he caught.) In the winter of 1864–65, Union soldiers who refused to re-enlist were kept in camp, while those who re-enlisted were given a 35-day furlough and a handsome bonus. As a Vermont private explained:

> Furloughs are the most precious privileges that the government allows their soldiers, and the prospect of going home has tempted a good many soldiers to re-enlist when nothing else would.[8]

The South needed re-enlistments too but was far less generous—giving furloughs to one soldier in ten in regiments that re-enlisted en masse. One reason for the importance of furloughs was the tensions between husband and wife, which most often involved sexual jealousies and fears of unfaithfulness. The Confederate government had a state reason to give more furloughs: the men could do farm work that was critical to the new nation's precarious food supply. The Yankees had a political motivation: in the 1862 and 1864 elections, Union soldiers from critical states were furloughed home to vote—especially to Indiana, where the legislature refused to allow voting in the field.

No one has tracked the patterns of furloughs in World War II, but we do know that frequent furloughs were a critical ingredient in bonding soldiers and their wives and were important for morale. Furloughs from the overseas battlefields were very hard to obtain, of course, but most of the soldiers were stationed in the States until late 1944. With the training camps located in remote areas, they were allowed frequent furloughs home—a process that overloaded the railroad system. From 1940 to 1943 the number of train passengers doubled, as did the average length of journey.

The critical ingredient in the furlough was the opportunity for the soldier, his family, and his community to reinforce their mutual solidarity. The men had so much to do, and so little time, that they moved double time (leading to fears they would be permanently changed psychologically). Indeed, when they returned, they often hurried to make up for "lost" time, as in the cases of the G.I.s who returned to school. A second element of the furlough was the implicit contract that the legalistic and individualistic American soldiers have always assumed they had with the government. Especially during the Civil War, soldiers had a sense that the army "owed" them a furlough, and when a deserved leave did not materialize, they were ready to mutiny or go A. W. O. L. The soldiers felt they were not "deserting" because they more-or-less planned to return. Deserters faced prison, though frequently the Confederacy offered amnesty for the tens of thousands of unaccountably missing soldiers.

Before 1863, in the Civil War, there was a legitimate way to force a furlough: surrender! By 1864, forty-nine regiments of the Confederate Army of the Tennessee, 28 percent of the total, had surrendered at least once and been "exchanged." Soldiers who were captured were given their release under an "exchange" agreement. They could go home and wait for their nation to arrange the paperwork of "exchange," then they would have to return to duty. Some soldiers perhaps voluntarily surrendered (as individuals) to take advantage of the system. The exchange system broke down on the race question (the Confederacy refused to exchange captured black Union soldiers), and, more subtly, on Grant's realization that the Confederacy needed its prisoners back much more urgently than he did.

After the summer of 1863, the rebel armies began to evaporate away slowly, with desertions and absentees without leave claiming up to half the nominal soldiers, and with new enlistments trickling off. When the home-front morale broke, the Confederate soldiers had to desert. If soldiers represented their communities—not just the Confederate nation itself—then the demands of their communities came first. That is, they competed with the demands of family. Indeed, the demands from women that their husbands return immediately to protect them from starvation or slave insurrection had become important by Gettysburg, and grew more insistent month by month. Confederate recruiters reported as early as 1863 that in backcountry parts of South Carolina:

> The tone of the people is lost; it is no longer a reproach to be known as a deserter; all are ready to encourage and aid the efforts of those who are avoiding duty, and to refuse information to and thwart and even resist those who seek to make arrests. . . .[9]

Historian Albert Kirwan concludes: "Thus had morale on the homefront deteriorated to the point where armies could not be kept in the field. The thread of life for the Confederacy was almost spun out."[10]

HOMEFRONT ECONOMICS

In the Civil War women contributed to the war effort in several ways. Some moved into the paid labor force, and others did volunteer work raising funds (as at Sanitary Fairs) or helping in hospitals. Women inside the home found time to make certain supplies for soldiers, such as clothing and bandages. More than a thousand Confederate ladies' relief societies were spontaneously created; the more modern, more organizationally minded Yankees established perhaps twenty thousand women's societies. Similar relief societies existed in World War II—many of which, like the U. S. O.-sponsored groups, provided valuable recreation to traveling soldiers. Others, like the tens of thousands of local Red Cross chapters that hand-rolled bandages, were artificial efforts to provide society women a semblance of patriotic participation. Housewives managing the domestic economy reduced their consumption patterns. Some of the reduction enabled food and supplies to be diverted to the military. Most of all, women diverted time—they rescheduled household duties. "I find that I can manage my housework and job without trouble," explained a welder in New York. "I wash on Mondays, iron on Tuesdays, and cook one night for the next."[11] Many women gave up hours of precious sleep. In both wars, reduced consumption was forced by a fall in purchasing power (that is, Washington and Richmond both printed paper money to pay contractors, with the resulting inflation hurting consumers). In the Confederacy, the faltering transportation and marketing systems caused reductions in household consumption with no compensating benefit to the war effort.

Given the fraction of Northern and Southern farming families, the role of women in the adjustment of the rural economy was perhaps as important as any other economic contribution. Some women replaced soldiers by taking on farm jobs not customarily done by women. How many and in what roles—this is the sort of answer that letters will provide, as women asked questions and soldier spouses sent back detailed instructions on farm management. Young men below military age probably expanded their work roles. So did young unmarried women. Some farm work was reduced or postponed (like maintenance and expansion); in the North, new machinery like reapers replaced some soldiers. In every section, some farms reduced the scope of operations or shifted the mix of crops and animals. In many cases (especially in the South), the women abandoned the farms and merged into the households of relatives, or even became refugees. We lack even rudimentary quantitative estimates of exactly what mix of strategies farm families used.

We know much more about the economic roles of women in World War II; the government had excellent statisticians. Furthermore, thanks to new polling techniques, we have public-opinion surveys that tell a good deal about what women thought of the war (or at least how they answered questions put to them in a standardized fashion). The challenge to historians of the war decade is to weigh the carrot and the stick—to estimate how women balanced inducements (like patriotism and money) against structural factors manipulated by the government. Women who preferred to spend their time caring for family members discovered the allotment paid to soldiers' wives was so small they had to find paid jobs. As a Schenectady, New York, war worker told a state investigator, "After the war, I want to be a housewife and to take care of our baby . . . but the allotment isn't enough to live on and I have to work now."[12] The money women earned can be calculated to the penny, and the surveys tell us a great deal about patriotic impulses. What is hard to gauge is the effect on women's roles during World War II of permanent structural factors (like class, age, race) and malleable factors (like geography and public services).

At two points during World War II a coalition of government agencies made a systematic effort to reach ALL the women in a particular community, to sign them up for war jobs, or to enlist them in the WAC or WAVES. The recruiters used media barrages by radio, newspaper, billboard and poster. They worked through clubs and community groups. They made personal face-to-face calls on 75,000 families in Cleveland, for example. Both campaigns ended in failure; in Cleveland, only 168 women enrolled in the WAC. The second drive targeted Akron, Milwaukee, Buffalo, Syracuse, Detroit, and some New England mill towns, appealing to women to take paying jobs. In Akron, interviewers talked to 87,000 housewives, of whom 630 in fact took jobs. Women simply were not willing to respond to propaganda barrages organized by strangers. Women set their own agendas and would not be moved. The result was a humbling learning experience for advertising agencies which had long held as an article of faith that given enough time and effort they could sell anything to anybody. American advertising learned that it had to rethink its basic proposition. They had to ask what is it that people wanted, then try to demonstrate that their product answered those needs—needs that had been autonomously generated by consumers themselves.

MARRIAGE

The most dramatic contradiction between patriotic and private lives came with marriage. Marriage was an inconvenience for the war effort. The custom of the 1940s called for new brides to quit their paid jobs, and set up housekeeping. The government wanted the women to stay on the job; and by stopping the construction of houses, apartments, house trailers, furniture and appliances, made it difficult indeed to get a marriage started. The surge in marriages and births that followed Pearl Harbor was not authorized ("If the Army wanted you to have a wife," old-timer sergeants explained to recruits, "it would have issued you one"). Until late 1944, most men in uniform were still stationed in training facilities and bases in the States, and if they were married without children, their wives tried to be near them. About half the wives succeeded. The government refused to build emergency housing for these wives near military stations, and tried generally to send the camp followers back home—that is, back to where they would find a paid job in a war plant. The camp followers, of course, were annoyed. "The war worker's wife gets a house and a big salary," they fumed. "What do we get?" Nothing—that was the point.[13] The government wanted them to go back home. To make sure they took a job when they did go back, Washington kept soldiers' pay scales and dependent allowances low, and refused to establish the sort of enlistment bonuses that were so important during the Civil War. With the draft running so smoothly, there was no need in World War II to offer financial incentives to prospective enlistees. In the Civil War, officers' wives occasionally followed their men to war, but enlisted men's wives rarely visited or stayed long. After 1862, respectable women rarely stayed with Confederate troops. Indeed, apart from prostitutes and nurses, it was an unusual sight to see a woman anywhere near most army camps. The soldiers had to get their familial support long distance.

In 1941, from the private point of view, after a dozen years of Depression, disappointment, and delay, it was time to get married and start a family. Marriage, and parenthood was the normal route to adult stature, and postponing it became harder and harder. Setting up a new household required ingenuity and help, given the shortage of apartments, furniture, and appliances. Servicemen's wives typically returned to their parents' home, a doubling up that would not be relieved until around 1948 when the postwar housing boom finally caught up with demand. Worse than the inconvenience and the delay was the loneliness. Young couples had discarded much of the tradition that had separated husbands and wives into different spheres and they sought equalitarian marriages focused on nuclear relationships. The long enforced separation of the affiancéd and newlyweds in World War II seems to have produced not divorce but a more intimate, companionate partnership—a phenomenon that can also be detected on a much less pronounced level during the Civil War. Despite the myth of an upsurge in divorces (in fact, divorce rates changed little in the 1940s), 27 percent of the wartime marriages eventually ended in divorce, compared with 26 percent for the late 1930s and 26 percent for the late 1940s. Couples were child-oriented, and in 1940 they began a "baby boom" that lasted until 1960. Between 1940 and 1942, the rate of first births jumped from 293 per 10,000 women to 375 (the rate of subsequent births went from 506 to 540). The increase in childbearing took place among all groups of young women, but was greatest among the best educated, who had the most resources and the most opportunities to understand and control their lives.

The family orientation in both wars was reflected in the conscription laws. In the Civil War, the Yankees' substitute system allowed families to choose which member went to war and which stayed home. The Confederacy was less flexible, leading to a heavy flow of appeals from womenfolk that the particular man or boy drafted or enlisted be spared to them. In World War II, there was almost no flexibility at the individual level, though a man could volunteer ahead of the draft and get some choice of how he served. Much of the debate on the World War II draft focused on fathers and eighteen-year-olds. Public opinion strongly opposed sending either one to combat. Indeed, very few fathers ended up in combat.

In the Civil War, the patriarchal family system was the norm in the South, and very prevalent in the North as well. How did patriarchal families cope with the absence of the patriarch? Some historians have suggested severe strains resulted, that letters and furloughs could only partially overcome. As in World War II, a doubling up with parents was common for soldiers' wives. The inability of traditional patriarchal families to provide for minimal needs of wives and children was pronounced in the South, but also was a factor in the North. In the North, the needs of impoverished soldier-families were met by locally organized relief programs. Often the help was orchestrated by Republican party operatives, as in Muncie, Indiana, at Thanksgiving 1864, when all able-bodied Unionists went into the woods to chop a winter's wood supply for soldier-families.

PATRIOTISM

Sacrifice and self-abnegation were central to the roles of women-at-war. The first duty of patriotic women was to send their men off to war, as explained by the editors of the *Boston Evening Gazette* in May of 1861:

The affluent send their sons and the fondest mothers shed tears of joy as boys leave for the field. Wives smother their emotions of tenderness and gird on the sword of their husbands for the fight, while the maiden who was but the gay butterfly of society takes the needle and ends in equipping troops for the contest.[14]

When the Confederate cause appeared problematic in Kentucky in 1862, invading rebel armies failed to enlist the number of volunteers they sought. "Enthusiasm is unbounded," Confederates discovered, "but recruiting at a discount; even the women are giving reasons why individuals cannot go."[15]

Acceptance, or willingness to send the menfolk off to war, involved not just the original departure. Perhaps more important was the continuous flow of support from the women toward their soldiers. The question of re-enlistment was especially critical. Veterans who felt they had performed their patriotic duty wanted to come home. Would the women also want it or send them back to war? How many women echoed the Massachusetts mother who instructed her sons in February 1864:

> Dear boys dont be discouraged. Yours is a holy cause a just cause and may the God of battles watch over and protect you is my constant prayer.[16]

When Vermont private Wilbur Fisk went absent without leave from his hospital bed to spend more time at home, his bride insisted he return. Frequently during the Civil War, Yankees reported with amazement, or amusement, that the Southern women were more ardent Confederates than the menfolk. The Yankee reports usually came from victorious invaders, who had already defeated the rebel men, and who now co-occupied the same public spaces as the rebel women. Nannie Haskins said in Clarksville, Tennessee, in 1863, "[I] never see [a Yankee] but what I roll my eyes, grit my teeth, and almost shake my teeth at him, and then bite my lip and turn away in disgust."[17] In the case of New Orleans, the solution found by Ben Butler (in treating hostile Confederate women as prostitutes) was an act of symbolic rape that stunned the Confederacy (and Europe as well). Yankees thought that the Southern she-devils by rebelling had forfeited their feminine claims.

In World War II there were fears that women were too private, insufficiently bloodthirsty, and that this might lead to demands for a premature peace. Perhaps the military was especially cognizant of the 1920s, when a strong public sentiment in favor of peace and pacifism—led by women—had hamstrung the military, or as late as the isolationist debates of 1940–41, when women were conspicuously opposed to intervention. The morale of the men was a major concern of the army; it produced many surveys of attitudes. The evidence is fairly strong that most enlisted men, and many officers, were motivated primarily by private individual goals rather than patriotic goals. The army told them to do their job right and they would all get home safely. When men worried, they worried about their health and their homes—far less often were they concerned with death or injury. The flow of letters from home reinforced this private view: rarely were soldiers urged to fight harder. The private correspondence was nothing at all like the government posters. Most letters reflected a nostalgic sentimentality of good times past, and always the urgent inquiry, when are you coming home? That indeed was the foremost question on the minds of soldiers as well.

FIGHTING WOMEN

The Confederates had a deeply rooted fear of pillage, mayhem, murder, and rape at the hands of deserters, Yankee invaders, or—most fearful of all—rebellious slaves. As early as January 1862, Georgia leaders issued a dire warning: the foot of the oppressor is on the soil of Georgia. "He comes with lust in his eye, poverty in his purse, and hell in his heart. He comes a robber and a murderer. . . ."[18] Southern rhetoric was worried:

> Neither life nor virtue is sacred from these northern barbarians; the old and infirm perish by their bloody hands, while lovely women—our wives and daughters—are reserved for a fate even worse than death.[19]

With the able-bodied white men away at war, self-defense became a female responsibility. Many thousands moved their families into safer areas. Most had to stay home—and the question is, how did the Confederates prepare their women for self-defense? Or did they prepare them at all? Georgia leaders advised women to practice scorched earth as the Yankees approached:

Let blackness and ruin mark your departing steps, if depart you must, and let a desert more terrible than Sahara welcome the Vandals. Let every city be levelled by the flame, and every village be lost in ashes. . . . Let, then, the smoke of your homes, fired by women's hands, tell the approaching foe that over sword and bayonet they will rush only to fire and ruin.[20]

There is no evidence that a scorched earth policy was ever followed. In the case of Sherman's March that strategy would have been counterproductive anyway, since Sherman could have turned in any direction. We have occasional statements by women who volunteered to set up female drill units, and scattered references to having a pistol or shotgun readied for self-defense. But we seem to be lacking any evidence of systematic arming or training of homefront women to prepare them for self-defense or defense of their homesteads. Was this an oversight or was, in fact, the Southern culture of violence restricted by custom solely to males? Women rarely went hunting or target shooting—before, during, or after the war. Armed self-defense is perhaps a theme of the 1990s that is being projected back onto a different era.

The American army, navy and marines in World War II created women's units, but, with an eye to public opinion, prohibited them from taking any weapons-training. When some WAVES handled sentry duty at Hunter College, the *New York Times* with alarm reported, "Hands Destined to Rock the Cradle Now Wield Billies with Lethal Power." The British, short of manpower, used women in combat roles, in anti-aircraft units. The women were able to handle all the duties, but were never allowed to pull the trigger, even when the target was a Luftwaffe pilot. The Germans had women's units in semi-combat roles, and also trained some civilian women in self-defense against the Russian invaders. The Russian army, serious about winning their war, used women in many frontline combat positions. Clearly, as late as 1945, there was deep ambivalence about training women to shoot men—indeed, the intense debate over women in combat in the 1990s shows the issue is still alive.

In the Civil War it was simply assumed by everyone that warfare was synonymous with manhood, and that women could never be soldiers. Women who located themselves near military encampments were labeled as sexually immoral—including the nurses. A Philadelphian wrote home in 1862, "There is a spirit of criticism & I might say sort of *slur* thrown out to those young ladies which attend the Hospitals."[21]

In World War II the nurses were not denounced and repudiated; they represented life, and the soldiers welcomed them. Other women in uniform were a different matter. While generals and admirals, after much initial reluctance, learned to appreciate the value of WACs, WAVES, SPARS, and Women Marines—and at the end of the war they pleaded, and demanded, that Congress make permanent the women's services— the women veterans were much more ambivalent. And the GIs never learned to appreciate servicewomen. Those who were gung-ho fighters felt their masculinity degraded—if "girls" could do their jobs, then being a soldier was not very masculine. Men in larger numbers were quite happy with their non-combat jobs, and were alarmed that women would replace them and force them into combat units. Women in uniform represented death. Rank and file opinion normally carried little weight in the military—but this time the men had a weapon they were not afraid to use: they created and circulated false rumors about the sexual promiscuity of the servicewomen. They warned their sisters and friends to avoid enlistment at all costs. Four decades after the event, one woman was still unable to hide her anger and shame:

> I joined the Waves and went to West Coast to be near my childhood sweetheart. While in Boot Camp, he sent a letter, ashamed of me for being in the service (called me a whore), I cried every night of Boot.[22]

The ugly stories had a devastating impact on recruiting; instead of the million WACs that the Pentagon had hoped for, the total came to 140,000, along with 100,000 WAVES, 13,000 SPARS, and 23,000 Women Marines. In fact, the service women were much less promiscuous or sexually active than servicemen, or than civilian women back home. But the scandal campaign soured their enthusiasm, and the vast majority quit as soon as possible after the war. When the Pentagon wanted to make the women's services permanent after the war, at least half the senior women officers opposed the idea. They had been humiliated at the hands of this man's army.

DEATH

War and death seem inextricably linked. This linkage, however, might be a historians' conceit, or an artifact of how we think about warfare today. The question is how people at the time thought of death, and how they linked the question of death to war in general and their own circumstances in particular. During the mid-nineteenth century, death meant something very different from what it did in the 1940s. People then were familiar with death at first hand. Infant mortality was high; there were far more fatal diseases that struck during youth and middle age; and death normally occurred at home, rather than in antiseptic hospitals or speeding ambulances. The gothic dimension of the romantic religiosity of the nineteenth century included a liturgy of death. The cemetery caught the popular imagination; even soldiers would visit them in their leisure hours, reading the epitaphs, contemplating the tombstones. Wakes, funerals, eulogies focused on the question of a "good death." Death was omnipresent, and the rituals surrounding death were central to the notion of family and community. Everyone knew they were to die—preachers reminded them weekly that they knew not the hour. The challenge was to be prepared for death, to die in a suitable way, and to be buried by the community. (The anonymous pauper's burial was the cruelest fear.) Civilians, however, seldom died unexpectedly. Normally there was sickness, with a prescribed ritual for how the sufferer should prepare, and how family and friends should behave. When the sad news arrived from Spotsylvania, Margaret Scott wrote her sister:

> He was shot in the head and died instantly, oh how like a knell it rings in my ears. . . . He lays in a battle field far away without one moment's warning and could not send no message to the wife he loved so well.[23]

Sudden, unexpected death was a horrible thing to contemplate—a person would not have time to prepare. Yet sudden death from bullet or shell became the normal way young men died in 1862.

Soldiers on the Virginia battlefronts routinely encountered freshly dug graves, shipments of coffins, new burial grounds, or fragments of bone and flesh. The challenge for the soldiers—and for their communi-

ties—was how to redefine the proper death so that the casualties of war
could be fitted into their rituals, and the agonies of bleeding to death upon
the battlefield could be incorporated into the concept of a good death. The
Yankee solution was to expand the religious rhetoric to make the death of
a soldier a heroic community sacrifice for a higher cause. Two of the most
dramatic literary statements of the era helped make the soldier's death a
sacred event. Lincoln used the occasion of the dedication of the first
national cemetery at Gettysburg to rededicate the nation to a new birth of
freedom—it was the dead who had given their lives that the nation might
live. It was the duty of the living to finish the work for which they had given
the last full measure of devotion. Theologically, Yankee soldiers were
mostly postmillennialists, which meant they understood the need to purify
the nation before Christ's Second Coming. Fighting—dying—helped
hasten the day. Besides the Gettysburg Address, the second literary
statement which captures the spiritual context of this war was Julia
Ward Howe's "Battle Hymn of the Republic." The stanzas echo the religious message, "Mine eyes have seen the glory of the coming of the
Lord. . . . As He died to make men holy, let us die to make men
free."

In the Confederacy, religious meaning took a different form, with a
premillennial theme. Theologically, it was not possible to predict the
Second Coming, nor was it necessary to purify society before it could
happen. It was necessary instead to prepare the individual soul for death
and personal salvation—a theme taken up by wave after wave of soldiers in
a series of revivals that pointed them to a fatalistic acceptance of death and
the promise of heavenly reward. Hope for spiritual immortality replaced
fear of earthly death. "I do not fear to die," cried out General William
Dorsey Pender, mortally wounded at Gettysburg. "I can confidently re-
sign my soul to God, trusting in the atonement of Jesus Christ."[24] Religion served perhaps as a compensation for separation from loved ones—
an alternative reference point. During the late stages of the war, and
especially after it, white Southerners helped redefine their cultural and
national identity in terms of the sacrifices their fallen foldiers had made
for the "lost Cause." Thus, in August 1864, Milton Barrett wrote to his
sister to console her on the death of her husband:

Your husband is gone to a world of rest where there is no tumult of war. . . . He will suffer no more hunger nor thirst, so Dear Sister, grieve not at your loss, for your loss is his gains. He died an honorable death; he gave his life, a sacrifice for his country's rights.[25]

In demographic terms, about one-tenth of the Yankee soldiers died in uniform, and one-fourth of the Confederates. In sharp contrast to the images conjured up, however, only 22 percent of the deaths came on the battlefield; 66 percent were due to disease and accident, and 12 percent to complications from wounds. Thus most deaths took place in hospitals— and were more likely witnessed by women nurses than by male comrades. Some historians have suggested the high Southern casualty rates helped create religious revivals—religion as an escape mechanism. Whether the Civil War soldiers were in fact so fatalistic about death is unclear, and it has been suggested that a surge of female piety may have produced the revivals. Perhaps most of the concern with death came from civilians, while the soldiers themselves focused more upon being wounded. Death might be in Fate's domain, but not non-fatal wounds. By 1862 death for the soldier had been incorporated into community and religious ritual. Whereas non-fatal wounds were never part of it; some Republican politicians were known for years to "wave the bloody shirt," but they were talking about battle deaths not injuries. As for the Confederacy, an alarming risk had to do with civilian deaths through murder, pillage, or starvation. There was no glory in that; it was not sanctified by the community. The civilians became increasingly terrified that such dishonorable death might indeed be their fate if their menfolk did not desert and rush to take care of them. As one wife wrote:

Last night I was aroused by little Eddie's crying . . . and he said "Oh Mamma! I am so hungry." And Lucy, Edward, your darling Lucy; she never complains, but she is growing thinner and thinner every day. And before God, Edward, unless you come home we must die.[26]

Twentieth-century Americans have been obsessed not with dying but with living. Motivations for achievement and self-esteem rarely include plans to die well in a community setting. In World War II, combat infan-

trymen welcomed the "million dollar wound," which, if it preserved the
family jewels, provided a sure escape from the threat of death. Indeed, the
suffocating censorship of World War II guaranteed that while enemy
death was treated in exquisite detail, the fact of American deaths were
covered up or treated euphemistically. Nurses, for example, were trained
to hide death from dying patients: "I don't believe he is going to make it.
Honestly, it tears your heart out by the roots, but we don't talk about that.
The morale must be kept high. No one dares to let down."[27] Some G. I.s
were indeed fatalistic, but the evidence is mixed as to the extent of resig-
nation to battle casualties and death. In World War II, in sharp contrast to
the Civil War, relatively few soldiers in all were in great danger—although
riflemen, fliers, and submariners had far higher risks than the remaining
three-fourths of servicemen. Willingness to serve in combat varied greatly
in World War II. Rural men were much less willing to enter combat than
were city men, which seems to have been the reverse of the Civil War
pattern. In the 1940s the better educated, younger, unmarried city men
were the ones eager to fight.

CASUALTIES AND STRATEGY

For the historians of the state, the central question is how leaders
took into account the likelihood of deaths and casualties in making military
decisions. It has often been said that the British, with searing memories of
the blood-filled trenches of the Western Front in the 1914–18 war, were
reluctant to invade France in 1942 and 1943. It has been suggested that
Dwight D. Eisenhower refused to move on Berlin in 1945 because of his
unwillingness to incur hundreds of thousands of casualties—might as well
let the Russians capture the Nazi capital—in what proved to be one of the
bloodiest battles in modern history. The Japanese in late 1944 discovered
how to fight the Americans psychologically: fight not just to win battles
but to inflict casualties. The Japanese were willing to die for their country;
the Americans were not. It can be argued that the navy was so stunned
by the losses resulting from kamikaze attacks off Okinawa that Admiral
Ernest King opposed an invasion of the home islands and proposed
instead to strangle Japan to death by a tightened blockade rather than
plunge so deep into harm's way again. The army in 1945 supported

invasion plans for Japan because it ignored the very high American casualties at Iwo Jima and Okinawa and looked instead at the much lighter losses Douglas MacArthur had incurred in New Guinea and the Philippines. Furthermore, General George Marshall seems to have felt that the American public would not tolerate a long drawn-out blockade solution—which would have kept millions of men in uniform for another year or two. The public wanted their men back and soon. Secretary of War Henry Stimson and President Truman intervened in the debate and decided to go with the atomic option because they feared that Marshall and King were both right. The best way to end the war with minimal American casualties was to hit the Japanese with one stunning shock: drop the atomic bomb.

In the Civil War, fear of death could enter high strategy. When Grant began hammering Lee in the Wilderness campaigns, with fearful casualties and plunging public opinion, there was doubt whether the home-front—or indeed the frontline soldiers themselves—would tolerate much more of the slaughter. Lincoln was nervous about casualties at first, he then caught fire and ordered Grant to "hold on with a bull-dog grip, and chew & choke, as much as possible."[28] He pledged reinforcements to cover Grant's attrition strategy and mobilized the Republican/Union campaign machine to drum up support for the war. When, in August 1864, Republican leaders were pessimistic and even defeatist about the impact of the huge death toll on the fall elections, Lincoln secretly pledged himself and his cabinet to a resolute course. In a memorandum he had each cabinet member countersign—but not read—Lincoln swore that if McClellan and the Democrats won the November election, Lincoln would do absolutely everything in his power to guarantee a Union victory on the battlefield before the new President would be sworn into office in March of 1865. Lincoln and Grant realized that Lee was unable to replace the losses of the Army of Northern Virginia, and that a campaign of attrition would eventually crack the fortress of Confederate Richmond. In July 1864, Jefferson Davis told Lincoln, "This war must go on till the last of the generation falls in his tracks . . . unless you acknowledge our right to self-government."[29] Despite that avowal, the Confederate leadership made a decision in 1865 to accede to defeatist public opinion and surrender (or flee abroad) rather than wage guerrilla warfare. Throughout the border region, large-scale bushwhacking and murderous guerrilla warfare had indeed taken place for years, but it took place primarily in areas with low slave concentrations. Guerrilla warfare in the deep South perhaps threatened a race war that as an option for the white South, was no longer tolerable.

Comparative history—in this case comparisons across time—can be as problematic as comparative history across space and culture. However, it can also be as revealing. The nature of patriotism and community, of life and death, can be explicated by comparisons across North and South, and across a century of time. Perhaps historiography is moving into a post-modern stage focused on how people felt—in this instance, not how they felt good, but how they felt bad. If so, comparative history of the human psyche can reveal yet another stratum of the ways the American psyche responds to crisis.

6

Fighting on Two Fronts: War and the Struggle for Racial Equality in Two Centuries

IRA BERLIN

I N the African-American's struggle for racial equality, which to a re-markable degree has coincided with the history of the United States, few generalizations carry greater weight than the reality that black people have made more rapid progress toward that elusive goal in time of war than in peacetime. The outbreak of war has signaled an opportunity for black people to press their case for rights denied them in quieter times. The sad fact is that whenever the American Republic has been on the defensive, whenever its white rulers desperate for assistance and its white majority fearful for its security, black people have been able to exchange their loyalty, their labor, and often their lives for a more substantial stake in American society. Often they have done so by playing upon the founding ideal—"all men are created equal"—which inevitably re-emerged as a byproduct of wartime pressure for unity in the face of foreign enemies and internal division. But behind the leveraging of national ideology stands a more direct calculus—the exchange of blood for rights. That calculus rests upon a notion that military service validates claims to citizenship, an idea that even the most violent opponents of racial equality found difficult to deny.

The bargain was as old as the nation, for the initial trade was made in the War for Independence. In fighting for American liberty, black people gained their first substantial taste of freedom on the North American mainland. The American Revolution opened the door to freedom for African-American peoples, signaling the beginning of the end of slavery in the Northern states and the rise of a large free black population in the Southern ones. Subsequently, progress toward equality—admittedly uneven and always incomplete—can be observed with the enlistment of soldiers in the nation's ranks during the War of 1812, the various campaigns against Native Americans in the trans-Mississippi West, the Spanish American War, and the First and Second World Wars. More recently, the relation between military participation of African-Americans and the advance of racial equality can be traced further in the effects of the Cold War and the hot conflicts that accompanied it in Korea, Vietnam, and the Persian Gulf.

In each of these conflicts, at crucial moments, American success rested in some part upon the incorporation of black men—and later women—into the national army. As black men became soldiers, the American army became an army of liberation, and white Americans recognized—however reluctantly—the rights of black people, if only because black soldiers in the field—and their families and friends at home—would accept nothing less. Thus, the advance of racial equality and the participation of black people in the American military marched side by side.

War transformed black men into liberators in a variety of ways. Some of which were related to the formal recognition that accompanied military service, recognition that began with enlistment and extended to pensions, veterans' parades, and monuments on the courthouse green. But the influences of military service were numerous and complex. In dramatic and undeniable ways, military service reshaped relations between whites and blacks—placing in direct contact men and women who had previously known each other only as hollow stereotypes. These meetings opened the possibility for peoples of European and African descent to meet on new ground and to reshape their relationships in strikingly novel ways. While such confrontations often affirmed the old status quo, they sometimes opened the door to new thinking.

Such new possibilities could be revolutionary, for they presaged not only institutional reconstructions but also the most basic social and psychological transformations. The changes that accompanied military service reached deep into the psyche of individual black men and women, countering the degradation that had undermined the self-esteem bred by centuries of servitude and second-class citizenship. Battlefield confrontations with the enemy exhilarated black soldiers by demonstrating in the most elemental manner the essential equality of men—in the eyes of their fellows, their families, their communities, and ultimately the entire society. Pride in the martial achievement of black men resonated throughout the African-American community.

For such reasons, black soldiers coveted the liberator's role. But from the Revolution to the Gulf War, soldiering in the service of the United States was a complex, often contradictory experience whose effects moved in many directions. If many black men rushed to join American armies and stand in the front ranks, others entered military service reluctantly, often at the point of a bayonet. Once enlisted, moreover, black soldiers frequently found themselves enmeshed in yet another white-dominated hierarchy which, like the one they were seeking to escape or transform, assumed their inferiority. Generally, black soldiers were organized into separate regiments. Sometimes they were paid at lower rates than white soldiers and denied the opportunity to become commissioned officers. Often they were abused by commanders whose mode of discipline resembled that of the slave master, and frequently they were assigned to menial duties rather than battlefield roles. Black soldiers thus learned forcefully of the continued inequities of American life. Although they wore the same uniform as white soldiers, observed the same articles of war, answered to the same system of military justice, and confronted the same enemy, black soldiers always fought a different war. They continued to face enemies on two fronts, battling the foe within and the foe without to achieve freedom and equality. Indeed, again and again, black people have employed the metaphor of "Fighting on Two Fronts" to describe the unique character of the black military experience. Moreover, the duality did not end with the war, for upon their return to civilian life, black soldiers found themselves assaulted for the very service they rendered, precisely because progress toward equality on the warfront threatened the old status quo.

Nonetheless, military service gave black soldiers far more than an ambiguous duality—no matter how limited the official acceptance of their contribution or slight the recognition of their valor. Inevitably, in military service black soldiers gained new skills and a wider knowledge of the world. Fighting and dying in the nation's service undermined stereotypes of inferiority and advanced the claims of black people to all the rights and privileges of citizenship. Victory bred confidence, which black soldiers carried back to civilian life and which permeated the entire black community. The success of black soldiers in their struggle within the army politicized them and their families, and prepared all for the larger struggle ahead.

An analysis of the effects of war on the struggle for equality in two different centuries has large implications that literally march across American history. The wartime struggle for equality must be viewed first within the bounds of military life itself, for the soldier's struggle began within the ranks. Its effects soon spread beyond the bounds of the battlefield, boot camp, and barracks—as fighting for freedom touched the lives of the families of soldiers and their communities. It did so because the military service of black soldiers infused all black people, civilians as well as soldiers, with a fresh determination to seek full justice for themselves and their posterity. Indeed, the implications of war for the struggle for racial equality certainly outlasted the shooting and deeply influenced the course of post-war life.

The broad influence of war on the struggle for racial equality can be observed in every conflict in which the Republic has engaged, but nowhere were the transforming effects more direct than in the Civil War and World War II. Both conflicts required a complete mobilization of the material and moral resources of American society in which notions of freedom and equality became central to the nation's war aims. Indeed, as the Union in the mid-nineteenth century and the United States in the mid-twentieth century distinguished themselves from a foe that celebrated a racially based social order, American leaders elevated the principle of equality in the pantheon of American ideals. With Abraham Lincoln's Emancipation Proclamation and Franklin D. Roosevelt's Four Freedoms, ideas of universal liberty and equality took center stage. The nation's determination to meet its own high standard grew, as well as its sensitivity to charges of ideological hypocrisy.

While the ideological dynamics of the Civil War and World War II pressed the United States toward a full commitment to equality, there were other commonalities of a more practical sort. Both conflicts saw people of African descent play crucial roles in securing victory, and both allowed black people and their allies to secure substantial gains in the struggle for equality: the Civil War secured full liberation from bondage and, in time, a recognition of the rights of black people as citizens; World War II marked a fuller realization of those rights as citizens.

Both the Civil War and World War II opened the door to a larger struggle for racial equality—pressing the color line as never before. The Civil War initiated a profound revolution in race relations. That revolution destroyed forever a way of life based upon the ownership of human beings and restored to former slaves proprietorship in their own persons, forcibly substituting the relations of free labor for those of slavery. In designating the former slaves as citizens, changes that accompanied the Civil War placed citizenship upon new ground and led to an intense period of social reconstruction, closely supervised by the victorious North, which in many places lasted over a decade. During the period, former slaves challenged the domination of the old masters, demanding land and the right to control their own labor. In time, former masters, abetted by a complaisant President, defeated the freedpeople's bid for economic independence and imposed on them new legal and extra-legal constraints. But whatever the outcome, the struggle—deemed "Reconstruction"—transformed relations between white and black people.

World War II initiated a second revolution in race relations, and the years following it have been denoted the "Second Reconstruction." It too was a period of profound change in the standing of black people and the relations of white and black. It too was accompanied by great turmoil, political change, and constitutional revolution. If the Second Reconstruction, like the first, left the nation far short of the ideal of equality, it nevertheless marked a period of commitment during which the nation moved closer to the ideal.

The commonality of the struggle of black soldiers in two centuries gave black soldiers a common voice. Listen, for example, to Corporal William Henry Gooding protest the federal government's refusal to pay black and white soldiers at the same rate.

> Now the main question is. Are we *Soldiers*, or are we LABOURERS. We are fully armed, and equipped, have done all the various Duties, pertaining to a Soldiers life, have conducted ourselves, to the complete satisfaction of General Officers, who, were if any, prejudiced *against* us, but who now accord us all the encouragement, and honour due us: have shared the perils, and Labour, of Reducing the first stronghold, that flaunted a Traitor Flag: and more, Mr President. Today, the Anglo Saxon Mother, Wife, or Sister, are not alone, in tears for departed Sons, Husbands, and Brothers. The patient Trusting Decendants of Africs Clime, have dyed the ground with blood, in defense of the Union, and Democracy. Men too your Excellency, who know in a measure, the cruelties of the Iron heel of oppression, which in years gone by, the very Power, their blood is now being spilled to maintain, ever ground them to the dust. But When the war trumpet sounded o'er the land, when men knew not the Friend from the Traitor, the Black man laid his life at the Altar of the Nation,—and he was refused. When the arms of the Union, were beaten, in the first year of the War, And the Executive called more food. for its ravaging maw, again the black man begged, the privelege of Aiding his Country in her need, to be again refused, And now, he is in the War: and how has he conducted himself? Let their dusky forms, rise up, out the mires of James Island, and give the answer. Let the rich mould around Wagners parapets be upturned, and there will be found an Eloquent answer. Obedient and patient, and Solid as a wall are they. all we lack, is a paler hue, and a better acquaintance with the Alphabet. Now Your Excellency, We have done a Soldiers Duty. Why cant we have a Soldiers pay?[1]

Gooding's eloquent plea to President Lincoln was echoed by an anonymous black soldier stationed at Fort Logan, Colorado, writing to the *Pittsburgh Courier* some eighty years later.

We are colored soldiers who have been discriminated against terribly to the extent where we just can't possible stand any more. We're supposed to be representing part of the Army in which we're fighting for equality, justice and humanity so as all men, no matter of race, color, or creed, can be free to worship any way that they please.

Here on the Post we're treated like dogs. We work on different positions, sometimes for 9 or 10 hours daily. In the mornings we report to one particular job and at noon we are taken from the former one into a complete new one by orders of the white N. C. O.s and at these jobs we work at a very tiresome task, one that is unfit for even a dog. And yet the whites which are supposed to be a labor battalion just sit down and watch us do their work.

Even in eating time we were told to remain at attention outside the mess hall until the whites have finished eating, then we go and eat what's left over—food which is cold, tasteless and even sometimes dirty from sitting on tables from left overs.

Why can't we eat, live and be respected as the whites? We're constantly being cursed at, and mocked. But yet we too have to die as well as them, and even perhaps beside them. We have now come to the conclusion that before we'd be a slave, We'd rather be carried to our graves and go home to the Lord and be saved. In fact we'd rather be carried to our graves and go home to the Lord to be saved. In fact we'd rather die on our knees as a man, than to live in this world as a slave, constantly being kicked around by other just because we happen to be of the darker race.[2]

The similarities between the struggles of some 179,000 African-American soldiers who fought in the Civil War and the 700,000 who fought in World War II are so manifest as to make any discussion seem more like sociology than history—as black soldiers in the two eras struggled over the same questions of access to military service, the same rights to promotion within the ranks, the same denial of equality to treatment in the field and access to the prerogatives of military life, the same desire for justice, and—at war's end—the same prerogatives as veterans. The effects of the two wars were likewise similar, making visible the hypocrisy of inequality in the land of liberty, elevating the federal government to the role of the black man's surest advocate, and enlarging the constituency for racial equality.

The struggle over the right to serve suggests eerie parallels in the experience of black soldiers in the Civil War and World War II. At the beginning of the Civil War, few Union policy-makers foresaw a military role for black men—either free or slave. In the eyes of most Northern leaders and most white Northerners, the conflict would be a war for Union—not against slavery—fought by white men of each section. Most federal policy-makers and Union army commanders followed the same line of reasoning, as the prospect of arming black men—free as well as slave—raised fundamental questions about the place of black people in American society, questions that went far beyond the immediate demands of the war. White Americans deemed bearing arms in defense of the Republic an essential element of citizenship, and federal legislation dating from 1792 restricted militia enrollment to white men. They were not about to share the right with black men.

For just this reason, African-Americans and their abolitionist allies challenged these proscriptions as denial of both the fundamental rights of man and the rights of citizens. They protested such discrimination vigorously in the black and abolitionist press, from the pulpits of churches and lecterns of antislavery meetings, and in the person of the most visible black leaders: Frederick Douglass, Martin Delany, George Downing, and Henry M. Turner. To these men and their constituencies, enlisting black men into the Union army would not only embody a measure of equality most white Northerners refused to concede, but also enlarge the claims of black people to full citizenship. They challenged the racial basis of Northern society at a time when civil war threatened to redefine racial lines. If federal officials resisted this logic, blacks and their allies pressed it all the harder. Eventually black men—slave as well as free—gained entry to the Union army, but only as grim military necessity made manifest the importance of the Sable Arm.

On the eve of World War II, black men had secured a place within the American army—although, in sharp contrast to the Civil War, they had but limited place in the American navy, and no place in the Marine Corps. Still, the battle to secure equal access to military service in the mid-twentieth century followed a path similar to that of the Civil War struggle. Black men and their allies sought a connection between full citizenship and full participation while federal officials—reflecting the sentiment of most white Americans—were reluctant to allow equal access to military service lest it provide access to a larger equality.

Even before the United States entered the worldwide conflict, black leaders had organized the Committee for Negro Participation in the National Defense and begun a campaign to enroll black men in the air corps—an effort capped by the successful creation of the famous Tuskegee Black Eagles. Once the war was under way, the issue shifted to equity in conscription, as the rate of induction of black draftees was lower by some 50 percent—a difference officials attributed to higher rates of venereal disease and lower standards of education among black Americans. Black people and their white allies protested this inequity with all the fervor an earlier generation had used to challenge the refusal to enlist black men in the Union army. The pages of the *Pittsburgh Courier* and the *Chicago Defender*, the preachers in African-American churches, and speakers for civil-rights organizations like the NAACP and National Urban League blistered the federal policy much as the abolitionist press, the black churches, and antislavery meetings had earlier criticized the denial of black enlistment. Black leaders like Walter White, William H. Hastie, and A. Philip Randolph took up the soldiers' cause much as Douglass, Delany, Downing, and Turner had done in an earlier era. In time, black leaders gained the parity they desired, and black men were inducted into the army in rough proportion to their numbers in the population.

As in the Civil War era, it took the mobilization of black people and their allies on the homefront and military necessity on the warfront to secure equal access to military service. But, suggesting the distance between the full incorporation of black soldiers in the American army in 1941 and their enlistment in 1863, there were also differences. Even before the start of World War II, a black man—Benjamin Davis—wore a general's star; a black man—William Hastie—sat as an aide to the Secretary of War; and black men served in greater numbers than ever before. Still, numerous inequities remained, and the parallels in the experience of black soldiers in two centuries did not disappear with their enlistment into the Union army.

Of all the inequities faced by Civil War soldiers, none angered them more than the policy of paying black soldiers less than white ones. While not necessarily more blatant or inequitable in intent or effect than other discriminatory actions by the federal government, this policy fully revealed the unfairness of the federal military services—and American society.

Black soldiers were promised equal pay by numerous federal officials, including the Secretary of War and his representatives. But, with the
admission of black men into federal service in 1862, the War Department
ruled that the legal basis for the service of black soldiers lay in the 1862
Militia Act and paid all black soldiers according to its provisions: $10 per
month, minus $3 for clothing, rather than $13 per month, plus clothing,
which white privates received. Even black commissioned and non-
commissioned officers received the same $7 monthly pay, so that the
highest ranking black officers gained barely half the compensation of the
lowest ranking white enlisted man.

The practice of paying black soldiers less violated what black soldiers
believed to be one of the first assurances they had received from those who
recruited them: they would receive the same remuneration as white soldiers. Unequal pay imposed severe strains on the families dependent upon
black soldiers for their support, but the principle mattered at least as
much. It provoked massive protests by black soldiers and their abolitionist
allies, causing black soldiers—free and slave, Northern and Southern—to
make common cause, while also capturing the attention of the Northern
public generally.

Black men in the army and their antislavery allies viewed the discriminatory pay rates as yet another vestige of second-class citizenship and
then determined to eradicate it. Led by black soldiers recruited in the free
states and encouraged by sympathetic white officers, several regiments of
black soldiers refused to accept the monthly $7, regarding it as an affront
to their dignity as Union soldiers. Rather than submit to inferior treatment
some went for over a year without pay. The 54th and 55th Massachusetts
Volunteers—whose story has been put on the screen in the movie *Glory*—
refused even the Commonwealth's offers to use state funds to increase the
compensation to the amount white privates received. In the meantime,
black soldiers fought and died, dug fortifications and fell ill, and fumed at
the progressive impoverishment of their families. By late 1863, the protest
boiled over into open revolt when men in the 3rd South Carolina Volunteers under Sergeant William Walker stacked their arms and refused to
perform duty until the army granted equal pay. Walker's superiors
charged him with mutiny and executed him as an example to other black
protestors. But Walker's death did not stem the protest. Black soldiers

stationed in other parts of the South began to agitate for change. Many regiments teetered on the brink of mutiny, until in the spring of 1864 Congress passed an act equalizing the pay of black and white.

Black soldiers received the same pay as white ones during World War II, but it was just one of the matters of discrimination that had been resolved. Numerous inequities—the product of policy as well as the execution of policy—remained, stigmatizing military service in the eyes of black soldiers who saw the traditional mores of the white South incorporated into the practices of the American military. The segregationist regime manifested itself in all aspects of the daily life of black soldiers whether on duty or off. To the black men who entered the World War II army, Jim Crow wore khaki as earlier he had worn Union blue. Segregation shaped military life whether on the parade grounds or in the recreation halls. For all black soldiers, the second-class citizenship that segregation represented was as galling as unequal pay had been a century earlier.

Black soldiers assaulted segregation with the same determination they attacked unequal pay in the earlier conflict. Progress was slow, and the continued existence of Jim Crow practices, especially in recreational facilities, caused great tension—tension that often broke out in violence. But, under unrelenting pressure, the army slowly relaxed its segregationist regimen. Sometimes military policy-makers acted through the incorporation of such visible tokens as heavyweight champion Joe Louis. Sometimes they moved with half-measures, as in 1943 when "White" and "Colored" signs were replaced by designations of "No. 1" and "No. 2"—classifications which changed practice not one whit. Only rarely did the army officially take a principled stand against the inequity of racial separation. Change came slowly.

Because the spirit of segregation remained, so did the tension and the protests. Protests continued to beget violence and, in extreme instances, led to full-blown mutinies—as at Alexandria in Louisiana, Camp Stewart in Georgia, and Port Chicago and Camp Rousseau in California—that more than rivaled William Walker's action some eighty years earlier. These mutinies were followed by courts-martial and more than a few exemplary punishments.

As in the Civil War, the system of military justice exacerbated the feelings of frustration of black soldiers. In both conflicts, black soldiers found themselves punished more quickly and severely than white soldiers. Still the relation between military justice and the black military experience was a complex one, whose effects resonated in a number of different ways. Army regulations ordered nearly every aspect of a soldier's life, and all soldiers found themselves in a system that demanded absolute obedience. But obedience took on special meaning for black soldiers, for, with few exceptions, their superiors were white. The weight of American race relations thus was woven into the fabric of army life.

This was especially true in the Civil War. Federal officials allowed for the commissioning of few black officers, and most black soldiers answered directly to white commanders. For these men, particularly for former slaves, the distance between unquestioned obedience to a white army officer and a white slave master was small. Wielding great power, some officers abused their authority, lording it over black men with excessive zeal and even sadistic cruelty. Since many of the punishments used to discipline soldiers—the lash, the stocks, the gauntlet—had been regularly employed by slaveholders, black soldiers frequently found it difficult to separate the old and the new forms of white domination.

Still, even in the midst of the Civil War, most black soldiers recognized a fundamental change in the source of authority that enlistment in the army had presaged, and they pressed white commanders with their own understanding of their new condition. While the rule of slavery had been personal and arbitrary, the rule of the army rested, at least in theory, on abstract law. If black soldiers stood answerable to military law and regulations, so did white officers. Furthermore, army regulations demanded obedience only to the *lawful* orders of superiors. The same regulations that imposed obedience upon soldiers required officers to exercise military command "with kindness and justice to inferiors," specified that punishment be "strictly conformable to military law," and forbade superiors "to injure those under them by tyrannical or capricious conduct, or by abusive language." Black soldiers who listened daily to the readings of regulations held their commanders accountable to these restrictions and heeded them no less than the admonitions of obedience. As they did they became familiar with a new system of justice, which held all to be equal in theory even when in practice white persons might be superior to black ones. Such a system of formal regulations would serve black soldiers well as they moved from being armed soldiers to civilians.[3]

By the mid-twentieth century the lash, the stocks, and the gauntlet had been outlawed, but military justice in World War II was often as difficult for black soldiers to achieve as it had been in the Civil War. Although a large black officer-corps existed in World War II and black soldiers usually shared their color with their immediate superiors, they did not have to look far to find a white commander, many of whom abused their black inferiors in a tradition that harked back to slave days. There were important counterbalances, to be sure. Numerous watchdogs followed the course of relations between whites and blacks within the army. Military commanders, concerned with the morale of their diverse fighting force and sensitive to the political implications of racial disruptions, labored to reduce the tensions between the white and black soldiers, issuing directives to lower ranking officers not to "injure those under their authority by tyrannical or capricious conduct or abusive language."[4] But the problem remained, and such orders, although repeated with increased frequency and greater force as the war dragged on, never secured the desired equality of treatment. Military justice in World War II seemed no less immune to the pressure of American racism than it had been nearly a century earlier.

But if progress was slow during World War II, the system of abstract law provided black soldiers with a measure of protection much as it had during the Civil War. As soldiers came to appreciate how the law could be used to protect them as well as to abuse them, they gained a firmer grasp on the rights of citizens. This was particularly true for young black men raised in the shadow of the plantation and under the heavy hand of rural paternalism. In both the Civil War and World War II, soldiering served as a school for citizenship.

Could they fight? Would they fight? Despite the military record of black soldiers in the American Revolution and the War of 1812, these questions haunted black soldiers mobilized in the war against slavery. The record of valor compiled by black soldiers in the Civil War and that subsequently amassed by black soldiers on the American frontier, in the Spanish-American War, and in World War I did little to answer these questions for white commanders. Black men who took up arms after 1941 still confronted the old skepticism. Doubts about their martial ability and commitment burdened black soldiers, and they longed for the opportunity to test their mettle on the field of battle. Yet, as always, armies needed large number of soldiers to do everything but fight. That need complemented the widespread belief that black soldiers could better handle shovels than guns; that black men should serve in rear positions rather than in the frontlines; that the real business of the war was a white man's affair. As a result, in World War II as in the Civil War, black soldiers in general found themselves serving as nothing more than uniformed menials, with the heavy physical labor of fatigue duty wearing out their bodies as it eroded their morale.

The response of black soldiers and their advocates—including nineteenth-century antislavery champions and twentieth-century civil-rights leaders—followed the same logic. They protested discriminatory labor assignments which neither military strategy nor the dignity of soldiers seemed to require. But the struggle to gain equal treatment was a difficult one. It was not until June 1864, near the end of the Civil War, that the War Department required labor to be detailed to black and white soldiers in proportion to numbers. Even then many commanders continued to work black soldiers more like beasts of burden than national defenders. Similarly, World War II commanders found many reasons to exclude black men from combat. Not until 1943, with the deployment of the 99th Pursuit Squadron in North Africa, did black airmen see combat, and army commanders were even slower still in employing black ground troops. Often they publicly maintained that black soldiers were unable to master the complicated weaponry of modern warfare—an insult that stung the entire black community. Black infantry men were not incorporated into American combat regiments until the last months of the war.

When given the oppportunity—be it at Fort Wagner, Port Hudson, or Milliken's Bend in the Civil War or the Battle of Bastogne in the closing months of World War II—black soldiers performed with great courage and valor. But acceptance came slowly and uneasily. Self-inflicted pressure to perform often meant that black soldiers accepted impossible military assignments and were used as cannon fodder. Even then their sacrifices were given but back-handed recognition.

While combat—the spilling of blood—seemed to be the most certain validator of claims to equality, a good deal of the liberating force of the black military service in both the Civil War and World War II derived not from great battles with the enemy or even stark protests against federal policy, but from the minutiae of military routine. Black soldiers savored the dignity of standing picket with the right to challenge trespassers, no matter their rank or race. They gained a new sense of their own place in society while guarding captured soldiers, whose dejected demeanor and powerless situation contrasted markedly with former boasts of racial invincibility—although the special treatment given Confederate and German prisoners rankled. Even the most routine of activities—the mastery of the manual of arms, the deployment of complicated weapons, and the execution of complex evolutions—provided new sources of pride and accomplishment. In short, the greatest changes rose not from explicit policies but from the opportunities that neutralized the acid of self-denigration and demolished the long-held assumptions of American race relations.

Because such subtle, unspoken changes had such a powerful effect, the black military experience touched many more than those who wore the soldier's uniform. Soldiering altered the lives of the families of black soldiers from the moment of enlistment. Indeed, enlistment itself was a family decision with deep implications for wives, parents, and children of soldiers. After enlistment, the family followed the soldier's career carefully, as their own status and livelihood—as well as that of their loved one—depended upon it. The battle over equal pay was as much as battle on the homefront as on the warfront. The same was true of the struggle against segregation in the military. Such struggles, moreover, reverberated beyond the family circle, mobilizing the black community in letter-writing campaigns and protest meetings. The black community became deeply involved in the soldier's experience, gaining strength from the achievements of their liberators. Making the case for equality, leaders on the homefront from Frederick Douglass to Walter White drew on the soldier's exchange of blood for citizenship.

And, to a degree, the exchange held. Certainly it did in the Civil War. During 1862, nothing moved the nation more sharply toward a commitment to emanicpation than the growing dependency of the federal army on black labor. In time, the realization that men who could dig could also fight became manifest to all but the most obtuse federal officers. The incorporation of black men into the Union army was announced by the Emancipation Proclamation. Indeed, the primary difference between the much-celebrated proclamation and the long-forgotten Congressional confiscation acts was the fact that Lincoln's edict opened military service to black men. Following the promulgation of the Emancipation Proclamation on January 1, 1863, black soldiers entered federal service in large numbers, with the enlistment of free blacks in New England and former slaves in the occupied South. By May 1863, the Bureau of Colored Troops was established, and federal policy became one of enlisting black men—slave as well as free—with all due speed.

Black enlistment transformed the federal army into an army of liberation. The presence of black soldiers deepened a firm Northern stand for emancipation. Indeed, Lincoln's own determination to stand by emancipation—despite pressure to retract or modify his proclamation—grew along with the number of black men under federal arms.

In a similar fashion, the commitment to equality seemed to grow with the services of black men in World War II. The contradiction of fighting against Hitler's racism with a segregated army undermined the ideological structure of American racism and weakened its institutional buttresses. The enlistment of black soldiers eroded notions of racial inferiority, and stimulated civil-rights activity. Although seemingly the structure of American racism hardly budged during World War II, it had in fact been fatally weakened. Nothing presaged this change more than the altered role of the federal government. The Civil War and World War II transformed the federal government into the strongest friend of black people and their most dependable ally in the struggle for equality. That is not to say that that ally was always reliable, but, in its executive, judicial, and even legislative guises, the federal government—more powerful than ever in the wake of its great military victories—became the court of first resort to the friends of racial equality. In appealing for federal assistance, black people and their allies continued to play their strong card: black men had served the nation in its moment of need.

The exchange of blood for citizenship thus had a powerful effect on postwar events, the years historians have called "Reconstruction" and "the Second Reconstruction." For one thing, military service permanently altered the lives of black men, elevating many to new heights of glory and power, propelling them into political and entrepreneurial careers. Black men who entered the federal army as slaves or second-class citizens returned as national heroes in the nation's great triumphs. In both the post-Civil War and post-World War II United States, military service provided stepping stones for leadership within the black community. Drawing on their martial experience and the confidence it engendered, black veterans reframed the aspirations of all black people and gave direction to the reconstruction of black communities. They organized schools, built churches, founded fraternal societies, and established a host of enterprises. Within these organizations, and within the black community more generally, black veterans moved into positions of authority, taking up offices on school boards, in church conventions and synods, corporations, municipal councils, state legislatures, and eventually the federal government offices.

Reminding the nation of their wartime service, black veterans-turned-politicians pushed on the color line, driving it back or at least bending it in important ways. Probably no petition for civil rights, probably no speech for racial equality, probably no appeal for racial justice in the post-Civil War and post-World War II eras did not fail to mention the role of black soldiers. Calling for the suffrage—enfranchisement in 1865 and an end to disfranchisement in 1945—no black political meeting failed to celebrate the valor of black liberators. Much the same was true of the struggle for economic benefits, whether forty acres and a mule or equal access to employment. From the first Civil Rights Acts to the first March on Washington, military service was used to press the color line, often successfully. While the gains toward equality often found acceptance in the name of wartime necessity, they nonetheless supported the larger ideal of equality. That ideal lost its power in the post-Civil War era as Reconstruction waned and as sectional reconciliation grew in importance. But in the aftermath of World War II, the Cold War continued to validate the exchange of blood for citizenship, giving the connection between the national ideal and the hope for equality continued viability. The soldier's exchange of blood for citizenship has never been redeemed in full, but even discounted its value has been incalculable in the larger struggle for equality.

7

War and the Constitution: Abraham Lincoln and Franklin D. Roosevelt

ARTHUR M. SCHLESINGER, JR.

ODDLY, the Gettysburg Address made no great impression on November 19, 1863. Lincoln's bright and devoted young secretary John Hay casually noted in his diary: "The President, in a fine, free way, with more grace than is his wont, said his half dozen words of consecration, and the music wailed, and we went home through crowded and cheering streets. And all the particulars are in the daily papers."[1] It took time for the Gettysburg Address to become a classic statement of the American creed. Today one sometimes feels that Lincoln's crystalline words have grown so familiar that they are part of the mechanical ritual of our lives—words we hear and repeat but no longer attend to.

The more venerable among us may remember *Ruggles of Red Gap*, a 1935 film in which Charles Laughton, playing an English butler won in a poker game by an American rancher, electrifies his new employer—and movie audiences of the 1930s sitting in darkened theaters—by remembering the Gettysburg Address, when his new boss had forgotten it, and delivering it as if each stunning phrase had come fresh from his mind. Laughton made us listen anew and made us think anew. For the testing of which President Lincoln so wonderfully spoke—whether a nation conceived in liberty and dedicated to the proposition that all men are created equal can long endure—was not only the aspiration of 1776 and the challenge of 1863 but must remain the unending commitment of all Americans till the end of our days.

The republic has gone through two awful times of testing since the achievement of independence—two times when the life of the nation was critically at stake, two times when the nation was led by Presidents absolutely determined that government of the people, by the people, for the people, should not perish from the earth. The two Presidents had to confront the question whether the Constitution of 1787 was equal to the cruel emergencies of 1861 and 1941. History in these periods subjected our republican institutions to their severest trials—and, with the survival of the Constitution, saw their greatest triumphs.

The two Presidents were very different men in very different situations. Abraham Lincoln striding from the backwoods of the middle border was the common man incarnate. Franklin D. Roosevelt was a Hudson River patrician. Lincoln was self-educated. Roosevelt received the best education his country could provide. Lincoln was chosen to head a republic of thirty-four states with a population of thirty-two million; Roosevelt, a republic of forty-eight states with a population four times as great. Lincoln faced a civil war within the United States; Roosevelt, a foreign war threatening to engulf the planet. Lincoln operated a presidency of still largely undefined powers; Roosevelt, a presidency considerably more secure in its assertions of national leadership. Lincoln was enveloped by a tragic sense of life. Roosevelt breezed through life in confident and incurable optimism.

Yet they had many similarities. Both were men of mysterious and impenetrable reserve, concealing resolute purpose behind screens of fable, parable, and jocosity. Both had deep and irreversible moral convictions about freedom and human rights. Both were skilled, crafty, and, when necessary, ruthless politicians. Both were lawyers who, while duly respecting their profession, regarded law as secondary to political leadership. Both had faith that the Constitution, spaciously interpreted, could surmount crisis. Lincoln, following his hero Henry Clay, "my beau ideal of a statesman," in a broad reading of the national charter, said in his First Inaugural: "I take the official oath today, with no mental reservations, and with no purpose to construe the Constitution or laws, by any hypercritical rules."[2] Roosevelt, following his heroes Theodore Roosevelt and Woodrow Wilson in their robust conceptions of presidential leadership, said in his First Inaugural, "Our Constitution is so simple and practical that it is possible always to meet extraordinary needs by changes in emphasis and arrangement without loss of essential form."[3]

And both Presidents confronted national emergencies that demanded bold and peremptory action. Both assumed powers that led other Americans to charge that the Constitution had been transgressed and betrayed. Both provoked cries of dictatorship. Both, in responding to what they saw as the necessities of the day, risked the creation of dangerous precedents for the future. An examination of the manner in which Lincoln and Roosevelt met their emergencies may illuminate our understanding of the potentialities, limits, and perils of presidential leadership. I propose to discuss in particular the way these two Presidents handled first the war-making power and then threats to internal security once war had begun.

The men who drafted the Constitution in Philadelphia in 1787 had questions of national defense much on their minds. The remedy for the infant nation's international vulnerabilities was, they believed, a strong central government empowered to create a standing army and navy, to regulate commerce, to enforce treaties, and, when necessary, to go to war. But, given the separation of powers, how should foreign policy authority be distributed within the new national government?

Here the Framers were unambiguous in their decisions. The vital powers were to be reserved for Congress. Article I of the new Constitution gave Congress not only the exclusive appropriations power—itself a potent instrument of control—but the exclusive power to declare war, to raise and support armies, to provide and maintain a navy, to make rules for the government and regulation of the armed services, and to grant letters of marque and reprisal—the last provision representing the eighteenth-century equivalent of retaliatory strikes and enabling Congress to authorize limited as well as formal war. Even Alexander Hamilton, the convention's foremost proponent of executive energy, endorsed this allocation of powers, expressly rejecting the notion that foreign policy was the private property of the President. "The history of human conduct," Hamilton wrote in the 75th *Federalist*, "does not warrant that exalted opinion of human virtue which would make it wise in a nation to commit interests of so delicate and momentous a kind, as those which concern its intercourse with the rest of the world, to the sole disposal of a magistrate created and circumstanced as would be a President of the United States."

No one can doubt the determination of the Framers, in the words of James Wilson, to establish a procedure that "will not hurry us into war; it is calculated to guard against it. It will not be in the power of a single man, or a single body of men, to involve us in such distress."[4] Sixty years later, during the Mexican War, Congressman Abraham Lincoln of Illinois accurately expressed original intent when he wrote that the convention "resolved so to frame the Constitution that *no one man* should hold the power of bringing this oppression upon us."[5]

While reserving decisive foreign policy powers for Congress, the Framers did assign the executive a role in the conduct of national security affairs. Instead of giving Congress the exclusive power to "make" war, as the draft under consideration stipulated, James Madison moved to replace "make" by "declare" in order to leave "to the Executive the power to repel sudden attacks."[6]

The President, moreover, was constitutionally designated commander in chief of the armed services. The Framers saw this, however, as a ministerial function, not as a grant of independent executive authority. The designation, as Hamilton wrote in the 69th *Federalist*, "would amount to nothing more than the supreme command and direction of the military and naval forces." It meant only that the President should have the direction of war once authorized or begun. Hamilton contrasted this limited assignment with the power of the British king—a power that "extended to the declaring of war and to the raising and regulating of fleets and armies,—all which by the Constitution under consideration, would appertain to the legislature."

The Constitution, in short, envisaged a partnership between Congress and the President in the conduct of foreign affairs with Congress as the senior partner. Yet one may suppose that another consideration lingered in the Framers' innermost thoughts—a fallback position that, in acknowledging the hard realities of a dangerous world, justified a measure of unilateral executive initiative. This was the question of emergencies.

The Framers had been reared on John Locke. They were well acquainted with chapter fourteen, "Of Prerogative," in Locke's *Second Treatise on Civil Government.* While in normal times, Locke said, responsible rulers must observe the rule of law, in dire emergencies they could initiate extralegal or even illegal action. Sometimes "a strict and rigid observation of the laws may do harm." The executive, Locke contended, must have the reserve power "to act according to discretion for the public good, without the prescription of law and sometimes even against it." The test of whether prerogative was rightfully invoked, Locke said, was whether the emergency was a true one and whether the exercise of prerogatives tended "to the good or hurt of the people"—judgments to be made in the end not by the ruler but by the people.

Prerogative was the exercise of the law of national self-preservation. The doctrine was not conceded in the Constitution, except for a solitary provision permitting the suspension of the writ of habeas corpus "when in Cases of Rebellion or Invasion the public safety may require it" (Article I, section 9). The limitation of emergency prerogative to rebellion and invasion and to the single matter of habeas corpus implied less a standard that could be extended to other issues than a rejection of any broader suspension of constitutional guarantees even in emergencies.

Yet the notion that crisis might require the executive to act outside the Constitution in order to save the Constitution still lurked in the back of the minds of the men who won American Independence. Hamilton wrote in the 28th *Federalist* of "that original right of self-defence which is paramount to all positive forms of government"; and Madison in the 41st thought it "vain to oppose constitutional barriers to the impulse of self-preservation." Even Jefferson, the apostle of strict construction, affirmed the need for emergency prerogative. "On great occasions," he wrote in 1807, "every good officer must be ready to risk himself in going beyond the strict line of the law, when the public preservation requires it." There were, he said, "extreme cases where the laws become inadequate to their own preservation, and where the universal recourse is a dictator, or martial law."[7]

Nor was this a passing thought. Jefferson restated the point more fully after he left the White House. "A strict observance of the written laws," he wrote carefully in 1810, "is doubtless *one* of the high duties of a good citizen, but it is not *the highest*. The laws of necessity, of self-preservation, of saving our country when in danger, are of a higher obligation. . . . To lose our country by scrupulous adherence to written law, would be to lose the law itself, with life, liberty, property and all those who are enjoying them with us; thus absurdly sacrificing the end to the means." He understood the risks in this argument and therefore placed emergency power under the judgment of history: "The line of discrimination between cases may be difficult; but the good officer is bound to draw it at his own peril, and throw himself on the justice of his country and the rectitude of his motives."[8]

Jefferson's defense of Lockean prerogative was inspired by his passion to protect the republic against Aaron Burr. This was a doubtful case. No one can be sure what the Burr conspiracy was up to. The House of Representatives, in voting down a proposal for the suspension of habeas corpus, rejected any idea that the life of the nation was at risk. Neither Jefferson's contemporaries nor future historians have been convinced that Jefferson faced an emergency so imperative as to justify a laying aside of the law. Burr's acquittal by the courts helped limit subsequent resort to emergency prerogative.

It was not enough for a President personally to think the country was in danger. To confirm a judgment of dire emergency, a President had to have the broad agreement of Congress and public opinion. Emergencies considerably more authentic than the Burr conspiracy took place in the next thirty years. But Presidents as forceful as Jackson and Polk refrained from invoking emergency prerogative—even in face of the nullification crisis and the war with Mexico.

Jefferson himself had restricted prerogative to "great occasions." But in fact he was prepared to ignore Congress and to take unilateral action on lesser occasions as well. Thus he sent a naval squadron to the Mediterranean under secret orders to fight the Barbary pirates, applied for congressional sanction six months later, and then misled Congress as to the nature of the orders. He unilaterally authorized the seizure of armed vessels in waters extending to the Gulf Stream, engaged in rearmament without congressional appropriations, and not infrequently withheld information from Congress.

Others of our early Presidents imitated Jefferson's unilateral initiatives. As Judge A. D. Sofaer has shown in his magistral work, *War, Foreign Affairs and Constitutional Power: The Origins,* unauthorized presidential adventurism thrived in the early republic. But these Presidents did not assert it as their constitutional right to ignore Congress and strike out on their own. "At no time," Sofaer writes of the classical period, "did the executive claim 'inherent' power to initiate military action."[9] Sofaer's surmise is that our early Presidents deliberately selected venturesome agents, deliberately kept their missions secret, deliberately gave them vague instructions, deliberately declined to approve or disapprove their constitutionally questionable plans, and deliberately denied Congress the information to determine whether aggressive acts were authorized—all precisely because the Presidents wanted to do things they knew lay beyond their constitutional right to command.

The partnership between Congress and the executive in the conduct of foreign affairs was thus unstable from the start. President Polk, in getting into a war with Mexico that, according to Lincoln, had been unnecessarily and unconstitutionally begun, showed both the potentialities of presidential power and the limitations of legislative control. Despite his own strong opposition to the Mexican War, Lincoln had the advantage of Polk's vigorous example when he returned to Washington a dozen years later, now President himself, facing not foreign war but domestic insurrection.

Domestic insurrection raised a different set of constitutional issues, and this simplified Lincoln's problem. He did not—or at least so he believed—need congressional recognition of a state of war, as he would have done against a foreign state (four Supreme Court justices soon opined otherwise, however, in the Prize cases). He had only, he believed, to carry out his presidential duty of enforcing domestic law against rebellious individuals.

Still even this duty implied in the circumstances a warlike course that might well call for congressional approval. And that war-like course called for auxiliary measures that certainly required congressional action. Lincoln chose nevertheless to begin by assuming power to act independently of Congress. Fort Sumter was attacked on April 12, 1861. On April 15, Lincoln summoned Congress to meet in special session—but not till July 4. He thereby gained ten weeks to bypass Congress, rule by decree, and set the nation irrevocably on the path to war.

On April 15, he called out state militia to the number of seventy-five thousand. Here he was acting on the basis of a statute. From then on he acted on his own. On April 19, he imposed a blockade on rebel ports, thereby assuming authority to take actions hitherto considered as requiring a declaration of war. On May 3, he called for volunteers and enlarged the army and navy, thereby usurping the power confided to Congress to raise armies and maintain navies. On April 20, he ordered the Secretary of the Treasury to spend public money for defense without congressional appropriation, thereby violating Article I, section 9, of the Constitution. On April 27, he authorized the commanding general of the army to suspend the writ of habeas corpus—this despite the fact that the power of suspension, while not assigned explicitly to Congress, lay in that article of the Constitution devoted to the powers of Congress and was regarded by commentators before Lincoln as a congressional prerogative. Later he claimed the habeas corpus clause as a precedent for wider suspension of constitutional rights in time or rebellion or invasion—an undoubted stretching of original intent.

When Congress finally assembled on July 4, Lincoln justified his actions. The issue, he said, embraced more than the fate of these United States. The rebellion forced "the whole family of man" to ask questions going to the roots of self-government: "'Is there in all republics, this inherent and fatal weakness?' 'Must a Government, of necessity, be too *strong* for the liberties of its own people, or too *weak* to maintain its own existence?'" So viewing the issue, Lincoln continued, "no choice was left but to call out the war power of the Government; and so to resist force employed for its destruction, by force for its preservation."[10]

The phrase "war power" was novel in American constitutional discourse. John Quincy Adams, it is true, had contrasted in 1836 the "peace power" as something limited by the Constitution as against the "war power," limited only by the laws and usages of nations.[11] But Adams was speaking about the war power of the national government as a whole, exercised through and with Congress. He was not speaking, as Lincoln was, about the war power as a peculiar function of the executive.

The "war power" flowed into the Presidency, as Lincoln saw it, through the presidential oath to "preserve, protect, and defend the Constitution," through the constitutional commitment to take care that the laws be faithfully executed, and through the constitutional designation of the President as commander in chief. "I think," he later said, "the Constitution invests its commander-in-chief, with the law of war, in time of war"[12]—a statement that, if not altogether clear, was certainly pregnant. It must be noted, however, that Lincoln limited that investment of power to wartime, thereby excluding twentieth-century tendencies to argue that the clause bestows powers on the Presidency in times of peace.

Still, Lincoln's reading of the clause greatly enlarged presidential power in war. His most far-reaching action, the Emancipation Proclamation, began by invoking "the power in me vested as Commander-in-Chief of the Army and Navy" and ended by justifying emancipation as "warranted by the Constitution, upon military necessity." He later characterized the Proclamation as without "constitutional or legal justification, except as a military measure." He added: "I conceive that I may in an emergency do things on military grounds which cannot be done constitutionally by Congress." And: "As commander-in-chief of the army and navy, in time of war, I suppose I have a right to take any measure which may best subdue the enemy."[13]

Lincoln did not himself define the limits of the executive war power. An exculpatory opinion, extracted from his somewhat reluctant Attorney General, Edward Bates, contended that the national emergency justified Lincoln in suspending habeas corpus and disregarding subsequent judicial objection, even from so august a source as Chief Justice Roger Taney in *Ex parte Merryman.* The President, Bates added, was the judge of the gravity of the emergency and was accountable only through procedures of impeachment.

But Lincoln, though he had begun by acting without congressional authorization, had no intention of ruling Congress out of the game. His actions, he told Congress when it finally assembled, "whether strictly legal or not, were ventured upon under what appeared to be a popular demand

and a public necessity; trusting then as now that Congress would readily ratify them. It is believed that nothing has been done beyond the constitutional competency of Congress."

It was necessary to suspend habeas corpus, Lincoln added, in order to assure the enforcement of the rest of the law and thereby the protection of the state. "Are all the laws *but one* to go unexecuted, and the Government itself go to pieces, lest that one be violated? . . . In such a case, would not the official oath be violated if the government should be overthrown?" Would the very principles of freedom prevent free government from defending itself? As Lincoln explained his case toward the end of the war, his oath to preserve the Constitution imposed the "duty of preserving, by every indispensable means, that government—that nation—of which the constitution was the organic law. Was it possible to lose the nation, and yet preserve the Constitution?"[14]

Lincoln took that duty with utmost seriousness and assessed the internal threat behind the lines in the North with stern urgency. Rebel sympathizers, he said, "pervaded all departments of the government and nearly all communities of the people. . . . Under cover of 'Liberty of speech,' 'Liberty of the press,' and *'habeas corpus,'* they hoped to keep on foot amongst us a most efficient corps of spies, informers, supplyers, and aiders and abettors of their cause in a thousand ways." Conspiracy-mongers like the detectives La Fayette Baker and Allan Pinkerton inflamed the official imagination. Northern opponents of the war were denounced as Copperheads. Invoking his "war power," Lincoln set in motion a series of drastic though often inept *ad hoc* actions: martial law and military courts, some far from the fighting fronts; detectives (the twentieth century learned to call them secret police) and paid informers; military arrest and detention of untold thousands of persons; suppression of newspapers; seizure of property; denial of the mails to "treasonable correspondence"—all in the belief that "certain proceedings are constitutional when, in cases of rebellion or Invasion, the public Safety requires them, which would not be constitutional when, in absence of rebellion or invasion, the public Safety does not require them."[15]

Such actions, though tempered by Lincoln's restraint and humanity, provoked denunciations of despotism and cries of dictatorship. In 1862 the eminent lawyer Benjamin R. Curtis, who five years earlier had been a dissenting Supreme Court justice in the Dred Scott case and six years later would be Andrew Johnson's counsel in the impeachment proceedings, published a cogent pamphlet condemning Lincoln's proclamations and orders as "assertions of transcendent executive power" having the effect of placing "every citizen of the United States under the direct military command and control of the President."[16]

The exuberant Secretary of State W. H. Seward rejoiced in the situation. "We elect a king every four years," he told the London *Times* correspondent, "and give him absolute power within certain limits, which after all he can interpret for himself."[17] If anything, Secretary of War Edwin Stanton rejoiced more. Even so measured a commentator as Lord Bryce could write in a few years that Lincoln was "almost a dictator . . . who wielded more authority than any single Englishman has done since Oliver Cromwell."[18] The Civil War, Henry Adams wrote five years after Appomattox, "for the time obliterated the Constitution."[19]

Of course Lincoln was far from a dictator. The mechanisms of accountability—Congress, the courts, free elections, freedoms of speech, press and assembly—all remained in place. No dictator would have tolerated such fierce opposition in Congress and such bitter criticism in the newspapers. Nor would a dictator have submitted to a presidential election in the midst of war—and made preparations, in case he lost, to cooperate with his successor. Nor would a dictator have tolerated a Copperhead as Chief Justice of the Supreme Court. Lincoln did not even seek a Sedition Act of the sort Congress had given the executive in 1798, or an Espionage Act, as in 1917.

Still, in issuing decrees without legislative authorization, Lincoln assumed quasi-dictatorial powers. And no doubt he exaggerated the internal threat to national security. But civil wars are desperate affairs. The North did in fact have many persons opposed to the war. Some Copperheads were in fact Confederate agents. A responsible President could not afford to take chances. One might wish that Lincoln had acted at the time with the wisdom available to historians after the peril had passed. But Lincoln had to reckon with the gravest threat to the life of the republic, and he could not foretell the outcome. "It is very difficult to remember," wrote Maitland, "that events now in the past were once in the future."[20] We know how it all came out. Lincoln did not.

As usual, Lincoln found the homely analogy to defend his course. Human beings, he observed, wished to protect life and limb. "Yet often a limb must be amputated to save a life; but a life is never wisely given to save a limb. I felt that measures, otherwise unconstitutional, might become lawful by becoming indispensable to the preservation of the constitution, through the preservation of the nation."[21] One recalls Jefferson's point about absurdly sacrificing the end to the means; one hears the Lockean echo, even though the Locke to whom Lincoln most often referred was the lesser Locke who wrote under the name of Petroleum V. Nasby.

Lincoln secured congressional ratification of most of his unilateral actions. Such ratification might be taken as legislative obeisance to an imperial President—or as legislative affirmation that, despite the emergency, Congress retained its constitutional powers. With the war still on, a divided Supreme Court in 1863 in the *Prize* Cases rejected the contention that those actions Lincoln took unilaterally before Congress ratified them represented merely his "personal war against the rebellion." The majority ruled that the attack on Fort Sumter created a *de facto* state of civil war and that the President was "bound to meet it in the shape it presented itself, without waiting for Congress to baptize it with a name."[22] In the stress of war the judiciary too accepted what the executive had ventured upon under a popular demand and a public necessity.

The emergency Franklin Roosevelt faced eighty years later assumed a different form but presented almost as mortal a threat to the life of the nation. By the summer of 1940, Great Britain stood alone against Hitler. With nearly half the British destroyer fleet sunk or damaged, with a Nazi invasion of Britain darkly in prospect, Winston Churchill, the new British prime minister, asked Roosevelt for the loan of American destroyers "as a matter of life and death."[23] Weighing this anguished request, Roosevelt, for all his desire to aid Britain, was acutely mindful of the constitutional role of Congress.

When the French prime minister had asked earlier that spring for American assistance against the Nazi blitzkrieg, Roosevelt had replied that, while the United States would continue supplies so long as the French continued resistance, "I know that you will understand that these statements carry with them no implications of military commitments. Only the Congress can make such commitments."[24] To Churchill's plea for the loan of destroyers, Roosevelt initially responded that "a step of this kind could not be taken except with the specific authorization of the Congress, and I am not certain that it would be wise for that suggestion to be made to the Congress at this moment."[25] Not only would such a step enrage the isolationist opposition in Congress, but it was also an explosive issue to throw into the 1940 presidential campaign. As late as August of this dangerous year Roosevelt continued to believe that a transfer of destroyers would require congressional action.

In the meantime, able New Deal lawyers, notably Benjamin V. Cohen and Dean Acheson, construed the applicable statutes to mean that unilateral executive action would be legal if the transfer of destroyers could be shown to strengthen rather than to weaken American defenses. At first the President heard the new argument with skepticism. But the British plight grew more desperate and Churchill's pleas more urgent. Roosevelt now moved with careful, if informal, concern for the disciplines of consent. He consulted his cabinet. He consulted congressional leaders. Through intermediaries he consulted the Republican candidates for President and Vice President, Wendell Willkie and Senator Charles McNary. McNary, a public-spirited man, was also the Republican leader of the Senate, and he soon passed word to the White House that, while it would be hard for him to vote for a statute authorizing the transfer of destroyers, he would make no objection if persuasive grounds could be found for going ahead without resort to Congress.

Roosevelt then extracted from his somewhat reluctant Attorney General, Robert H. Jackson, an opinion telling him that he could by executive agreement exchange destroyers for bases in British possessions in the Western Hemisphere. Jackson mentioned the commander in chief clause only to note, "Happily, there has been little occasion in our history for the interpretation of the powers of the President as Commander in Chief." Instead of relying upon the "constitutional power" of the Presidency, Jackson found "ample statutory authority to support the acquisition of these bases." His opinion rested basically on a construction of laws passed by Congress, not on theories of inherent executive authority. Later Jackson observed that Roosevelt "did not presume to rely upon any claims of constitutional power as Commander-in-Chief" but made the transfer because, as he read the law, "Congress so authorized him."[26]

Critics thought the Attorney General's opinion strained, and Jackson himself years later made a semi-disclaimer. The great constitutional scholar E. S. Corwin called the opinion at the time "an endorsement of unrestrained autocracy in the field of our foreign relations," adding hyperbolically that "no such dangerous opinion was ever before penned by an Attorney General of the United States."[27]

Even great constitutional scholars can overreact, and in this case Corwin surely overreacted. The Jackson opinion was a response to a unique emergency; it received tacit congressional ratification when Congress appropriated money to build the bases; and to my knowledge it has never since been cited as justification for solo executive exploits in foreign affairs. The destroyer deal was compelled by a threat to the republic surpassed only by the emergency Lincoln faced after Sumter. It seems less a flagrant exercise in presidential usurpation than a defensible application of the Locke-Jefferson-Lincoln doctrine of emergency prerogative.

The destroyer deal was an unneutral act. Still, as international lawyers pointed out at the time, Hitler's own scorn for neutral rights weakened any claim he might make for the neutral rights of Nazi Germany. The deal did not (as some have said in recent years) violate domestic neutrality legislation. That legislation governed economic, not political, relations between the United States and belligerent states. It prohibited loans, credits, arms sale, and travel under specified conditions; it did not prohibit choosing sides.

The really decisive step away from neutrality, however, was not taken unilaterally by the President. It was taken with due solemnity by the President and Congress together in March 1941. Instead of relying on inherent presidential power, Roosevelt asked Congress to enact the Lend-Lease bill, a bill that, if it became law, would align the United States in the most unequivocal manner with Britain in its war against the Axis states. After two months of vigorous debate, Congress passed Lend-Lease by comfortable margins in both houses.

The Lend-Lease Act set the course for the months that followed. As Cordell Hull, the Secretary of State, told the American Society of International Law in April, the declared policy of the legislative and executive branches to give aid to Britain "means in practical application that such aid must reach its destination in the shortest of time and in maximum quantity. So ways must be found to do this."[28]

Once Congress had authorized the lending and leasing of goods to keep Britain in the war, did this authorization not imply an effort to make sure that the goods arrived? So Roosevelt assumed, trusting that a murky proclamation of "unlimited national emergency" in May and the impact of Nazi aggression on public opinion would justify his policy. In protecting the British lifeline, Roosevelt in the next months undertook a series of steps that by autumn had thrust the United States into an undeclared naval war in the North Atlantic. These steps—U.S. naval patrols that soon turned into convoys halfway across the ocean; the despatch of American troops to Greenland and soon to Iceland; cooperation with the British navy in tracing and sinking German U-boats; misrepresentation of the German attack on the destroyer *Greer*, the shoot-at-sight policy in patrol zones in September—were taken on presidential orders and without congressional authorization.

The question arises: by what authority did Roosevelt thus go to quasi-war in the North Atlantic? Looking back at the fiery debates of that ancient day, one is struck by the relative absence of constitutional argument. Isolationists denounced the Lend-Lease Act as an excessive delegation of legislative power to the President. But it was, after all, a statute duly passed by Congress after full debate. It was not a unilateral assumption of power by the President.

No isolationist had paid more attention to the Constitution than the formidable historian Charles A. Beard. Beard had made his name thirty years before with *An Economic Interpretation of the Constitution*, and in 1943 he published *The Republic*, a series of dialogues on the Constitution. But the two volumes of polemic against Roosevelt's foreign policy he wrote after the war turned on presidential violations of "covenants with the American people to keep this nation out of war"—covenants made in speeches and party platforms; not, except for scattered references in the epilogue to the second volume, on presidential violations of constitutional provisions and prohibitions.[29]

In Congress isolationists tended to make substantive rather than constitutional arguments. Senator Robert A. Taft of Ohio was an exception. At one point he objected that the President had "no legal or constitutional right to send American troops to Iceland" without congressional authorization. Congressional acquiescence, Taft said, might "nullify for all time the constitutional authority distinctly reserved to Congress to declare war." But only one senator supported Taft's constitutional protest.[30] The failure to invoke the Constitution probably expressed a sense of futility about constitutional argumentation once the passage of the Lend-Lease Act had made Congress an accomplice in Roosevelt's policy.

The constitutional question remained in abeyance. Roosevelt acted as if his policies derived from the need to execute the congressional mandate embodied in the Lend-Lease Act, not from independent presidential or commander in chief power. Why then did he not seek explicit congressional authorization?

Unlike Lincoln, who could count on congressional ratification for his early unilateral measures, Roosevelt faced a bitterly divided Congress. He had to balance risks: the risk of arguably illegal actions that would get Lend-Lease goods to Britain against the risk, should he seek congressional authorization, of a defeat that would imply repudiation of the aid-to-Britain policy and might thereby, in Roosevelt's profound belief, mean the capitulation of Britain and deadly danger to the United States.

In April 1941, as British shipping losses grew, Henry L. Stimson, the Secretary of War, urged the President to request convoy authority from Congress. Roosevelt responded, as Stimson noted in his diary, "that it was too dangerous to ask the Congress for the power to convoy. . . . If such a resolution were pressed now it would probably be defeated."[31] In May, Stimson handed Roosevelt a draft congressional resolution authorizing the use of force to protect the delivery of supplies to Britain. The President thanked him but again judged the time ill-chosen. In June, the President's Harvard classmate Grenville Clark, now an eminent lawyer, urged Roosevelt to ask Congress for a joint resolution approving measures necessary to assure delivery. Roosevelt replied in July that the time was not "quite right."[32] The renewal of selective service in August by a single vote in the House of Representatives would seem to vindicate the presidential assessment of the political odds.

Roosevelt's actions in the autumn of 1941, like Lincoln's in the spring of 1861, were, in a strict view, unconstitutional (though Lincoln's at least took place after war had begun). But, unlike later Presidents, Roosevelt did not seek to justify the commitment of American forces to combat by pleas of inherent constitutional power as President or as commander in chief. He thereby proposed no constitutional departures. Nor did he move behind a veil of secrecy. The debate between the isolationists and the interventionists was the most bitter in my lifetime. Roosevelt's major decisions were argued in the open and concluded in the open. With Hitler's cooperation, he brought the country along and kept it substantially united behind his policies.

He did not assert in the later imperial style that there was no need to consider Congress because the office of commander in chief gave him all the authority he needed. Jackson's opinion on the destroyer deal shows how undeveloped commander-in-chief theory was in those innocent days. In eighty-three press conferences in 1941 up to Pearl Harbor, Roosevelt never once alleged special powers in foreign affairs as commander in chief. When the title occurred in his speeches and messages, it generally signified only the narrow and traditional view of the commander in chief as the fellow who gave orders to the armed forces.

Pearl Harbor soon ended the policy debate. Thereafter Roosevelt, like Lincoln, had to cope with problems of internal security. Roosevelt had much the simpler task. It was easier to protect internal security in foreign war than in civil war. Moreover, civil liberties were themselves much more precisely defined and understood in 1941 than in 1861; and, as a result of the extension of the Bill or Rights by incorporation through the Fourteenth Amendment, civil liberties were in a much stronger constitutional position.

In 1941, while protesting his sympathy with Justice Holmes's condemnation of wiretapping in the Olmstead case, Roosevelt had granted to Attorney General qualified permission to wiretap "persons suspected of subversive activities against the United States."[33] Given the conviction Roosevelt shared with most Americans that a Nazi victory endangered the United States, he would presumably have been delinquent in his duty had he not ordered precautionary measures against Nazi espionage, sabotage, and "fifth column" penetration. Though we now know that the internal Nazi menace was even more exaggerated than the Copperhead menace had been, who could have been sure of that at the time? No more than

Lincoln could Roosevelt foretell the outcome. Events now safely in the past were then in the perilous future.

Roosevelt, like Lincoln, broadened his apprehensions to include Americans honestly opposed to the war. By prodding the FBI to investigate isolationists and their organizations, he blurred the line between enemy agents and political opponents. Harking back to the Civil War, Roosevelt even called his isolationist adversaries Copperheads; and in the conspiracy-obsessed J. Edgar Hoover he found an equivalent of Lincoln's La Fayette Baker and Allan Pinkerton.

There was, however, little serious government follow-up of Roosevelt's prodding. His prods were evidently taken by his subordinates as expressions of passing irritation rather than of constant purpose. In 1941 Roosevelt appointed Francis Biddle, a former Holmes law clerk and a distinguished civil libertarian, as Attorney General. "The most important job an Attorney General can do in a time of emergency," Biddle said on assuming the office, "is to protect civil liberties. . . . Civil liberties are the essence of the democracy we are pledged to protect."[34] Roosevelt kept Biddle on the job throughout the war despite Biddle's repeated resistance to presidential importunings that threatened the Bill of Rights.

Roosevelt's preoccupation with pro-Nazi activity increased after Pearl Harbor. "He was not much interested in the theory of sedition," Biddle later recalled, "or in the constitutional right to criticize the government in wartime. He wanted this anti-war talk stopped."[35] Biddle managed to avoid most presidential suggestions regarding the prosecution or suppression of the press. But in time, Roosevelt's prods forced a reluctant Biddle to approve the indictment of twenty-six pro-fascist Americans under a dubious application of the law of criminal conspiracy. A chaotic trial ended with the death of the judge, and the case was dropped.

Biddle also opposed the most shameful abuse of power within the United States during the war—the relocation of Americans of Japanese descent. Here Roosevelt responded both to local pressure, including that of Attorney General Earl Warren of California, and to the War Department, where such respected lawyers as Henry L. Stimson and John J. McCloy argued for action. Congress ratified Roosevelt's executive order before it was put into effect, so the relocation did not represent a unilateral exercise of presidential power. The Supreme Court upheld the program in the Hirabayashi and Korematsu cases, both decided, like the Prize cases, in wartime.

The most vicious assaults on civil liberties in the Roosevelt years resulted from private, not government, action—though private action spurred on by the Supreme Court. The Gobitis decision in 1940 upholding the compulsory salute and pledge of allegiance to the flag led to persecutions of Jehovah's Witnesses—who rejected flag worship as idolatry—mobs, arson, and even a case of castration.[36] Then in 1943, despite the high patriotic fervor generated by the war, the Court reversed itself and declared the compulsory pledge and salute unconstitutional. "If there be any fixed star in our constitutional constellation," Robert H. Jackson, now an associate justice, wrote on behalf of the Court, "it is that no official, high or petty, can prescribe what shall be orthodox in politics, nationalism, religion, or other matters of opinion."[37] One would like to hope that these words still express the national view.

For all Roosevelt's moments of impatience and exasperation, his administration's performance on civil liberties during the Second World War—the Japanese-American case aside—was conspicuously better, if also easier to accomplish, than the Lincoln administration's performance during the Civil War. In 1945 the American Civil Liberties Union saluted "the extraordinary and unexpected record . . . in freedom of debate and dissent on all public issues and in the comparatively slight resort to wartime measures of control of repression of opinion."[38]

Most of Roosevelt's actions to protect national security—even the relocation of Japanese Americans—observed constitutional requirements of due process. His most conspicuous deviation from the Constitution during the war came in September 1942, when he told Congress that, if it did not repeal a particular provision in the Price Control Act within three weeks, he would refuse to execute it. "The President has the power, under the Constitution and under Congressional Action," he declared, "to take measures necessary to avert a disaster which would interfere with the winning of the war."[39] Congress repealed the offending provision, averting a constitutional showdown.

The question lingers: by what authority did Roosevelt act? We are back again to Locke and emergency prerogative. Franklin Roosevelt had probably not looked at the *Second Treatise on Civil Government* since his student days at Harvard, if he had even looked at it then. But the doctrine of emergency prerogative had endured because it expressed a real, if rare, necessity. Confronted by Hitler, Roosevelt supposed, as Jefferson and Lincoln had supposed in the crises of their presidencies, that the life of the nation was at stake and that this justified extreme measures, using "the sovereignty of Government," as Roosevelt said in 1941, "to save Government."[40] Like Jefferson and Lincoln, Roosevelt did not pretend to be exercising routine or inherent presidential power. Unlike Jefferson's case of the Burr conspiracy but like Lincoln's case of the Civil War, Roosevelt's case had substantial public backing, and the electorate (and therefore, as Mr. Dooley had predicted, the courts) sustained his use of emergency prerogative.

Roosevelt in 1941, like Lincoln in 1861, did what he did under what appeared to be a popular demand and a public necessity. Both Presidents took their actions in light of day and to the accompaniment of uninhibited political debate. They did what they thought they had to do to save the republic. They threw themselves in the end on the justice of the country and the rectitude of their motives. Whatever Lincoln and Roosevelt felt compelled to do under the pressure of crisis did not corrupt their essential commitment to constitutional ways and democratic processes.

National crisis, the law of self-preservation, the life of the republic at stake, might thus justify Lockean prerogative and the consequent aggrandizement of executive power. Lincoln and Roosevelt embraced the grim necessity. But, regarding executive aggrandizement as but a means to a greater end, the survival of liberty and law, of government by, for, and of the people, they used emergency power, on the whole, with discrimination and restraint. Nevertheless, they risked the creation of precedent. As the Supreme Court said soon after Appomattox, the nation had "no right to expect that it will always have wise and humane rulers. Wicked men, ambitious of power, with hatred of liberty and contempt of law, may fill the place once occupied by Washington and Lincoln."[41] How to assure the recession of executive power when the emergency passed?

Henry Adams, reflecting on the obliteration of the Constitution during the Civil War, observed that the Framers "did not presume to prescribe or limit the powers a nation might exercise if its existence were at stake. They knew that under such an emergency paper limitations must yield; but they still hoped that the lesson they had taught would sink so deep into the popular mind as to cause a reestablishment of the system after the emergency had passed." The test, Adams wrote in 1870, was now at hand. "If the Constitutional system restored itself, America was right."[42]

Lincoln and Roosevelt, seeing the war power as a means to a higher end, understood the need to restore the constitutional regime and affirmed in the midst of the emergency that emergency prerogative must expire with the emergency. "The Executive power itself," said Lincoln, "would be greatly diminished by the cessation of actual war." "When the war is won," said Roosevelt, "the powers under which I act automatically revert to the people—to whom they belong."[43]

So indeed it happened, and the constitutional regime did re-establish itself. This was perhaps due less to renunciation by Presidents than to resistance by the People and resilience in the system. Lincoln had derived the notion that "the American people will, by means of military arrests during the rebellion lose the right of public discussion, the liberty of speech and the press, the law of evidence, trial by jury, and Habeas corpus throughout the indefinite peaceful future which I trust lies before them." He could not believe that, he said—once again the homely analogy—any more than he could believe that "a man could contract so strong an appetite for emetics during temporary illness as to perish in feeding upon them during the remainder of his healthful life."[44]

Once the crisis ended, the other two branches of government briskly reasserted themselves. The separation of powers sprang back to defiant life. A year after Lincoln's death, the Supreme Court held in *Ex parte Milligan* that the arrest and trial under martial law behind the lines of Lambdin P. Milligan, a venomously pro-slavery conspirator, violated the Constitution. Seward's elective kingship gave way in half a dozen years to a President at the bar of impeachment, followed by the period later famously characterized as one of "congressional government."

In the same fashion, the death of Roosevelt and the end of the Second World War were followed by a diminution of presidential power. A year after victory, Roosevelt's successor was so unpopular that voters said "To err is Truman" and elected a Republican Congress. The next year Congress gained posthumous revenge against the mighty wartime

President by proposing the Twenty-second Amendment and thereby limiting all future Presidents to two terms in the White House.

The instinctive dialectic of politics thus offers a measure of insurance against the possibility that emergency prerogative might lead to post-emergency despotism. Yet the danger persists that power asserted during authentic emergencies may create precedents for transcendent executive power during emergencies that exist only in the hallucinations of the Oval Office and that remain invisible to most of the nation. The perennial question is: How to distinguish real crises threatening the life of the republic from bad dreams conjured up by paranoid Presidents spurred on by paranoid advisers? Necessity, as Milton said, is always "the tyrant's plea."

The experience of Lincoln and Roosevelt suggests, I believe, the standards that warrant presidential resort to emergency prerogative. The fundamental point is that emergency prerogative cannot be properly invoked on presidential say-so alone but only under stringent and persuasive conditions, both of threat and of accountability, with the burden of proof resting on the President.

Let me try to define these conditions. Here, I would submit, are the standards:

1. There must be a clear, present, and broadly perceived danger to the life of the nation and to the ideals for which the nation stands.

2. The President must define and explain to Congress and the people the nature and urgency of the threat.

3. The understanding of the emergency, the judgment that the life of the nation is truly at stake, must be broadly shared by Congress and the people.

4. Time must be of the essence; existing statutory authorizations must be inadequate; and waiting for normal legislative action must constitute an unacceptable risk.

5. The danger must be one that can be met in no other way than by presidential initiative beyond the laws and the Constitution.

6. Secrecy must be strictly confined to the tactical requirements of the emergency. Every question of basic policy must be open to national debate.

7. The President must report what he has done to Congress, which, along with the Supreme Court and ultimately the people, will serve as judge of his action.

8. None of the presidential actions can be directed against the domestic political process and rights.

These standards, I believe, sufficiently distinguished what Lincoln did in the spring of 1861 and Roosevelt did in the autumn of 1941 from what Jefferson did in 1807, from what Truman did in seizing the steel mills in 1952, from what Nixon did in his use of "national security" to justify illegal acts in 1972–73, from what Reagan did in the mid-1980s with regard to Iran and the contras, from what the Bush administration threatened to do (until Congress saved him by passing a resolution he deemed unnecessary) in going to war against Iraq in 1991.

Lincoln's policy after Sumter, Roosevelt's in the North Atlantic, at least in the eyes of most Americans at the time and of most scholars in retrospect, represented a necessity—but not a precedent. By declining to use claims of inherent and abiding presidential power to justify their actions, Lincoln and Roosevelt took care not to give lesser men precedents to be invoked against lesser dangers. These two Presidents remained faithful to the spirit, if not the letter, of the Constitution: acting on the spirit to save the letter.

"If the people ever let command of the war power fall into irresponsible and unscrupulous hands," Justice Jackson said in dissent in the Korematsu case, "the courts wield no power equal to its restraint. The chief restraint upon those who command the physical forces of the country, in the future as in the past, must be their responsibility to the political judgments of their contemporaries and to the moral judgments of history."[45]

8

To Preserve a Nation: Abraham Lincoln and Franklin D. Roosevelt as Wartime Diplomatists

HOWARD JONES

A S DIFFICULT as it is to believe, historians have only recently begun to focus on the wartime diplomacy of Presidents Abraham Lincoln and Franklin D. Roosevelt. Indeed, the international threat faced by Lincoln has still received remarkably little attention. The most extensive treatment of Lincoln as diplomatist remains Jay Monaghan's beautifully crafted 1945 study, *Diplomat in Carpet Slippers: Abraham Lincoln Deals with Foreign Affairs;* but this work rests on thin archival research and, of course, lacks the insights afforded by the literature published in the last fifty years. Roosevelt's diplomacy has been the subject of much more scholarly work. In addition to numerous accounts of his policies during World War II, others have encompassed his entire relationship with foreign affairs. Nearly all studies of these two Presidents' diplomacy demonstrate that they were superb practitioners of *Realpolitik*. But none of them have concentrated on the moral and intellectual bases of their subject's foreign policy.

The two Presidents confronted different types of war, which necessitated two different approaches to diplomacy. Whereas Roosevelt grappled with clearly defined enemies from the outside (Japan, Germany, and Italy) and easily maintained his constituency, Lincoln dealt with a civil war that identified the enemy as inside the country and necessarily made attracting widespread support more challenging. The nation's domestic conflict of 1861–65 was in many ways an extremely bitter family affair in which the issues were deeper, more intimate, and much more fervent than those dealt with by Roosevelt decades afterward. On the one hand, Lincoln confronted an internal rebellion, which allowed him to claim extraordinary domestic police powers in guaranteeing a republican form of government; on the other hand, he waged a full-fledged war that permitted him to exercise his military powers as commander-in-chief. In the course of this fuzzily defined conflict, Lincoln had to focus on preventing foreign intervention while justifying a vicious contest requiring Americans to kill Americans. Any form of outside involvement, he knew, had the potential of escalating the conflict into an international war destructive to the republic itself. Hence, Lincoln sought to isolate the war from the outside world by devising a moral and intellectual justification for the struggle that rested on the freedoms highlighted in the Declaration of Independence.

Roosevelt, however, faced an external threat that required no such appeal to individual liberties. His diplomacy sought to unite disparate forms of governments against the Axis powers by assuring the Four Freedoms of life—freedom of speech and worship, and freedom from want and fear. Roosevelt told Congress in January 1941 that to defeat "the so-called new order of tyranny," Americans must strive for a "moral order" that exalted "the supremacy of human rights everywhere."[1] The President dealt with diverse peoples who did not always share his democratic ideals, leading him to focus on the goal of self-determination, or the right to choose the form of government desired.

Both wars took on one important similarity: they developed into moral crusades. Lincoln appealed to universal principles of right and wrong, and ultimately concluded that it was necessary to destroy the Southern government and way of life. Emancipation, he told an official in the Department of Interior during the autumn of 1862, meant that "the [old] South is to be destroyed."[2] Roosevelt likewise made the war he waged into a crusade against the Germans and, especially, the Japanese who had launched the surprise attack on Pearl Harbor. Roosevelt characterized the enemy as inherently inferior, evil, and even subhuman; Lincoln chose to focus on the good that could come from the war rather than to condemn the enemy (who was likewise American) as base and vile. After the war, he knew, would come the horrendous problem of knitting the nation together again. But both Presidents recognized that their righteous wars required total victories.

If Lincoln's diplomacy was quiet and unassuming, that of Roosevelt's was anything but unassuming. Lincoln had to place early constraints on the pugnacious diplomacy of his Secretary of State, William H. Seward. Matters came to a head in April 1861 when Seward wished to challenge Britain and other European nations in the Western Hemisphere in a specious effort to rally Americans around the flag and save the Union. The secretary had another purpose as well: to usurp Lincoln's authority and install himself as prime minister of what he regarded as a hopelessly inept administration. Lincoln kept the entire affair secret while pointedly reminding his upstart that he was neither the President nor a prime minister. Trouble did not disappear. On more than one occasion the President toned down Seward's strident language in diplomatic notes sent to England; in one instance, the mild-mannered and studious Union minister in London, Charles Francis Adams, discreetly held back delivery of a hotly worded note from his superior, choosing instead to summarize its contents to his counterpart in a measured way. Roosevelt served as his own counsel in foreign affairs. He himself handled the key areas of Europe and the Atlantic, leaving the rest of the world to his secretary of state, Cordell Hull.

After their initial problems, Lincoln and Seward worked together in a warm and accommodating relationship that found them virtually inseparable in policy-making but with the President maintaining control over those foreign issues that directly threatened the Union. During the *Trent* crisis with England in late 1861, Lincoln took the lead in steering the Union away from war. In November of that year, Captain Charles Wilkes of the Union navy acted without authorization in stopping the British packet ship *Trent* in the Caribbean and illegally removing two Confederate emissaries to Europe, James Mason and John Slidell. Threats of war thundered from England as its government and people denounced Wilkes's action as a violation of neutral rights and a calculated insult to national honor. Lincoln freed the two Confederates and resolved the crisis, but not until fellow northerners had celebrated their "victory" over the South as a much-needed palliative to the Union disaster at Bull Run. Seward, however, wrote the diplomatic note that salvaged some measure of American prestige. By acceding to England's demand to liberate the men, Seward declared in a broadly stretched interpretation of international law, the United States served notice of its agreement with the British in renouncing the right of search. On another occasion, when foreign intervention in the war appeared imminent during the fall of 1862, Lincoln almost single-handedly converted the war into a crusade against slavery and ultimately discouraged outside involvement. Yet it was Seward who convinced the President to delay the announcement of the Emancipation Proclamation until the Union had won a battle in the field.

The backgrounds of the two Presidents were strikingly different, and yet both Lincoln and Roosevelt had charisma, that magical quality of leadership which defies definition because it means different things to different people. Each President had the capacity to inspire his people, whether by word or deed, and to most observers took on the image of a forthright leader in command of a carefully devised plan for victory. Perhaps because of Lincoln's modest prairie upbringing, homely manner, and rustic physical appearance, he exuded a warm self-confidence tempered by a humble and self-deprecating style that moved others to follow him. Roosevelt, by contrast, was cosmopolitan in demeanor and never left the air of his Dutchess County New York background behind him. Yet he, like Lincoln, held onto enough popular support while surviving four arduous years of war during which the nation's future was at stake.

Lincoln and Roosevelt succeeded as wartime diplomatists largely because they were hard-line realists who were also gifted advocates of America's highest ideals. Though Lincoln did not have Roosevelt's public relations advantages of speaking over radio, appearing in newsreels, and attending summit conferences, he still quickened the popular pulse with written and spoken declarations that were eloquent and univeral in meaning. In his First Inaugural Address, The Emancipation Proclamation, and the Gettysburg Address, he appealed for a mystical and permanent union, the inherent rights of mankind, and the sanctity of republicanism. Roosevelt called for national self-determination, most notably in the Atlantic Charter, jointly declared with British Prime Minister Winston Churchill in August 1941. He did so again at Yalta in February 1945, joined by Soviet Premier Joseph Stalin.

Lincoln and Roosevelt relied heavily on idealistic pronouncements in promoting realistic goals. Neither President sought political martyrdom by sacrificing liberty; rather, they accomplished their objectives through compromise and common sense. But it is also clear that Lincoln's approach was more personal than Roosevelt's; whereas the former sought a government based on the principle of equality contained in the Declaration of Independence, the latter worked toward a generalized liberty in which the government guaranteed freedom *from* certain dangers such as fear, hunger, and oppression.

Lincoln was a man of deeper thought and purpose than Roosevelt. Doubtless a chief reason for their differences was their education: Lincoln studied the Bible; Roosevelt went to Harvard. Another part of the explanation lies in their different preparations for office. Lincoln was out of political office during most of the years preceding his Presidency, a situation he exploited by analyzing the issues propelling the nation into civil war. His many speeches and writings dealing with the growing national crisis reflected a keen understanding of the issues and their relation to timeless questions of right and wrong. Roosevelt, however, spent much of his pre-presidential career in public office, leaving him little time for philosophical reflection even if that had been his inclination. Caught up in the swirl of everyday politics, he dealt with most problems on a purely political level and never made an extensive examination into how the international issues pushing the world into war related to larger matters of morality. When writer John Gunther once asked Mrs. Roosevelt, "Just how does the President *think?,*" she replied: "My dear Mr. Gunther, the President never 'thinks'! He *decides.*"[3]

As President, Roosevelt employed a problem-solving approach, which led to what one historian has called "crisis-to-crisis diplomacy." Roosevelt often appeared indecisive toward the growing problems of Europe and Asia. As early as his first year in office, 1933, he developed a trademark in foreign policy that a contemporary called "an exercise in tight-rope walking."[4] Roosevelt continually sought the middle ground between nationalism and internationalism, between domestic and foreign issues.

No evidence suggests that Roosevelt gave much thought to the ideal of personal liberty that drove Lincoln. For Lincoln, the end of the war meant that the central task had just begun: he wanted to promote a personal brand of freedom that extended far beyond that ever to be contemplated by Roosevelt. The struggle, Lincoln insisted in 1862, was "not altogether for today. It is for a vast future" in that it "presents to the whole family of man, the question whether a constitutional republic, a democracy," as he asserted in the Gettysburg Address, "conceived in Liberty, and dedicated to the proposition that all men are created equal, . . . can long endure."[5] Roosevelt, too, looked forward to the postwar world, but his vision rested on national self-determination.

Lincoln detested war but rationalized its existence as a means toward a greater end. "It breathed forth famine, swam in blood and rode on fire; and long, long after, the orphan's cry, and the widow's wail, continued to break the sad silence that ensued." In 1863, twenty-one years after this public declaration, Lincoln noted other base characteristics of war: "Deception breeds and thrives. Confidence dies, and univeral suspicion reigns. Each man feels an impulse to kill his neighbor, lest he be first killed by him. Revenge and retaliation follow. . . . Every foul bird comes abroad, and every dirty reptile rises up." In attempting to explain the existence of war, Lincoln argued to a friend that God "permits it for some wise purpose of his own, mysterious and unknown to us; and though with our limited understandings we may not be able to comprehend it, yet we cannot but believe, that he who made the world still governs it." Might not "the awful calamity of civil war," Lincoln later asked, "be but a punishment, inflicted upon us, for our presumptuous sins, to the needful end of our national reformation as a whole People?"[6]

Roosevelt likewise expressed revulsion toward war—though, one senses, somewhat less convincingly, and certainly less eloquently. In his well-known Chautauqua address of August 1936, he declared (not entirely accurately): "I have seen war. I have seen war on land and sea. I have seen blood running from the wounded. I have seen men coughing out their gassed lungs. I have seen the dead in mud. I have seen cities destroyed. . . . I have seen children starving. I have seen the agony of mothers and wives. I hate war." And yet, was not this the same Roosevelt who reveled in occupying the world's center-stage with Churchill? "It is fun to be in the same decade with you," the President cabled the Prime Minister during the war.[7]

In any event, neither President was a pacifist: if wars *must* be fought, they must be won as quickly and decisively as possible, and for a higher purpose. Lincoln was hard-nosed in his pursuit of the war. The rebels must realize, he explained in July 1862, "that they cannot experiment for ten years trying to destroy the government, and if they fail still come back into the Union unhurt." Roosevelt, too, recognized the importance of convincing the enemy that it had lost the war. Rather than permit the Germans to escape total defeat (as he believed they had done in the Great War), he insisted on unconditional surrender. "It is of the utmost importance that every person in Germany should realize that this time Germany is a defeated nation,"he told Secretary of War Henry L. Stimson. To Secretary of the Treasury Henry Morgenthau, Roosevelt declared, "We have got to be tough with Germany and I mean the German people, not just the Nazis. You either have to castrate the German people or you have got to treat them in such a manner so that they just can't go on reproducing people who want to continue the way they have in the past."[8]

Lincoln sought only the gradual emancipation of slavery in the early stages of the war, concentrating instead on putting down the rebellion and restoring the Southern states to their rightful place in the Union. He never wavered from the constitutional guarantees protecting slavery; but he also worked toward emancipation by moving Americans in that direction one step at a time. Indeed, Lincoln told a black delegation in the White House that colonization appeared to be the only remedy because of the intense racial feelings held by whites toward blacks inside the United States. But as one historian explained, Lincoln used "the pernicious 'lullaby' of colonization" as an expedient intended "to allay his own uncertainties, and more importantly the fears of the vast majority of whites, concerning the eventual place of free black people in the United States." As late as August 1862 Lincoln again demonstrated his political acumen in offering the following assurance to New York publisher Horace Greeley in a letter printed in the *New York Tribune:* "My paramount object in this struggle *is* to save the Union, and is *not* either to save or to destroy slavery. If I could save the Union without freeing *any* slave I would do it, and if I could save it by freeing *all* the slaves I would do it; and if I could save it by freeing some and leaving others alone I would also do that." But as the war became protracted, so did its purpose expand. To preserve the Union, Lincoln ultimately declared, the Confederacy had to be destroyed, which meant that slavery itself had to die. As colonization had served its purpose, as one historian has noted, so did abolition become "an end as well as a means, a war aim virtually inseparable from Union itself."9

Controversy has risen over Lincoln's strategy during the war. According to one historian, Lincoln developed a "military strategy" intended to advance his "national strategy," and thereby subordinated military to political aims. As Roosevelt did in World War II, Lincoln demanded an "unconditional surrender" that necessarily entailed drastic social and political changes in the South. Another historian, however, refuses to accept the use of this term regarding the Civil War because, under international law, the words unconditional surrender automatically signified the existence of a war between nations. Even if one were to speak of "surrender" in terms of international law and not domestic troubles, this writer insists, Lincoln's "provisional emancipation proclamation was a *conditional*-surrender proposal: if states returned to the Union in the next several months, they would retain their slaves."10

This view, however, fails to consider the practical aspects of Lincoln's strategy: the President gave the South a mere hundred days to resume its normal status within the Union before the Emancipation Proclamation went into effect on January 1, 1863. In the interim, Lincoln remained open to compromise on slavery and racial issues that fitted the dictates of his Republican party; but he realized that there was little reason to hope for the Union's restoration within this short period. Fierce Confederate resistance continued, ensuring that none of the Southern states would willingly return to the Union on these or any other terms; only a Union military conquest in each Southern state would assure the end of slavery. The Union had no chance to achieve its goal within that brief time span. Emanicipation would therefore go into effect and doubtless take on a momentum of its own that would eventually undermine the peculiar institution everywhere—including the border states. Lincoln waged a war that could end only with the South's unconditional surrender.

Both presidents realized the importance of cloaking the ugliness of war with mythology and imagery, and thereby attempted to lift its meaning above the battlefield in an effort to sanctify the horrendous sacrifice. As one historian has perceptively pointed out, "It was a paradox of the liberal faith, that the lover of peace had to be ready to fight wars to defend the survival of that faith."[11] Though referring only to Lincoln, this testimony applies just as readily to Roosevelt.

A central point permeates both Presidents' thinking: if war has any worthwhile goal, it must be to guarantee liberty from oppression, whether that oppression comes from physical enslavement or from some form of bondage to a totalitarian government. In the Civil War, Lincoln viewed black freedom as an integral step toward securing liberty for all; not only must the South lose on the battlefield, but it must also lose its archaic views about race relations and the social order. Slavery, Lincoln had insisted to the Illinois legislature in 1837, rested on "injustice and bad policy." The enslavement of human beings, he publicly declared in 1854, was a "monstrous injustice." To deny liberty to any person, whether black or white, encouraged the eradication of liberty for all. Indeed, human bondage was double-edged in establishing tyranny. As Lincoln declared five years later, "he who would *be* no slave, must consent to *have* no slave. Those who deny freedom to others, deserve it not for themselves; and under a just God, can not long retain it." And, as President, Lincoln told Congress in December 1862 that, "In *giving* freedom to the *slave*, we *assure* freedom to the *free.*"[12] Roosevelt, as well, opposed any form of government that denied basic freedoms.

Both Lincoln and Roosevelt have been accused of dictatorial policies. According to one critic, Lincoln resorted to "more arbitrary power than perhaps any other President." But recent studies have softened this view. Lincoln defended the Emancipation Proclamation by declaring "that measures, otherwise unconstitutional, might become lawful, by becoming indispensable to the preservation of the constitution, through the preservation of the nation." Roosevelt was even more blunt in his readiness to sacrifice principle in the name of expediency. At one point in May 1942 he told a small group that "I am perfectly willing to mislead and tell untruths if it will help win the war."[13] Admittedly, both Presidents stretched the powers of their office by using their military commissions. Yet Lincoln and Roosevelt confronted their national crises by relying on the Constitution and a profound sense of moral purpose in preserving the nation.

Both Presidents were extremely adept in securing policies that in reality went even further in meaning than appearance. Lincoln assured a crowd in Chicago that he revered the Declaration of Independence as the very foundation of America. But when he declared that all men were created equal, he himself added the qualifying words, "let it be as nearly reached as we can." Human frailties undermined the drive for perfection, he knew, but mankind should continue striving toward that goal. "We can succeed only by concert," he told Congress. "It is not 'can *any* of us *imagine* better?' but 'can we *all* do better?'"[14] Roosevelt and Lincoln moved within severe social and political restraints, which forced them to recognize that imperfection was the reigning principle in the world and that a slow, steady advance toward a better place was preferable to demanding all and receiving nothing.

Let the focus now be Lincoln, who, it is clear, came to realize that the Civil War must assume a higher purpose than merely defeating the Confederacy. His religious convictions necessitated his belief in a divine plan in which he as President acted as God's instrument in effecting great social changes. That, it could be argued, was presumptuous if indeed not blasphemous, but the sentiment was heartfelt; and Lincoln went further. He believed that the Civil War could beget what one writer calls a "spiritual regeneration." Using Biblical imagery, Lincoln asserted that the Civil War was engendering a rebirth of spirit based on the "born again" concept found in the New Testament Gospel of John. "Our republican robe is soiled, and trailed in the dust," Lincoln declared. "Let us repurify it.

Let us turn and wash it white, in the spirit, if not the blood, of the Revolution."[15]

As Lincoln viewed matters, the same energy that permeated the great document of 1776 was now moving the American nation closer to the ultimate goal of freedom for all. The Declaration of Independence had provided the spirit of the Constitution, which itself served as the first real attempt to manifest that ideal, to be shaped in accordance with the steady progression toward the idea of univeral liberty contained in the Declaration. By converting the war into a moral crusade, Lincoln vindicated the massive suffering and suggested that divine intervention would assure Union victory. The war by the summer of 1863, according to a historian, "had gone on too long, its aspect had become too grim, and the escalating casualties were too staggering for a man of Lincoln's sensitivity to discover in that terrible ordeal no greater purpose than the denial of the southern claim to self-determination."[16]

In the Emancipation Proclamation, Lincoln used his power as commander-in-chief to implement the principles of the Declaration of Independence. The Constitution, Lincoln insisted to a member of his cabinet, justified the Proclamation as a "military necessity." In a national emergency, he automatically took on military powers not allowed to Congress. To a large public group, he asserted that "As commander-in-chief of the army and navy, in time of war, I suppose I have a right to take any measure which may best subdue the enemy."[17] The long-range result of this military measure would necessarily be the death of slavery.

In seeking his idealistic and realistic objectives, Lincoln assumed executive powers that only appeared to have been unconstitutional. Never before had a President referred to the war power as belonging to him. But he based his reasoning on his pledge as President to safeguard the Constitution. That document, he proclaimed in a letter intended for the public, made him "commander-in-chief, with the law of war, in time of war." Before a special session of Congress, he bitingly responded to the charge of wrongdoing by asking whether republics contained an "inherent, and fatal weakness"? Can they not defend themselves by any means available? "Must a government, of necessity, be too *strong* for the liberties of its own people, or too *weak* to maintain its own existence?"[18]

Lincoln did not act in a dictatorial manner. In issuing the Emancipation Proclamation he exercised his authority as commander-in-chief of the army and navy in putting down an armed rebellion against the U.S. government. Lincoln made no claim to a permanent acquisition of presidential power; he confined the use of military authority to the time of the rebellion itself. "Can it be pretended," he asked a friend, "that it is any longer the government of the U.S.—any government of Constitution and laws,—wherein a General, or a President, may make permanent rules of property by proclamation?" Lincoln also had not acted in any civilian capacity—which denoted his understanding that only Congress could end slavery. The basic platform of the Republican party, he told listeners during his famous 1858 debates in Illinois with Senator Stephen A. Douglas, was to halt the spread of slavery and place it "in the course of ultimate extinction." In his First Inaugural Address, Lincoln declared that "I have no purpose, directly or indirectly, to interfere with the institution of slavery in the States where it exists. I believe I have no lawful right to do so, and I have no inclination to do so."[19]

Lincoln had several purposes in mind in announcing the Emancipation Proclamation. First and foremost, he expected it to facilitate the military effort. But he also knew that emancipation would bring about a far-reaching series of social changes that, in turn, justified the use of force on ending slavery. Lincoln's enlistment of blacks in the Union army proved integral to eventual Union victory; his appeal to blacks to walk off the plantations aimed at destabilizing the South by pulling out that region's chief social, political, and economic cornerstone. In March 1863 Lincoln wrote Andrew Johnson, military governor of Tennessee, that "the bare sight of fifty thousand armed, and drilled black soldiers on the banks of the Mississippi, would end the rebellion at once." By August, the Union army contained 50,000 black troops, prompting Lincoln to declare to a friend that "the emancipation policy, and the use of colored troops, constitute the heaviest blow yet dealt to the rebellion."[20]

Not surprisingly, Lincoln's great document satisfied only those observers perceptive enough to discern the reality of the proclamation rather than its appearance. One historian criticized it as having "all the moral grandeur of a bill of lading." Another cynically dismissed the document as "more often admired than read," and insisted that neither the author of emancipation nor the document itself deserved praise for ending slavery.

Military and political considerations, this latter writer insisted, dictated the proclamation; moral factors played no important role in a policy that aimed only at preserving the Union. Had not Lincoln, though personally finding slavery morally repugnant, supported gradual emancipation with compensation to owners—or even colonization—in seeking to resolve the problem of slavery? But Lincoln's careful and even sterile wording of the proclamation was purposeful. It was, he declared, a "necessary war measure for suppressing said rebellion."[21] But it also turned the nation toward antislavery and thereby assured ultimate freedom for the slave.

The traditional arguments regarding Lincoln's use of emancipation as a military measure are sound; but they fail to note the international dimensions of his move. Lincoln also intended the proclamation to prevent foreign intervention in the war. To the Union minister in Spain, Carl Schurz, Lincoln declared in September 1861, "I cannot imagine that any European power would dare to recognize and aid the Southern Confederacy if it became clear that the Confederacy stands for slavery and the Union for freedom." A year later he told a group called Chicago Christians of All Denominations that "no other step would be so potent to prevent foreign intervention."Indeed, one historian has insisted that Lincoln declared the Emancipation Proclamation "with the European powers largely in mind." Ending slavery might win their support. "In some respects," the same writer concluded, "the Emancipation Proclamation was more important as a diplomatic document than as a domestic one; it elevated the moral cause of the Union to a higher plane."[22]

If this assessment is a bit strong, it nevertheless draws attention to a critical aspect of the Civil War. Lincoln reasoned that if the Union made the war a crusade against slavery, England could not enter the contest on the side of the slaveholding South. In a very real sense, his attempt to thwart outside involvement in the war constituted a vital part of his military effort to win that war. Within the most extreme of scenarios, the South could have negotiated a military alliance with one or more of the intervening powers and, during the tenuous first eighteen months of the war, tipped the balance in its favor and emerged triumphant. Even a mediation would have threatened the Union; *any* form of intervention would have legitimized secession, raised Confederate morale, and opened foreign markets and treasuries to leaders in Richmond. The foreign dimensions of the Emancipation Proclamation fell within Lincoln's argument for military necessity.

More than that, however, Lincoln had devised an effective wartime strategy that contained both realistic and idealistic overtones. He realized that the moral and political ramifications of such a move were incidental to the main military thrust of restoring the Union. He knew that the Constitution condoned property in slaves and thereby obstructed progress toward the realization of equality underlying the Declaration of Independence. He also recognized that his power as commander-in-chief was limited to putting down the rebellion. Consequently, he first reiterated his assurance to the South that he would not use his civilian power to interfere in its domestic institutions. A moral denunciation of the South, he realized, would obstruct his wish to govern that region of the country once the Union was whole again. And he made sure that emancipation through his military power did not cast moral aspersions on slaveowners in the border states. Top priority, of course, was to win the war; but if humanitarian ends derived from realistic means, so much the better. Lincoln fully realized that the best form of policy, whether domestic or foreign, emanated from a balance between the real and the ideal.

And yet, Lincoln's emancipation strategy regarding foreign affairs almost backfired: instead of solidifying England's support for the Union, the proclamation struck many Englishmen as the most sordid type of hypocrisy. Surely the Emancipation Proclamation signaled the Union's last gasp, they angrily declared. To escape imminent defeat, the Union had "played its last card," according to the *Times* of London.[23] The British chargé in Washington, William Stuart, bitterly denounced the document as a cheap, last-ditch effort to salvage victory by stirring up slave revolts throughout the South. A bloody race war would erupt, knowing no territorial bounds and soon dragging in other nations. If the Union truly opposed slavery for humanitarian reasons, it would have proclaimed abolition as the chief goal of the war. The irony is that the proclamation stimulated a British push for intervention that sought to end this most horrible of wars and assure the demise of slavery.

Fortunately for the Union, the forces operating against British intervention proved stronger than those working for that end. After the initial expressions of disgust for the proclamation, Englishmen came to realize that intervention meant war with the Union. Further, they began to see that emancipation had generated a movement toward abolition that would not end until every black person in America was free. Within a month of the preliminary proclamation of late September 1862 (and more than two months before its actual implementation), British working groups joined liberals in hailing the President's announcement as the death knell of slavery. Popular support for emancipation became so widespread that it undercut those Southern sympathizers in Parliament who had called for intervention. Such a move became much more difficult to consider now that Lincoln had lifted the war into a moral crusade for black freedom.

Emancipation therefore served first as a means for winning the war and then, finally, as a chief purpose of the war itself. Abolition became morally inseparable from the preservation of the Union—both a "military necessity" and "an act of justice," as Lincoln so rightfully declared in his Proclamation. Emancipation had provided more than 100,000 black men to the Union army by the summer of 1864. In an interview he insisted that "no human power can subdue this rebellion without using the Emancipation lever as I have done." That same summer he told Horace Greeley of his desire for a peace based on "the restoration of the Union and abandonment of slavery." In his Second Inaugural Address, Lincoln denounced slavery as "one of those offenses which, in the providence of God . . . He now wills to remove [through] this terrible war, as the woe due to those by whom the offence came. . . . Yet if God wills that it continue, until all the wealth piled by the bondman's two hundred and fifty years of unrequited toil shall be sunk, and until every drop of blood drawn with the lash, shall be paid by another drawn with the sword, as was said three thousand years ago, so still it must be said 'the judgments of the Lord, are true and righteous altogether.'" Thus "by embracing the cause of the slave," according to one historian, Lincoln "had found the war's ultimate justification and thereby a way to come to terms with his God and with himself."[24]

This is all well and good; but even this does not go far enough. Lincoln sought to undermine the contradictions between the ideal (the Declaration) and the real (the Constitution) by demonstrating that a nation built on liberty must continually hone its republican principles within the realities of life. The central premise of the Declaration—that of equality—took on greater stature as a result of the ongoing war. Indeed, the Declaration, like the blood of Christ, repeatedly washed the Constitution of its transgressions against humanity through the process of amendment. As Lincoln noted in his First Inaugural Address, the Union was perpetual and arose from the Articles of Association of 1774, the Declaration of Independence two years afterward, and the Articles of Confederation in 1781. The imperfect Union therefore came *before* the Constitution, whose aim was *"to form a more perfect union"* based on a government, he declared at Gettysburg in November 1863, "of the people, by the people, for the people."[25]

Consequently, at Gettysburg Lincoln argued that the Civil War provided a vital impetus to the great social and political changes born of the American Revolution when he expressed his fervent wish that all these Americans "shall not have died in vain—that this nation, under God, shall have a new birth of freedom." The war still raging in late 1863 had not yet completed the task of achieving liberty. Americans, he insisted, now faced "the unfinished work" of moving the nation closer to fulfilling the promises of its founders.[26]

Lincoln's Gettysburg Address, a mere 272 words in length, provided the moral and intellectual underpinning of the war, which, in turn, gave the President his realistic and idealistic justification for waging that war. Out of the Union victory at Gettysburg arose an opportunity to elevate the war's aims from the earthly to the heavenly realm. The butchery of the battle became the crucible from which arose the great test of the Republic—whether that experiment in liberty would survive. The bloodbath at Gettysburg became part of what one writer calls a "larger process" of universal change. "Words had to complete the work of the guns."[27]

At Gettysburg took place the epochal struggle between life and death, with Lincoln converting the horrors of the battle into the very apotheosis of death, into life. Lincoln's "funereal," melancholy presence, according to one historian, was part of the contemporary acceptance of the "culture of death" in which gloom and foreboding were desirable qualities that operated as intermediaries between heaven and earth. Lincoln deified death by making it serve life. As he himself wrote in one of his early pieces of poetry mourning the dead:

> O memory! thou mid-way world
> 'Twixt Earth and Paradise,
> Where things decayed, and loved ones lost
> In dreamy shadows rise.[28]

The Civil War served as an important transition between the destruction of human slavery and the continuing progress toward human equality. Thus, the war became a means rather than an end. In speaking of the Declaration of Independence, Lincoln thought it "contemplated the progressive improvement in the condition of all men everywhere." The Founding Fathers, he believed, "did not mean to declare all men equal *in all respects.*" They "meant simply to declare the *right,* so that the *enforcement* of it might follow as fast as circumstances should permit." Their ideal was a "free society . . . constantly looked to, constantly labored for, and even though never perfectly attained, constantly approximated and thereby constantly spreading and deepening its influence and augmenting the happiness and value of life to all people, of all colors, everywhere."[29]

Lincoln wanted black people to experience the "life, liberty, and the pursuit of happiness" emphasized in the Declaration of Independence. As one writer declares, Lincoln's ideal of liberty was "open-ended" in that it possessed "the capacity to expand toward notions of equity, justice, social welfare, equality of opportunity." Like Henry Clay, Lincoln believed that *"it is true as an abstract principle* that all men are created equal, but that we cannot practically apply it in all cases." Another historian declares that Lincoln supported "Clay's middle-of-the-road, pragmatic position" of "opposition to slavery in principle" and "toleration of it in practice." But this assessment misleadingly suggests that Lincoln's motivation was so heavily political that it left little room for either moral or practical considerations. Lincoln considered the advancement of individual liberty the primary motivation in life; but he also recognized the impracticality of attempting to abolish slavery at once. As Lincoln admitted in 1852, Clay realized that "slavery was already widely spread and deeply seated" and "did not perceive, as I think no wise man has perceived, how it could be at *once* eradicated, without producing a greater evil, even to the cause of human liberty itself."[30]

On a practical level, Lincoln recognized that social and racial equality was out of the question during his lifetime. "I have already said the contrary," he publicly asserted in 1854. "I am not now combating the argument of NECESSITY, arising from the fact that the blacks are already amongst us." Slavery, Lincoln insisted during his debates with Douglas, was a form of despotism that violated the natural right of self-government found in the Declaration of Independence. Every human being had the inherent right to freedom; but this did not automatically mean racial equality. "I have no purpose to introduce political and social equality between the white and black races." But he did not rule out such changes in the future. Lincoln viewed the move toward a better place as part of "the eternal struggle between . . . right and wrong—throughout the world."[31]

Emancipation thus became the principal avenue though which individual freedom might manifest itself to the fullest degree possible during the nineteenth century. "On the side of the Union," Lincoln asserted before Congress in July 1861, was "a struggle for maintaining in the world, that form, and substance of government, whose leading object is, to elevate the condition of men—to lift artificial weights from all shoulders—to clear the paths of laudable pursuit for all"—white *and* black—"to afford all, an unfettered start, and a fair chance, in the race of life." In freeing the slave, he later insisted to Congress, "we *assure* freedom to the *free.*" Only by preserving the Union could Americans save the form of government that offered "the last best, hope of earth."[32]

Lincoln sought to fulfill the dream of his long-time favorite in the Senate, Daniel Webster, who in 1830 had uttered the famous words, "Liberty *and* Union, now and forever, one and inseparable!" To Lincoln, liberty could not exist without the Union, for the Union was the chief guarantor of republicanism. Preservation of the Constitution, he declared to a friend, carried with it the "duty of preserving, by every indispensable means, that government—that nation—of which that constitution was the organic law. Was it possible to lose the nation, and yet preserve the constitution?" The sanctity of the Union, Lincoln insisted, was the chief prerequisite to the destruction of slavery. "I could not feel that, to the best of my ability, I have even tried to preserve the constitution, if, to save slavery, or any minor matter, I should permit the wreck of government, country, and Constitution all together." He drove home the point by admitting that "general law" called for the protection of "life *and* limb." So "often a limb must be amputated to save a life; but a life is never wisely given to save a limb."[33] Liberty and Union must mesh, Lincoln proclaimed, providing his paramount aim in the war and afterward.

To Lincoln the wartime diplomatist, foreign affairs were inseparable from domestic affairs, both in terms of the diplomatic and military aspects of the war as well as its central objective of preserving the Union as a bastion of individual freedom. The struggle to prevent foreign intevention in the war was of profound importance to Lincoln. During the first critical year and a half of the war—when its outcome hung in the balance—he feared a foreign involvement that would doubtless have assured Southern independence and thereby subverted the ideals found in the Declaration of Independence. Only a Union victory in the war could preserve the republic and assure its continued progress toward equality. Lincoln thus personified the diplomatist *par excellence* in seeking a wartime goal built on moral and intellectual principles while having the common sense to work toward that goal by measured, practical, and realistic means.

Roosevelt's own realistic approach to foreign affairs first became clear in his move from a Wilsonian League of Nations resting on moral obligations. According to the traditional interpretation, Roosevelt was a Wilsonian who considered collective security the key to America's security. But Roosevelt gave up the League of Nations idea for both practical and political reasons. Although his enthusiasm for Woodrow Wilson was genuine, he came to believe that the League's underlying assumption of equality among nations did not fit with reality. Then, in the presidential campaign of 1932, Roosevelt completed his steady drift from the League idea by caving in to pressure from influential publisher William Randolph Hearst, who rigidly opposed American participation in the League and refused to support any presidential candidate favoring the idea.

Ensuing events led Roosevelt to support an international peace organization based on power. Ultimately called the "Four Policemen" idea, the new order revolved around the establishment of spheres of influence in which, he declared to the British, "the real decisions should be made by the United States, Great Britain, Russia and China, who would have . . . to police the world." The Great Powers, he publicly insisted, "were in complete agreement that we must be prepared to keep the peace by force." Roosevelt believed that other nations would emulate America once given the chance. "It was the city-on-a-hill/an-example-for-all-the-world-to-follow approach that FDR preferred," one historian declares, "even if coercion and force were sometimes legitimate means to the end." The postwar world would rest on "peaceful coexistence, even if the peace officers had to be armed." Another historian agrees that Roosevelt was more interested in a Big Four power arrangement than "a federation acting for the brotherhood of all mankind."[34]

A second indication of Roosevelt's realism came with his decision to extend diplomatic recognition to the Soviet Union in 1933. The United States, he believed, had ill-advisedly alienated the Soviets after the Great War by morally condemning the Bolsheviks. The President favored recognition for a mixture of realistic reasons. Not only did it seem rational for two large countries to maintain official communication, but the establishment of diplomatic relations would permit a commercial arrangement beneficial to both. Even more important was Roosevelt's hope that Soviet-American cooperation might slow Japan's penetration of China. Finally, he realized that Russia would someday be a major determinant in international concerns.

A third sign of Roosevelt's realistic approach to foreign policy came with his effort *before* the Pearl Harbor attack to move the United States more deeply into international affairs. "Revisionist" historians have argued that he practiced the art of deception in outwardly supporting neutrality while secretly maneuvering a reluctant American nation into the European war. In August 1941, Roosevelt and Churchill proclaimed the Atlantic Charter, which advocated "the right of all peoples to choose the form of government under which they will live."[35] This joint call for national self-determination as a wartime objective took place, critics pointed out, nearly four months *before* the United States had entered that war.

As in most history, however, the truth was more complex than believed. Roosevelt began his presidency determined to keep out of the war, but ultimately realized—even *before* Pearl Harbor—that there was no alternative to entering the war. Like many Americans of his day, he attributed the Great War to arms-makers and other businessmen who had tied the nation so tightly to the belligerents that it had no choice but to enter the fighting to protect investments. He refused to make the same mistake. Even when Roosevelt later sought a moral embargo on aggressor nations, his real purpose was to stay out of the conflict by exerting economic pressure on the belligerents. Roosevelt feared that a strict adherence to neutrality might push the United States *into* the war rather than keep it out. He preferred what he termed "permissive legislation" that allowed him to place an embargo on the aggressor and *not* the victim.[36]

Appearances and realities began to diverge as the crisis built in Europe during the late 1930s. Roosevelt began a slight shift toward internationalism in October 1937, when, in his controversial "Quarantine Speech" of October in Chicago, he condemned "the epidemic of world lawlessness" and advocated "positive endeavors to preserve peace." Roosevelt, however, intended that his speech buy time to facilitate his continued search for peace. Sanctions, he knew, were out of the question because of American domestic opposition. During the Munich crisis of 1938, Roosevelt remained unsure about what action, if any, the United States should take and therefore did nothing. By the close of that year, however, he had concluded that the threats posed by Germany, Italy, and Japan to Europe and Asia had direct bearing on U.S. security as well. During the 1940s, one writer concludes, Roosevelt became the "reluctant internationalist" who had finally accepted his responsibilities as a world leader.[37]

Controversy has raged for some time over Roosevelt's devious policies toward the growing crisis in Europe. No question exists that a vast gulf developed between appearances and realities. But it also seems clear that, after the disillusioning effect of appeasement at the Munich Conference, the President engaged in several moves intended to preserve American security. During the debate over whether to lift the arms embargo, Roosevelt tried to keep the country out of the war by observing a pro-Allies neutrality. There can be no doubt that the President deliberately misled Americans in an effort to help England and France. To journalist and friend William Allen White in late 1939, Roosevelt admitted that "my problem is to get the American people to think of conceivable consequences without scaring the American people into thinking that they are going to be dragged into this war."[38]

Roosevelt's most distinct turn toward internationalism came in his highly publicized commencement address at the University of Virginia in June 1940. Italy had that same day declared war on France, darkening the ceremonies in Charlottesville and pushing him to more direct action. Most attention has gone to his rebuke of Italy—"the hand that held the dagger has struck it into the back of its neighbor."[39] But this dramatic statement obscured the President's promised assistance to England and France—the last two countries seemingly capable of stopping the Nazi juggernaut and thereby safeguarding American security itself. After the fall of France to Germany that same month, only Britain stood between America and Hitler. And only the United States could provide the means by which the British could withstand the German war machine.

The destroyers-bases deal with England the following September further revealed Roosevelt's furtive and yet expanding foreign policy. According to terms, the President traded fifty outdated destroyers for ninety-nine-year leases on eight British bases in the Western Hemisphere, extending from Newfoundland south to British Guiana. Churchill negotiated this unique arrangement which Roosevelt enacted by a highly controversial executive agreement. The President at first thought that Congress had to approve the deal and he followed his cabinet's advice to seek bipartisan support from Republican Wendell Willkie, who would be that party's standard-bearer in the approaching presidential election. Though Willkie refused to garner Republican support in Congress for the idea, he agreed to leave the issue out of the campaign. Roosevelt realized, however, that the situation was an emergency requiring swift action and, arguing that isolationists and other critics would block the measure in Congress, acted without its approval and in an unneutral manner. Little question exists that aid to England violated neutrality and hence constituted a hostile act against Germany. Most important, however, Roosevelt believed that failure to support the arrangement would endanger his own nation's security. The transaction, he declared, constituted "the most important action in the reinforcement of our national defense than has been taken since the Louisiana Purchase."[40]

Another example of Roosevelt's wily approach to diplomacy came during the presidential election of 1940. Despite Willkie's early reluctance to make foreign policy an issue in the campaign, he abruptly shifted tactics when it seemed he might not win. If Roosevelt won reelection, Willkie warned a large and exuberant crowd in Baltimore, the President would soon take America into the European conflict. In Boston on October 30, Roosevelt responded with words that have remained famous for their calculated impact: "And while I am talking to you mothers and fathers, I give you one more assurance. I have said this before, but I shall say it again and again and again: Your boys are not going to be sent into any foreign wars." Missing from his speech was a passage originally to be read: "except in case of attack." When speechwriter Samuel Rosenman inquired about this important omission, Roosevelt testily remarked that he saw no reason for including those words. "Of course we'll fight if we're attacked. If somebody attacks us, then it isn't a foreign war, is it?"[41]

Even more unneutral was Roosevelt's support for the hotly contested Lend-Lease Act of March 1941. By its provisions, the United States would lend or lease any defense item to any nation that the president considered critical to America's own welfare. "We must be," he declared in one of his many fireside chats over radio, "the great arsenal of democracy." In testimony before the Senate, historian Charles A. Beard urged that body to oppose the bill and "preserve one stronghold of order and sanity even against the gates of hell."[42] Beard's warnings about the administration's interventionist course were not unjustified. Lend-Lease made the United States a not-so-silent partner of the British in the war.

As in all interventions, the first move led to a deepening involvement. To protect the sea routes to England, the White House ordered American soldiers to Greenland and Iceland, and then assisted British naval vessels pursuing German submarines. When Secretary of War Stimson recommended seeking Congressional authorization for a convoy system designed to escort merchant vessels passing through submarine-infested waters, the President decided against this approach for fear that the deeply divided Congress would vote it down and thereby undermine the British war effort. Instead, Roosevelt secretly approved a measure permitting the U.S. Navy to patrol the waters beyond the 300-mile neutrality zone established in the Atlantic shortly after war had broken out in 1939. But as Stimson recorded in his diary, the President's real purpose was to "follow the [British] convoys and notify them of any German raiders or German submarines that we may see and give them a chance to escape."[43]

Then, without Congressional approval, the President authorized a shoot-on-sight policy in the Atlantic, which soon involved the United States in an undeclared naval war against Nazi submarines. A German U-boat, he told Americans over nationwide radio in September 1941, had attacked the U.S.S. *Greer* in a blatant act of piracy. Though Roosevelt knew at the time that the *Greer* itself had instigated the encounter, he exploited the incident to justify a convoy system. German submarines, he declared, had become the "rattlesnakes of the Atlantic," forcing the U.S. Navy to escort "all merchant ships—not only American ships but ships of any flag—engaged in commerce in our defensive waters."[44]

The most bitter controversy over Roosevelt's policies centered on the Japanese attack on Pearl Harbor. Nothing has matched the ferocity of the charges made by "revisionist" historians who claimed that the President, unable to convince the American public of the German threat, actually *welcomed* a Japanese attack because it took the United States into the war through the "back door."[45]Convincing refutations came from several writers, who admit to numerous mistakes by the White House but deny the existence of a purposeful policy based on the back door theory. One historian demonstrates that numerous conflicting intelligence signals— "noise"—created a chaotic situation not conducive to calm analysis.[46] Another writer interviewed Japan's wartime leaders and found that they were *not* mere pawns of a duplicitous President who manipulated them into the Pearl Harbor assault; rather, they were determined to attack the United States. Further, Roosevelt had to oppose *all* forms of fascism— both German and Japanese—and unavoidably adopted policies that hurt Japanese interests in China and hence charted the course to Pearl Harbor. Though some critics remain, the conspiracy theory regarding Pearl Harbor deserves little scholarly attention.

With the United States in the war, its earlier recognition of the Soviet Union now proved integral to their wartime collaboration. Indeed, Roosevelt extended Lend-Lease aid to the Soviets, demonstrating his realistic diplomacy in the face of stern opposition from his own military and diplomatic advisers, who believed it impossible for the Soviets to ward off the German onslaught and that America could never reconcile its principles with those of the Soviets. Aid to the Soviet Union also led to a wartime unity conducive to a postwar situation that might have been more dangerous than it actually turned out to be. The assistance program, one writer declares, opened a "window of trust and cooperation" that later allowed the Kremlin to argue during *glasnost* that ideological differences did not preclude great power collaboration during a crisis.[47] Ever the realist and pragmatist, Roosevelt pursued one chief objective throughout the war: defeat the Nazis by any means at his disposal. But he also kept a wary eye on the postwar world.

Still another example of Roosevelt's *Realpolitik* came with the democratic principles he advocated in the Atlantic Charter and the Yalta Declaration on Liberated Europe. A year after the Atlantic Charter, in 1942, Roosevelt sent an anniversary message to leaders of the United Nations, which affirmed "their faith in life, liberty, independence and religious freedom, and in the preservation of human rights and justice." In harmony with the Atlantic Charter, the Yalta Declaration of early 1945 called for Big Three cooperation in "the earliest possible establishment through free elections of governments responsive to the will of the people."[48] The ideal of self-determination permeated both documents and heralded an end to colonialism; but much more did the reality of peace rest on the combined military strength of the Great Powers.

According to one criticism, Roosevelt's makeshift and indecisive leadership during the war helped bring on the Cold War. The bulk of the President's efforts to win the Soviets' trust came apart in the face of Secretary of State Cordell Hull's rigid adherence to the Atlantic Charter; from Stalin's viewpoint, the right of self-determination did not guarantee friendly neighbors. Roosevelt's premature assurances to the Soviets of a second front further raised their suspicions of the West; repeated delays by the United States and England in drawing off the German invasion of June 1941 seemed like a cynical effort to allow both belligerents to destroy each other. On the issues of boundaries and sovereignty relating to Poland, according to one writer, Roosevelt at Yalta appproved "an ambiguous and elusive paper agreement" that reflected his lack of concern for the beleaguered country and his failure to see the connection between the war and its aftermath. If the President had worked toward a definite western boundary, the same writer speculates, "he might have limited postwar Soviet influence in Central Europe and achieved a fairer territorial settlement." The result was that "Poland, more than any other issue, gave rise to the Cold War, and Roosevelt, through his misleading diplomacy, must bear a share of the responsibility."[49]

Admittedly, Roosevelt's wartime policies toward not only the Soviets but the British as well widened the gap between hope and reality and contributed to the Cold War. Yet these policies now appear to have been unavoidable. Documents show that Roosevelt was not Stalin's fool, and, as one writer demonstrates, the President and his advisors believed that "Britain epitomized much of what was wrong with the world." Indeed, the White House argued that British colonial policies were chiefly responsible for the international rivalries that brought on *both* world wars. During the interwar period, the British had encouraged the outbreak of economic depression and war through a closed economic system conducive to commercial and political rivalries. The Roosevelt administration wanted to replace the British system of imperial preference with a Wilsonian program of world interdependence based on a liberal commercial network resting on the principle of reciprocity. In this manner, the President could satisfy Wilsonian idealists while realistically involving the United States in international affairs. The White House wanted to redesign the postwar global economy into one based on the end of colonialism and the institution of free trade that, the writer correctly argues, meant "equal commercial opportunity" and "the elimination of discriminatory trade practices."[50] But the United States fell victim to events beyond its control: Soviet expansion, civil war in China, and a rash of colonial revolutions.

The President had a fairly specific vision of the postwar world when he formulated wartime policy. Contrary to traditional accounts, one writer insists, Roosevelt had "a conscious, structured foreign policy" that perhaps left a great gulf between "concept and implementation" but nonetheless did not bend to every whim of domestic opinion. As idealist and realist, Roosevelt sought both short- and long-range objectives by attempting to implement Wilsonian principles in accordance with global realities. Another writer declares that Roosevelt sought a "world citadel of freedom" by acting as a "soldier of freedom" during World War II.[51] When Roosevelt advocated that the projected United Nations Organization place Nazi-liberated territories under the trusteeship of member nations until the freed peoples were capable of governing themselves, he used idealism to cloak the reality of power politics by assuring national self-determination while guaranteeing strategic bases for the United States and its allies.

Roosevelt slowly but surely adopted internationalist princples to lead the United States into a wartime alliance that ultimately brought victory over fascism. Given his wartime need to placate the Soviets, he was in no position to make demands of Stalin. By the time Harry Truman became President in April 1945, the Red Army occupied many of the areas in eastern Europe that the West expected to benefit from Yalta's promise of self-determination, and Stalin's quest for security virtually assured no governing voice except his own. Even Roosevelt's chief critic allows that the President "met these challenges boldly, playing a key role in ending the Nazi tyranny and making a valiant if unsuccessful effort to avert the Cold War."[52]

Like Lincoln, Roosevelt found that foreign and domestic affairs were inseparable. Only an Allied victory in the war could preserve the right of national self-determination and thereby sanctify the American republic. Roosevelt thus joined Lincoln in exemplifying the effective wartime diplomatist who sought goals resting on moral and intellectual principles while recognizing the practical limitations involved in reaching such goals.

Both Lincoln and Roosevelt assumed wartime powers that stretched the Constitution but were nonetheless justified by national emergencies threatening the republic. On matters of domestic security, Lincoln's task was less clear-cut than that encountered by Roosevelt. By the time Roosevelt became President, the Fourteenth Amendment had solidified the status of civil liberties by anchoring them in the Constitution. But like Lincoln, Roosevelt did not distinguish between enemies of the state and political opponents of the administration. *All* opposition endangered the war effort and became subject to governmental practices not always falling within the letter of the law. Lincoln suspended the writ of habeas corpus; Roosevelt authorized mail tampering and wiretapping. Roosevelt also approved the establishment of relocation centers for Japanese-Americans in the United States—a measure that grew out of long-standing racial animosity for Orientals as well as the widespread fear of sabotage. The wartime expedient nonetheless won the support of numerous lawyers (including Stimson), members of Congress, and the U.S. Supreme Court.

Lincoln would have agreed with Roosevelt's January 1941 declaration before Congress that he had used "the sovereignty of Government" in an effort "to save Government." Neither man subverted the Constitution in preserving the Republic; the wartime crises they faced had necessitated extreme presidential actions deemed vital to national survival. They never wavered from the central objective of protecting both liberty and law. As Arthur Schlesinger wrote in Chapter Seven, both Presidents "remained faithful to the spirit, if not the letter, of the Constitution: acting on the spirit to save the letter."[53]

Their methods must have been just: after the emergencies were over, the governments themselves resumed the normal constitutional process. Lincoln forecast this eventual outcome when he assured Congress that "the Executive power itself would be greatly diminished by the cessation of actual war." Roosevelt alike publicly declared, "When the war is won, the powers under which I act automatically revert to the people—to whom they belong."[54] Soon after Lincoln's assassination, Congress regained power so quickly that it came close to removing his successor, Andrew Johnson, from office. And, shortly after Roosevelt's death the American people turned sharply against his successor, Harry Truman, by voting in a Republican Congress and proposing the Twenty-second Amendment to the Constitution, which limited a President to two terms in office.

Lincoln and Roosevelt perceived real dangers to the nation and reacted in ways that focused on the very best in diplomacy: they kept the grand vision of freedom before the American people while dealing realistically with the problems threatening that ideal. The national danger that confronted each President did not always allow for Congressional deliberation; consequently, they took unilateral actions that invited probing constitutional questions not answerable in a satisfactory way to every American. But even though both men at times resorted to secrecy, they kept the wartime goals themselves before the public and therefore subjected foreign policy to continual discussion and debate. Both Presidents realized that in a republic their actions would come under the careful scrutiny of Congress, the Supreme Court, and the American people.

Lincoln and Roosevelt preserved the nation by safeguarding liberty as the very essence of the republic. As wartime diplomatists, they recognized that sound moral and intellectual leadership provided the vital underpinning to an effective and realistic brand of diplomacy. Deceptions, distortions, diplomatic falsehoods—even the diplomatic lie—all have a habit of catching up to the perpetrator at some time, whether through the efforts of contemporary observers or historians later rummaging through the evidence. Roosevelt has stood vulnerable to such charges; Lincoln has also, though to a lesser degree. Fortunately for Americans, however, both Presidents developed a moral and intellectual justification for their foreign policies that rested on republican ideals, and kept that vision uppermost while preserving the nation in its two most perilous times.

9

Retelling the Tale:
Wars in Common Memory

MICHAEL C. C. ADAMS

WHEN Studs Terkel used *The Good War* in the title of his 1985 oral history of World War II, he made all other titles of books on that conflict pale by comparison. He also implicitly challenged us to think about a wider theme, namely, why some wars are thought of as good and some as bad. I think most people would agree that, within this framework, the Civil War and World War II are good wars, Vietnam (and possibly Korea) is a bad war.

There are some clear reasons why this should be so. Both the Civil War and World War II came after periods of self-doubt when the very existence of accepted national foundations appeared in jeopardy. The sectional animosities of the 1850s threatened to divide America permanently. Southerners increasingly rejected unconditional loyalty to the Union, while some Northerners seemed too apathetic or cowardly to fight for the nation's life. Abolitionists said "let the wayward sisters depart in peace," quarantining slavery at the expense of federal unity.

In the 1930s the Great Depression cast doubt on whether capitalism was a viable economic system. Politicians seemed inadequate to address the crisis, while European "strong men" like Adolf Hitler and Benito Mussolini converted people to the idea that a healthy state required authoritarian leadership. Americans seemed too jaded by World War I and too paralyzed by the effects of the Depression to offer help to the European democracies in their struggle for survival.

But in April 1861 with Fort Sumter, and December 1941 with Pearl Harbor, the nation sprang to life. "A nation hath been born again / Regenerate by a second birth!" wrote W. W. Howe after Lincoln's call for volunteers. There was "a unity," proclaimed one member of Congress shortly after Pearl Harbor, "never before witnessed in this country." Columnist Russell Baker said the war gave people a sense of community, of purpose and belonging, after the long gray years of the Depression.[1]

Both wars seemingly left America more united, purposeful, sure of its course. Both wars boosted business enterprise, bringing prosperity for some, particularly of the white middle class, in the giddy era of the Gilded Age and the suburban comfort of the 1950s. Not least, both wars enhanced America's status as a military and diplomatic power.

Vietnam, by contrast, came after a period of relative unity, the 1950s, and appeared to divide the nation. America's forces were not victorious in the field, and the war boosted taxation and inflation rather than prosperity. At its height, the war cost the taxpayer $1,000,000 per day. Americans became less confident about using their military power to intervene in international disputes. A poll carried out for *Rolling Stone* magazine in April 1988 showed that 65 percent of respondents opposed further serious overseas military commitments. Respondents said Vietnam had lowered faith in the U.S. government and America's contemporary world role, whereas "the victory of World War II was not only a glorious triumph for the nation, but it taught deeper lessons about what one could expect in life. The United States could stand up for just causes, and if everyone pulled together, it could win."[2]

The view of Vietnam as a bad war was furthered by the fact that

America's aims were essentially defensive, to protect rather than to take ground, to defend a regime rather than conquer an enemy power. Objectives were often nebulous. The most clear-cut offensive, Tet, was an enemy victory, if not on the ground, at least in the mind. As one veteran put it, "There were no Normandies or Gettysburgs for us, no epic clashes that decided the fates of armies or nations." Or, as another said, there was "no Patton rushing for the Rhine, no beachheads to storm and win and hold for the duration."[3]

All this is in some sense true. But it is not the whole truth. There is in our popular culture a selective recall of war's features that makes the conflicts seem either better or worse than they were. To this degree, our wars have been mythologized. Often this retrieval of the past is to serve a didactic purpose: to point a moral about how virtuous we once were or to decry the recent follies of ourselves and our government. As Keith Walden, a student of myth, comments, what many people want from history is not greater understanding of what actually happened, but, rather, contact with familiar patterns that provide fundamental reassurance about the validity of basic values in the culture. In our context, good wars show us the benefits of unity and sacrifice for a well-understood cause, bad wars show what happens when we are disunited and our purpose is unclear. Good wars are supposed to have toughened our moral fiber, purged the selfishness of peace, and placed us higher on the road of national destiny. In this sense, as Haydon White argues, the process by which we retell our history is subjective and somewhat akin to fiction.

There are more than 90,000 books and articles on the Civil War, but they tend to retell the same story about the bravery of North and South, the epic clashes of major armies, the rivalries of Ulysses S. Grant and Robert E. Lee, Abraham Lincoln and Jefferson Davis. We have drastically narrowed the area within which discussion of the conflict can take place and within this boundary we say more and more about less and less. Our understanding of the war has hardened around what are taken to be the climactic moments in the massive saga of redemption through war. We have volumes on a single day at Gettysburg or, even more remarkable, a single action, such as Culp's Hill, within a single day's fighting. I have sometimes likened this to medieval warriors sitting around the great fire in the mead hall, listening to *Beowulf* or *The Song of Roland,* great tales that reaffirm male bravery and grand tribal destiny. Epic films such as *Gettysburg, The Longest Day, Patton* seem to fit this category.

Meanwhile, important parts of the past are omitted, ignored, and finally lost to memory. We do not know enough about the homefront in the Civil War. When the film *Glory* appeared, people said they had never heard the story of the black regiments. There had been scholarly studies, but only with *Glory* did black soldiers enter mainstream awareness. Thus the film served a purpose, but the 54th Massachusetts is now being co-opted into the Civil War/good-war myth, part of selective recall. For re-enactors the regiment is a vehicle for expressing contemporary middle-class black pride; most people don't know that one reason for black recruitment was to save trained white mechanics from the draft by taking advantage of the black man's low value to industrial society.

Bad-war myths, like good-war myths, also obscure the full past. In the case of Vietnam, it is popularly held that many veterans suffer post-traumatic stress disorder (PTSD) because this was an ugly war and they didn't get a parade, whereas most veterans of other wars adjusted quickly to peace. Also, we have the MIA (missing in action) myth. According to careful scholars, the idea that captured American service personnel were being hidden in Asia originated during the presidency of Richard M. Nixon and was used by the administration to help justify carrying on the war after it had promised peace through a secret plan: we had to fight on until our boys were free. But by now the myth has taken on a life of its own: in a recent poll, 69 percent of Americans believed that U.S. prisoners are still held in Asia, perhaps as many as 2000. There is no evidence for this. Under the conditions these men would have endured, they would be long dead. In fact, all save two or three American prisoners were accounted for when the war ended. Most of the MIAs were lost in water or inaccessible jungle, or were blown to pieces; they can never be reclaimed.

But this is not the point of the myth. It is not about real missing persons. We had no such obsession after World War II, when there were 79,000 MIAs, 19 percent of Americans presumed dead in the war. In Vietnam there were only 2300 MIAs, or 4 percent of American losses. The issue is not even about treatment of the dead; Confederate graves at Chantilly have been bulldozed for town houses without causing a national scandal. The MIA myth is about two things: First, deliberate public ignorance; despite all the books available on war, most people don't care to think honestly about what happens to a body hit by a projectile. Second, the myth makes tangible our resentment that our boys were lost in a doomed war in a far-off country we don't care about. The myth is about negative emotions. Unfortunately, it also painfully misleads relatives of MIAs.

Myths of good and bad wars handicap the garnering of knowledge because they constrain the historian in looking at crucial questions which fall outside the canons of the myths. Bad wars may be less harmful here because they let us look at problems like PTSD. Good-war myths prevent our exploring negatives. Thus, the rigid censorship of World War II, in conjunction with Hollywood's glamorized portrait of the war, denied Americans knowledge of that war's reality, which came to be seen as a lightning contest of lean fighting machines and young men who became hardened veterans under sage leaders like John Wayne's Sergeant Stryker. Admiral Gene LaRocque, who served throughout the war, said of war movies: "I hated to see how they glorified war. In all those films, people get blown up with their clothes on and fall gracefully to the ground. You don't see anybody being blown apart." Film, in combination with re-enactors, is also removing us from the reality of Civil War combat. It may be fun to camp out in antique uniforms, and re-enacting may have educational value, but unless we load with ball ammunition, we do not reproduce the substance of battle.[4]

With regard to combat, there are no good or bad wars. Some soldiers in any war find fighting exhilarating, but its essential nature is destructive, cruel, horrific. At least 50 percent of men in action in World War II soiled themselves. A last order before action was, "Keep your assholes tight." Many Civil War soldiers were so green and frightened that in their misery they fouled their weapons. Some 18,000 muzzleloaders retrieved from the field of Gettysburg were loaded with two to ten rounds. In World War II, a team of U.S. army researchers headed by Samuel Stouffer found that 75 to 85 percent of men were so revulsed by the killing, they could not fire their weapons in combat. The killing was done by unaimed fire from heavy-weapons platoons, artillery and bombers, a storm of brute-force firepower.

Projectiles do not impact politely as in the movies. Private Nick

War's Essential Nature is Destructive, Cruel, Horrific

The anguish of combat, as seen by Howard Brodie. Charcoal-pencil sketch, 1945. (Courtesy of the U. S. Army Center of Military History)

Weekes of the 3rd Alabama, describing the effect of canister hitting his unit at Chancellorsville, saw "an arm and shoulder fly from the man just in front, exposing his throbbing heart. Another's foot flew up and kicked him in the face as a shell struck his leg. Another, disemboweled, crawled along on all fours, his entrails trailing behind, and still another held up his tongue with his hand, a piece of shell having carried away his lower jaw."[5]

Ernie Pyle, a war reporter, saw the D-Day coast of Normandy for a mile out littered with shattered boats, vehicles, and body parts floating in the water. William Manchester, in the Pacific, was wounded when body parts blew into his spine. One GI was killed by a flying head, another by the ring on a severed finger.

Many soldiers die by burning; in World War II because they were hit by napalm or phosphorous rounds, which made them flare up like Roman candles, or because their planes or tanks caught fire (the Sherman was called a Ronson because it flamed so easily). In the Civil War, wounded were roasted alive when muzzle flashes set the undergrowth on fire. William T. Sherman never forgot how, at Shiloh, "our wounded men, mingled with rebels, charred and blackened by the burning tents and grass, were crawling about begging for someone to end their misery."[6]

Any field after a battle is a charnel house. Souvenir hunters and hungry animals picked over the Civil War dead. R. L. Dabney, of Stonewall Jackson's staff, noted that after Cross Keys many "dead, with some, perchance, of the mangled living, were partially devoured by swine before their burial." Wild pigs, dogs, and land crabs fed on the casualties of World War II. Civil War wounded might lie out for days. Charles B. Haydon of the 2nd Michigan recorded during the Peninsular fighting of June 1862 that "There were not a few [wounded] in the last battle who were literally eaten alive by maggots." The faces of the dead became "a smooth, dark shining mass of putridity, nearly as large as a half bushel." Breeding in this garden of decay and excrement, the diseases that accounted for two of three army deaths flourished. Haydon noted on June 14, "A dead rebel soldier was today fished out of the well where we got what was supposed to be the best water." Nineteenth-century technology could not cope with the harvest of the dead: earth was scooped over men where they fell, to be uncovered by the elements or animals, or removed by civilians who wanted the dead away from their houses.[7]

Although treatment of the wounded improved immensely by the late stages of World War II, with sulfa drugs for shock, penicillin for infection, portable hospitals for emergency surgery (MASH units), life for the combat soldier remained dirty, uncomfortable, debilitating. In action, he lived largely on processed field rations and cigarettes; the front lines stank of tobacco and vomit from soured stomachs. He could not bathe or defecate in comfort. For, despite our image of mobile battlefronts, much of World War II (in Italy, Normandy, the Philippines and Central Pacific) was a brutal slogging match over difficult terrain. Eugene B. Sledge, a marine, has described how in a Pacific foxhole he lived in slime and decay, scooping excrement out in a ration can, enduring the sight, stench, and touch of decomposing bodies. Cleaning up after the Peleliu campaign, his muddy hair ripped the teeth from his comb and his festering socks pulled flesh from his feet. The combat soldier was forced into the most intimate knowledge of our animal mortality. "Set fire to him and he'll burn. Bury him and he'll rot like other kinds of garbage," said bombardier Joseph Heller of the casualty.[8]

Contrary to the myth that in good wars boys become men, veterans who go on to the end, as illustrated in *The Red Badge of Courage* and *Sands of Iwo Jima*, boys in fact become veterans who burn out. Stephen W. Sears has said that many men were not the same after Antietam. The same was true of other engagements. Most soldiers didn't serve throughout the war, and some went home disillusioned to discourage others from volunteering. The Stouffer team found that prolonged exposure to combat destroyed the GI's usefulness. After thirty days of continuous fighting, a soldier was exhausted; after forty-five he might need hospitalization. The two soldiers Patton slapped were veterans who had endured too much.

Men willed their own deaths, to end the agony of combat. Audie Murphy performed the feats of apparent daring that made him America's most decorated man in World War II during a period of despair in which he was trying to get killed. When he starred as Henry Fleming in "The Red Badge of Courage," he saw the flag-waving heroics in the final sequences as bitterly silly. He was emotionally spent: "Before the war, I'd get excited and enthused about a lot of things, but not any more," he said. During breaks in production he would stare "as though lost in a distant dream." In 1952, Murphy still had the "two-thousand-yard stare" of the damaged combat veteran.[9]

We know from Vietnam that the ordeal of combat in a bad war leads to substance abuse. We acknowledge this less freely with good wars. Yet alcoholism was a chronic problem in Civil War armies and made parents reluctant to let boys enlist. A wife seeking to separate from her husband in 1866 said that he had enlisted from Buffalo, New York, in 1863 and, "like many of our brave and noble soldiers yielded to the demon intemperance rendering him unfit for work, for society, and too soon unworthy of a wife's care, forgiveness, or endurance."[10]

To try to prevent abuse, booze was denied to enlisted men in World War II. But they scrounged it or brewed their own. Aqua Velva from the PX (post store) and grapefruit juice was popular, reminiscent of a Tom Collins. Some GIs got hooked on pep pills. At least 10 percent of American troops took amphetamines at some time. Benzedrine was popular;

about 25 percent of men in field prison were heavy users. The pain killer morphine also produced addiction among some wounded.

Civil War soldiers went to opium and cocaine for physical and mental release. We have yet to evaluate the role of laudanum, an opium solution that Thomas De Quincey, an English addict, said induced a dream state like a theater of the mind. Was Braxton Bragg's erratic behavior in 1863 partly a result of being sedated with opium? Were John Bell Hood's 1864 rash battles before Atlanta partly stimulated by heavy use of alcohol and laudanum to ease his maimed body?

The veterans of good wars do suffer PTSD. Twenty-five percent of men still in veterans' hospitals from World War II have mental wounds. In 1992 a woman recalled of her brother who had fought in the Pacific: "We never understood him when he came back from the war. He left as this bright, energetic eighteen-year-old and returned languid and somewhat of an alcoholic. He got married, then quickly divorced, and died of cirrhosis of the liver at thirty-four. I never knew what happened to him over there to make him so sad." That enervating sadness could have been seen eighty years earlier in the "aimless young men in grey" witnessed by journalist Whitelaw Reid in the defeated South, veterans who "stared stupidly" and had "a played-out manner."[11]

In neither the Victorian era nor the "quiet man" culture of 1940s America could veterans share the anguish of combat. "Even the simplest soldier," said GI J. Glenn Gray, "suspects that it is unpopular today to be burdened with guilt." Suppression produced moodiness. The wife of Joshua L. Chamberlain, the hero of Little Round Top, considered divorcing him when he came home a distant stranger. Suppression also resulted in abuse: A paratrooper's wife would "sit for hours and hold him while he just shook"; later, he hit her and the children. "He became a brute" and they divorced.[12]

Many Civil War veterans who couldn't adapt ended in jail. The *North American Review* estimated in October 1867 that "there cannot be less than five or six thousand soldiers and sailors who fought for the Union now confined in the state prisons" and "tens of thousands" more in local jails. Pennsylvania's Eastern Penitentiary reported in 1866 that many inmates were veterans who "had fought in the war and were shattered." Other maladjusted soldiers ended in bar fights or were killed by police-

Some Civil War Soldiers Became Homeless Drifters

The Straggler, by Alfred R. Waud. Wood engraving in *Harper's Weekly*, 1863. (Courtesy of the Library of Congress)

men, as was Sam Hildebrand, a partisan ranger from Missouri, shot by an Illinois constable after a bar fight in March 1872. Some became homeless drifters, many of the thousands of tramps who infested American roads in the dislocation produced by war. They were like the Vietnam veterans still living in the North Woods or the GI in Italy who said, "I want to live so far back in the hills that I'll never see another human being." As late as 1878 one police chief still believed that "This tramp system is undoubtedly an outgrowth of the war," a legacy of soldiers "bumming" from civilians.[13]

After World War II the GI Bill helped to offset prejudice against hiring veterans. But many Civil War soldiers had to conceal their military experience to get jobs: they were assumed to have loose habits and to be unreliable. As Reid Mitchell has noted, Union and Confederate troops came to feel undervalued. They were even ordered off sidewalks by policemen as though they were unclean. Likewise, a World War II returnee said, "Nobody really cared about you whatsoever. It was a big surprise to everybody when you came home. What are you doing here?" they implied. Another said, "when you come back they treat you just like scum. If you ever get the boys all together they will probably kill all the civilians."[14]

Rejection was worst for the physically maimed. The Union army carried out 29,980 amputations, the Confederacy about 25,000. By July 1866 the war office had issued 3,981 false legs, 2,240 arms, 9 feet, and 55 hands. One veteran, without arms, begging aid, was told by a prosperous citizen that "he was a _____ fool for going to the war." "Wouldn't you think she'd know better than to marry a cripple?" was the 1940s verdict on a woman who married a one-legged GI. We shut away the disquieting human damage of war. When patients from the plastic surgery hospital in Pasadena, California, went downtown, the paper got letters asking, "Why can't they be kept on their own grounds and off the streets?" Mangled men, shrouded in bleak Civil War hospitals, retreated from society's gaze to the recently invented hypodermic syringe, which caused shooting-up to be called "the army disease."[15]

A tenacious popular belief is that successful wars, by eliciting patriotism, selflessness, and community solidarity, strengthen traditional values and return society to its roots, usually projected as being in a past golden age when everything was simpler, government was smaller, and the individual mattered more. In fact, wars tend to have the opposite effect: they loosen traditional mores, promote radical change away from the past, encourage bigness and complexity in government and economic life. For example, we think nostalgically of rural America, before the era of urban-industrial glut. The Civil War, by eroding the power of the Southern planter class, a major exponent of agrarian values, helped to kill that world. Huge government contracts stimulated business and the related urban growth. Chicago's packing industry tripled in size from 1861 through 1863. This produced major corporations, big unions, and the angry labor disputes of 1876 and beyond. Government increased in size and intervened in the life of the individual through war taxation and the draft. Soldiers got used to ready-made clothing and brand-labelled goods in the army; they bought them after the war, encouraging the dominance of national brands and consumer conformity.

The same is true of World War II, only more so. America's biggest fifty-six companies got 75 percent of war contracts. The small went under: two months after Pearl Harbor, *Business Week* noted the death of 200,000 small businesses. Small farmers went under, too, as defense plants ate their land, and high wages attracted rural labor to the cities. The number of U.S. farms declined by 17 percent. Uncle Sam put his hand in America's pocket and many paid income tax for the first time; he put citizens in uniform—ten million Americans entering military service through the draft.

These wars enormously enhanced the organization culture with its top-down direction. Presidents Lincoln, Franklin D. Roosevelt, and Harry Truman all used emergency war powers to enhance the executive. When Lincoln declared emancipation and Truman dropped the atom bomb, no matter how wise the decisions, they were not debated in open forum. The fates of nations were placed in the hands of individuals. Lincoln gagged his conservative opponents and some were exiled to the Confederacy, including Copperhead leader Clement L. Vallandigham. Censorship in World War II was severe, but most people conformed willingly. This led William H. Whyte to rail against organization culture in which people conform, hide behind committees, and accept unquestioningly directives from above. His favorite target was Herman Wouk's *The Caine Mutiny* (1951), a story of mutiny on a World War II minesweeper. Wouk argues that the crew should not have questioned the captain's judgment, even though he was unstable and would probably have sunk the ship. In 1869, John William De Forest, a Union veteran, had made a similar point to Whyte's. He bewailed the triumph of democracy in the Civil War, monotonous and "remarkably uniform in degree and nature." He regretted the killing off of Southern aristocrats, individuals of strong character.[16]

Wars usually loosen sexual mores and shift gender-based social roles. The Civil War and World War II saw upswings in marriage rates. But some marriages undertaken in haste before a departure for the front broke up on sober reflection; others fell victim to infidelity by both sexes. In August 1861, some 645 members of the 7th Louisiana were reported sick, complaints included opium addiction, mumps, measles, and venereal disease. In World War II, some 75 percent of GIs overseas admitted to having sex. VD caused more casualties in northern Europe than the V2 rocket. Often men seduced women whose husbands were serving away. Willie Couch, a rebel from Orange County, North Carolina, divorced his wife in May 1865 because the war had made her a "lewd woman and common prostitute." An officer overseas in World War II wrote, "Everyday or so a soldier comes in to find out how he can stop his allotment to his wife or get a divorce. So many of the wives are doing their husbands wrong."[17]

Abortion rates went up as women sought to hide the evidence of adultery. In 1866 the New York Prison Association reported that some army wives "have lapsed from virtue, and naturally desire to obliterate the evidence of their guilt." Other women aborted because, on army pay or a widow's pension, they couldn't feed more mouths. Major cities caught up in war, Washington and Richmond, or Naples, London, and Paris, developed armies of prostitutes. In Richmond, in 1864, "you may see the women promenading up & down the shady walks jostling respectable ladies into the gutter." Often the so-called whores were starving women forced to trade sex for the necessities of life. Mrs. E. Jett wrote in September 1864 that federal soldiers had offered her "anything to eat I wanted" if "I wod comedate them." She refused but neighbors were "horin" for food.[18]

Women did respectable work in the Civil War as clerks, seamstresses, farmers. They gained self-confidence; a popular song ran,

> Just take your gun and go;
> For Ruth can drive the oxen, John,
> And I can use the hoe.

Not all wanted to quit when the war ended. "Why are all the women of 1865 so discontented?" asked a female columnist as Union war work evaporated. Some stayed on; by the early 1890s women held 5600 of the 17,600 positions in the Washington bureaucracy. Male admiration for women's role as volunteer nurses and workers in the war helped the cause of woman suffrage in some Northern states. Henry W. Bellows of the New York Sanitary Commission said women's contribution meant more "than a whole library of arguments and protests."[19]

In World War II women also took paid work and staffed voluntary organizations. By 1944, nineteen million had paying jobs. Many willingly stepped out when peace came, but some resented being laid off. A female worker fired at the Tacoma navy yard said she was glad to quit, but "many women in here are plenty unhappy though. The taste of independence has spoiled 'em."[20]

In addition to shaking gender roles, both wars changed race relations permanently. The Civil War ended slavery but left the hard work of molding an equal society to be done. World War II brought the issue to a head when black soldiers were placed in segregated units, forced to sit at the back of buses and behind German prisoners of war at service shows. This produced the first sit-ins and an anger that writer James Baldwin predicted correctly would bring "the fire next time," the civil rights movement which is usually erroneously seen as originating in the bad war era of the 1960s.

The turmoil of war also bred generational conflict and increased juvenile delinquency. When 1860's fathers and elder brothers donned uniform, youngsters were left without a male hand in an era that stressed discipline. Women, too, might be away from home working. Elizabeth Custer saw in Washington an "army of black [clad] and weary creatures who had lost their husbands or sons in the war and were working for daily bread for themselves and their children." At night they hurried home to cook dinner, but many children had little supervision during the day. Some ran wild. A Massachusetts prison official estimated that 25 percent of juvenile offenders "have near relatives in the army." Other young offenders were ex-soldiers who had enlisted as adolescents before their characters had formed and who came to age believing in the free life of violence. A majority of offenders in the Kansas State Penitentiary in 1867 were juveniles undermined by "absence from home, exciting circumstances of the war, the false idea that 'jayhawking' was not a crime."[21]

The tradition of ill-discipline and violence among youth contined after the war. Armed youths were heavily represented in the striking mobs of 1876. In 1878, William Graham Sumner, a leading educator, bemoaned the catering to aggression and wildness in boys' magazines. Stories encouraged violence, defiance of authority, truancy, even carrying guns. A growing ethic said that "Every youth who aspires to manliness ought to get and carry a revolver."[22]

Juvenile delinquency increased in the 1940s, and for some of the same reasons. As parents entered the services or war plants, children enjoyed unusual freedom. When kids also had unprecedented cash to spend, irresponsible behavior was inevitable. With young men in the forces, jobs usually unavailable, such as bowling alley attendant, opened to young teens. New work areas, such as baby-sitting, needed by female workers, were created. By 1942, three million teenagers 14–17 were employed.

Kids with money and time stayed up all night in movie theaters, smoking reefers of tobacco and marijuana. Barred from the war effort, bored, they joined gangs, roughed up adults, vandalized public property, and stole cars to joyride. One disgusted adult wrote to the Indianapolis *News* that youth "must have thrills, speed, excitement; that's one reason why they break laws." By 1944 teens were estimated to have a spending power of $750,000,000 per annum. Business got on the bandwagon, helping to create a teen world separate from adult life, with its own culture fed by fads, fashions, magazines, pop music. Comic books, with a monthly circulation of 12,000,000 by 1942, were the only reading for some adolescents. Schools accommodated teens' demand for work time by cutting school hours. Even then, one state experienced a 17 percent increase in the dropout rate 1940–44 as teens took jobs. Schools lowered academic standards and offered more vocational training to hold students. Philip Wylie, a government official, charged in 1942 that the schools were failing and most students couldn't think.[23]

Adults were outraged by so-called Victory Girls, kids too young to be volunteer workers, who made a patriotic contribution by giving sex to boys in unifrom. It was estimated that 85 percent of girls near army bases who had frequent sex with soldiers were not prostitutes but Victory Girls. One was fourteen when Pear Harbor was bombed. Her father went away on war work and her mother was distracted by younger children. Neglected, she started seeing soldiers. This became promiscuity and led to three failed marriages. Looking back in 1985, she felt that the war had given youth too much freedom. The shock of social change and instability helped to foment "red scares" after all America's major wars. The loss of felt security in traditional values at home was exacerbated by revolution abroad, giving a sense of living in an unpredictable world. The Paris Commune of 1870, the Bolshevik Revolution of 1917, and the Chinese Communist victory in 1949, each itself a product of war and its aftermath, fueled American anxiety in a changing world.

The aftermath of war should be seen as part of the conflict. Our good war myths, which climax in the moment of victory, obscure the continuing costs of war. We remember that the Civil War and World War II boosted business enterprise. We neglect the long-term fiscal costs, which do not peak until two generations later, due to the interest on the debt contracted in the war and the payment of veterans' benefits—40 percent of the federal budget in the 1890s went for war pensions. The original cost of the Civil War to the Union, 1861–65, was $3.07 billion (the cost to the Confederacy was a further incalculable sum). By 1967, when 1,353 pensions were still being paid, the taxpayers' bill had risen to $8.57 billion, or 2.79 times the original sum. Ths cost of World War II is even greater. The national debt quintupled during the war from $50 billion to $260 billion. The interest on that amount was about $200 billion, which was not paid off before 1975. Veterans' benefits will peak around the turn of the century. In 1990, there were 7.2 million recipients of medical and pension benefits as a result of World War II service, including more than half the men over age sixty-five.

In addition to the fiscal cost, there is the lingering cost to human lives. We have noted the veterans' adjustment problems. We should remember too the women whose menfolk died or were wrecked, women who often lived incomplete lives. Nathaniel Hawthorne wrote of widows who "will pine and wither, and tread along many sour and discontented years, and at last go out of life without knowing what life is. . . . Every shot that takes effect . . . kills one and worse than kills the other." At the start of the Spanish-American War, Theodore Roosevelt's troops marched through Southern towns to the embarkation point for Cuba. Along the route men and young girls came out to cheer for a splendid little war, but the old women held back and wept, surely for young men long dead and others about to die.[24]

We should think, too, of the war orphans. Pennsylvania alone raised 2000 in its public institutions after the war for the Union. A whole generation of Southern children matured in a society of blighted hope, poverty, and stunted education. The war robbed them of youth and promise. Emma LeConte, a seventeen-year-old, wrote in 1865: "How dreadfully sick I am of this war. . . . We have only the saddest anticipations and the dread of hardships and cares, when bright dreams of the future ought to shine on us." We should think, too, of the children of veterans who were subject to depression, drinking, and violence.[25]

There is a further, profound cost to wars in desensitization to human suffering, a moral hardening often allied to a sense of national destiny arising from success in war. Appalling devastation and acts of dubious morality come to be accepted as the price of human progress. The blunting of human sensibility through war troubled Henry James, who got at it in a chilling ghost story "The Jolly Corner" (1908). This tale, essentially autobiographical, is about a New Yorker who has spent much of his adult life in England and so has missed the Civil War and the following boom years. He returns to his ancestral home, the Jolly Corner in New York City, to determine what America is now like and what he has missed. In the empty house, the sepulchre of what might have been, he meets his alter ego, the ghost of himself on a different path. The ghost is successful, a Union officer turned businessman, one of the type who served on Grant's staff and then swarmed to power and profit during his presidency. But he is not happy: he is maimed physically and mentally by the war; he is hard and cruel. Life in the pursuit of power has dehumanized the ghost, and he tries to kill the living man, his alter ego. The protagonist decides that he would have been a tougher man had he served in the war, a mover and shaper of great events, but he would have sacrificed part of his humanity.

Wars, particularly total wars like the Civil War and World War II which pit basic values of whole peoples in opposition, produce a ruthless brutality in the quest for total ememy submission. Though Americans embrace unconditional surrender as a national style and the only sure way to peace, it has caused immense suffering, not always justified by military necessity. Total wars tend to undermine the humanity of the combatants, who become inured to committing cruelties that they denounce in others. Thus, both North and South treated prisoners callously. Although we think of the Civil War as a gentlemen's war initially, by 1862 it had turned cruel. John Pope's orders regarding treatment of hostile civilians are one instance. Thomas J. Jackson advocated taking no prisoners, even extermination of the enemy population to win an ideological fight to the death.

We understand that in wars with cultures of different ethnicities, such as Vietnam, mutual ferocity is intensified by misunderstanding. But the ferocity of mutual suspicion also characterized the Civil War. Perhaps the destruction was made worse not because this was a brothers' war, as we often say, but because it was between perceived strangers. Southerners saw themselves as descendants of the English aristocracy, Cavaliers holding in check the vulgar barbarism of ill-bred Yankees, descended from canting Puritan Roundheads and an Anglo-Saxon underclass conquered by Norman chivalry in 1066. The British visitor G. W. Featherstonhaugh found that South Carolina planters despised Northern middle-class merchants "whom they consider to be by the nature of their avocations, incapable of rising to their level."[26]

For their part, Northerners often acknowledged that Southerners had a certain aristocratic manner and charm, but their leisured style was actually decadent idleness, built on slave labor. Their civilization, said *Harper's Weekly* in 1858, "is a mermaid—lovely and languid above, but ending in bestial deformity." Frederick Law Olmsted, the great landscape architect, traveling the antebellum South, thought it was behind the improving capitalist spirit of the age. "There, work is not only painful: it's shameful," he wrote. "To ride, to hunt, to smoke like a Turk in the sunshine: there is the destiny of the white. To do any other kind of manual labor is to act like a slave."[27]

This was anathema to bustling Yankees. As they invaded the South, they mistook the physical decay of war for further evidence of shiftless character. "This is a queer country and queer people," said a Union soldier about Virginia. "I sometimes wonder if I am not in a foreign

Cartoon in *Harper's Weekly*. Wood engraving, 1860.

country," commented another. Dislike of Southern slovenliness led to arguments that the people should be removed to make way for Northern immigrant labor. The wife of an Ohio soldier said, "banish them forever" and "confiscate their property to the use of the government or to the use of poor loyal citizens."[28]

Most Americans had expected a short war. When it dragged on, an emotional rage grew against the incomprehensible opponent causing this pain. John Esten Cooke, rebel and historian, said: "From the summer of 1862, the war became a war of wholesale devastation. From the spring of 1864, it seemed to have become nearly a war of extermination." We think here of William Tecumseh Sherman. His march to the sea has been seen as the crucial forerunner of *Blitzkrieg*, the lightning thrust breaking the will to fight. But it has been argued, notably by Charles Royster, that Sherman went beyond military necessity to a wanton level of destruction. Although neither Sherman nor Sheridan in the Shenandoah ordered the killing of women and children, they did condemn thousands to extreme suffering. General Smith D. Atkins boasted that homeless women in Georgia had to beg crusts: "O it was glorious to see such a sight . . . you women keep up this war. *We* are fighting *you.* " Another soldier wrote after the march through South Carolina: "We burnt every house, barn, mill that we passed. . . . We took just what we wanted, cry or no cry."[29]

Rage at the hateful alien across the lines produces atrocities. Some Civil War soldiers killed the wounded and took ears, scalps, teeth, even jaws as trophies. The worst behavior was where rules failed, in guerrilla fighting against raiders and bushwhackers. A soldier fighting Mosby's partisans in Virginia felt as a grunt in Vietnam was to feel, surrounded by hostiles "all around you watching your movements," "citizens in the day and Bushwhackers at night." In this milieu both sides showed little mercy and little discrimination about whom they shot. When Mosby's men derailed trains, prominent citizens were tied to locomotives by federals.[30]

Brutality characterized the war in the borderlands between Kansas and Missouri. The sack of Lawrence, Kansas, by William C. Quantrill in August 1863, included the killing of civilian men and boys, some by torture and burning. Women were not killed but were "symbolically raped," in Michael Fellman's term, by the violation of their homes and butchery of their men before their eyes. In response to Quantrill, Senator

James Lane called for genocide: "for self-preservation there shall be extermination." General Thomas Ewing, commanding the district, created a free-fire buffer zone by depopulating the Missouri border counties. "Those lingering in the void after September 9 would be considered Rebels and hence guilty until proven innocent, if they were given the chance," much as in Vietnam.[31]

Many of the same phenomena occurred in World War II. As that war progressed, our urge to destroy increased, and finally we merged military and civilian targets. In Europe this eventuated in the British and American fire-bombing of Dresden, an undefended city of no military significance, where up to 135,000 people were killed on February 13 and 14, 1945. On the ground, Axis and Allied soldiers showed a minimal restraint absent from the Russian front. But dehumanization of the enemy still occurred, leading to the murder of prisoners. Occasionally men lost control, as they did later at My Lai: in June 1944 an American battalion went awry, killing everything in a French village. The Canadian James Bacque has argued that in 1944–45 American and French rage at the Nazis led them to deprive German POWs of food and shelter, causing hundreds of thousands to die. Stephen Ambrose, a biographer of commander Dwight D. Eisenhower, disputes the allegation. But American camp guards have endorsed Bacque. "I witnessed the atrocities Stephen E. Ambrose tries to gloss over," said one. "We sometimes stepped over the boundary of civilized behavior and resembled to some extent what we were fighting against," admitted another.[32]

In the Pacific, mutual racist hatred created a war of horrors. Both sides tortured and killed prisoners, mutilated corpses, took ears, hands, even heads as souvenirs. Slaughter of Japanese neared genocide as Axis soldiers rejected or were refused mercy. On Okinawa, attacked April 1, 1945, almost the entire 120,000-man Japanese garrison died in a frenzy of death. The incendiary bombing of Japanese cities, begun early in 1945, devastated sixty-one cities and caused 672,000 casualties, even before the atom bombs killed more than 265,000 more. Much of the killing was necessary but, as John Dower notes, we felt little for the victims—a loss of our own humanity.

The desensitization to the suffering of others—war psychosis—leaves a legacy. The Civil War enhanced the habit of easy violence, with

In the Pacific, Mutual Racist Hatred Created a War of Horrors

Louseous Japanicas

The first serious outbreak of this lice epidemic was officially noted on December 7, 1941, at Honolulu, T. H. To the Marine Corps, especially trained in combating this type of pestilence, was assigned the gigantic task of extermination. Extensive experiments on Guadalcanal, Tarawa, and Saipan have shown that this louse inhabits coral atolls in the South Pacific, particularly pill boxes, palm trees, caves, swamps and jungles.

Flame throwers, mortars, grenades and bayonets have proven to be an effective remedy. But before a complete cure may be effected the origin of the plague, the breeding grounds around the Tokyo area, must be completely annihilated.

Cartoon in *Leatherneck Magazine*, 1945. (Courtesy of the Marine Corps Association)

millions of firearms in circulation. Violent crime escalated: New York saw a 50 percent increase in 1864–65. Vigilance committees usurped the law to bully blacks in the South, tramps in the North. Crucially, violence had become associated with righteousness and providential mission. The nation in victory was arrogant. Colonel James F. Rusling, writing in the *United States Service Magazine,* boasted that the crushing of the South proved the superiority of Northern manhood. And the poet James Russell Lowell crowed: "Who now shall sneer . . . Roundhead and Cavalier!" The *New York Herald* went a note higher, envisaging the Union armies marching on to establish republics all across the globe, "on—till the soldiers of Grant, Sherman and Sheridan have saved the world as they have saved the Union." Here is the nascent idea of America as world's policeman, American military intervention justified by America's superior righteousness and power.[33]

This sense of surety in America's mission led in part to the destruction of the Native American tribes. If the image of the Canadian West is of a lone "Mountie" keeping the peace between Indian and white on an even footing, in America it is of bluecoats herding Indians into barren rural ghettos and slaughtering them when they resisted. The mass destruction of the buffalo, the Indians' subsistence base, was justified by analogy with the 1864 ravaging of the Shenandoah as a necessary adjunct to progress. And both Sherman and Sheridan, practitioners of total war, argued periodically for the extermination of Native Americans who got in the way of white destiny. Thus Sherman: "We must act with vindictive earnestness against the Sioux, even to their extermination, men, women, and children." In the age of Social Darwinism, it was easy to look back and see Union victory in the Civil War as the survival of the fittest, the inevitable course of nature, justifying an even greater destiny through violence in the postwar era of westward expansion.[34]

Having opposed aggressive militarism in Germany and Japan, America at the end of World War II had a justifiable sense of righteousness. But the danger again is in moral complacency, as war veteran Paul Fussell has pointed out: "If for years you fancy that you are engaged in fighting utter evil, . . . before long you will come to believe that therefore you yourself must incarnate pure goodness." If you are perfect, then what you do is justified by your purity, even if the same actions carried out by others would be reprehensible. When the Axis bombed Rotterdam or Shanghai, we called these war crimes. But the *New Yorker* justified the massive civilian deaths inherent in fire bombing as, "Americans working for a high and common purpose, with leadership based on brains and goodness and faith in human endeavor. . . ."[35]

This argument that our ends justify our means puts us on the slippery moral slope that in the Cold War (surely a postscript to World War II) led to the commission of acts that violate our stated ideals. We have connived at the assassination of foreign leaders and the overthrow of sovereign governments, we have financed terrorism, waged undeclared war, and attacked peaceful coastal installations, despite our outrage over Fort Sumter and Pearl Harbor. We have lied publicly, even to our own people. Experiments with radiation and sterilization have been tried on soldiers, prisoners, the indigent. We have carried out illicit nuclear tests and hidden from our citizens the dangers of leaking nuclear waste. Our self-righteousness about our right to use force led 81 percent of Americans polled by *Newsweek* at the time of the 1989 Panama invasion to believe that the U.S. has the right to remove unilaterally a foreign head of state of whom it disapproves. This has led political commentator Wade Huntley to argue that America (as well as the Soviet Union) could not attain victory in the Cold War, because we "were willing to compromise American principles and ideals (not to mention laws) in the name of fighting Communism."[36]

The moral certainty arising from complete victory in our good wars has diminished intellectual skepticism and made it difficult to question accepted verities. Since the Civil War, it is impossible for Americans to consider, as citizens of other states such as the Soviet Union, Canada, and Great Britain have had to do, the break-up of current geopolitical arrangements and boundaries. Only foreign observers, such as the French commentator William Pfaff, will ask if the world might be better off if the Confederacy had become independent, creating "a North America composed of two medium-sized and one large but not gigantic nation." In this situation, "North Americans today might be more comfortable with themselves and with the world."[37]

As the popular version of history becomes settled, certain viewpoints are canonized. It is an article of faith that the 1938 Munich agreement was a disaster, proving that aggressors can never be appeased. This axiom came to dominate American Cold War thinking, leading ultimately to the decision to fight in Vietnam. Clark Clifford, presidential adviser and Secretary of Defense 1968–69, said: "We were conscious of the grievous default on the part of the European nations that had permitted Adolf Hitler and the Third Reich to gain power and control over most of Europe. We felt that aggression in Southeast Asia had to be stopped at its inception, or it would spread into the Pacific, to the Philippines, and even as far as Australia and New Zealand." Thus the Munich analogy played into the Domino Theory.[38]

In fact, Munich offered no such simple moral. Was Czechoslovakia, debatably not a model democracy but a pastiche of competing ethnic groups, the best place to stand against Hitler? France needed time to rearm: its military was capable only of a defensive stance in 1938. Britain, facing the prospect of a three-ocean war against Germany, Italy, and Japan, sought to postpone hostilities as long as possible. By 1939, Italy's military capacity was waning as Britain's peaked; and by 1940 the Royal Air Force had radar, which helped to win the crucial Battle of Britain. Further, the Munich agreement lasted only six months so that its long-term significance can be overrated.

Codifying wars into good or bad prevents us from looking at the commonality of experience between conflicts popularly seen as polar opposites. The Civil War and Vietnam evoked more of a sense of high adventure, of embarking on a "hero quest," than did World War II. Men in the 1940s tended to see the war merely as a job to be done. Their songs were rarely inspirational, and their aim was to get back to normality in the shape of new cars, girls, baseball, and home-cooking. Most could not define fascism or democracy and, despite the current rhetoric of an American crusade against Nazism, many had no hatred for Germany. (Germany finally declared war on America, not vice versa, and many Americans thought Japan, not Europe, should be the primary target of American arms.) Combat soldiers, unlike those of the Civil War and Vietnam, had little chance of going home before the war ended, and they resented it. The Stouffer team found that 75 percent of combat troops thought they should be replaced by fresh men. We usually think of Vietnam as the reluctant war but military historian Martin Van Creveld has found that a higher percentage of grunts in Vietnam could define the political ideals they were defending and may have had a higher ideological commitment to their fight than the GIs of World War II.

Many Civil War soldiers freely admitted they weren't sure where the right lay. Ambrose Bierce, later a famous writer, said in June 1864 that he was engaged in the Union "cause which may be right or may be wrong." Buying substitutes to avoid service became respectable. The *New York Times* defended the practice as "the only means of sparing that class . . . who work with their brains—who do the planning and directing of the national industry." Grant estimated in September 1864 that desertion was robbing the army of 80 percent of men recruited. Nevertheless, within this framework of ebbing commitment, there seems to have been among the soldiers of the 1860s and 1960s a shared sense of war as the ultimate male experience. Soldiers in both wars referred to themselves as knights in armor, an image almost inconceivable among Americans in World War II.[39]

Perhaps the earliest war novel in the English language was John William De Forest's *Miss Ravenel's Conversion from Secession to Loyalty* (1867). In this, a young Northerner, Edward Colburne, is turned by the Civil War from a shy, retiring youth into a confident mature man. In the process, he beats out his Southern rival, Colonel Carter, for the hand of Miss Ravenel. De Forest, a Northerner, concludes that "he is a stronger and better man for having fought three years, out-facing death and suffering."[40] He will return home to be a leader in his community. World War II novels tend to have less hopeful endings. Consider Norman Mailer's *The Naked and the Dead* (1948) in which a decent American officer is killed by his own authoritarian superior and we are led to believe that a form of neo-fascism will triumph in postwar America.

Contrast this with Oliver Stone's *Platoon* (1986), also a work in which Americans kill one another, but one in which a good American, Chris Taylor, survives. Stone has said elsewhere that he believes veterans are best prepared to lead America, a reiteration of De Forest's theme after the Civil War. Stone relates the quest in Vietnam back directly to the great quests of the nineteenth century. The best soldier in the platoon is Sergeant Robert E. Lee Barnes. His stature is so great that Stone links him to the greatest quester in American fiction, Captain Ahab in Herman Melville's *Moby-Dick*, (1851). Whatever else Vietnam may have been, Stone sees it as a male saga to be set alongside the real and fictional epics of America in the seminal period of the mid-nineteenth century.

If Stone believes that the grunts followed in the steps of Lee and Ahab, others thought they followed the great celluloid heroes of World War II. As one veteran put it, he went to Vietnam to "kill a Commie for Jesus Christ and John Wayne." In the impact of World War II film lore on the Vietnam generation, we are reminded again of the continuity between wars and the cause and effect relationship that is hidden when we pigeonhole events.[41]

In other senses, Vietnam may be seen as the culmination of trends developed earlier. We are sensitive to the massive level of destruction in Vietnam: the U.S. dropped more bombs on its ally, South Vietnam, than on its enemies in World War II. But this emphasis on bludgeoning tactics has earlier roots. Alan T. Nolan accuses Lee of wasting his army in questionable frontal assaults. Caleb Carr generalizes the point, charging the leading generals with an unimaginative brute-force approach, using grinding attrition. He compares Civil War leaders unfavorably to the Revolutionary War generals who had few resources and won by finesse; or the Prussian generals who used the same technology that produced butchery in 1864 to crush France with lightning speed in 1870. Taking the point further, it has been argued that Civil War generals thus set up the reliance on weight of fire and force of numbers that produced a needless destruction in World War II, where American forces, far from performing lightning strikes, obliterated everything in their path, damaging the environment to such a degree that it had not recovered in some areas twenty years later. Because of over-reliance on blanket firepower, American losses from friendly fire have risen in the nation's last four wars.

In this essay, I have tried to argue that the retelling of our wars has narrowed our conception of them, distorting their good or bad points and radically constraining the ways in which discussion of the conflicts and their characteristics can take place. This presents problems for the historian who must seek to demonstrate the complexity of the past. Most importantly, the costs and failures of our so-called good wars have been largely ignored. The Civil War guaranteed the Union, and it ended slavery. But it did not end inequality; it cost the South a century of poverty; and it changed the pattern of the American political and economic landscape forever. World War II stopped Nazism, fascism, and Japanese imperialism. But it, too, did not end inequality at home, and its legacy was the Cold War, fought under the shadow of nuclear annihilation.

History can teach lessons and can possibly suggest models for future action. But caution must be exercised in not simplifying the lessons of the past. Munich has been used too often and too glibly to argue that great powers must always use force against their ideological opponents; this argument helped to produce the Vietnam War. Could we not argue with equal force that the refusal of Britain and France to enter the Civil War on the side of the Confederacy suggests that great powers should usually leave others to sort out their own affairs? The Civil War and World War II may be models for future action, but again they may not. Both were total wars fought after the flag had been fired on and American national life was in some sense at stake. This is not likely to be the situation in the immediate future. In lauding past military victories, we can forget that arms were a last resort, an admission that peaceful means of adjusting disputes have failed utterly. The Civil War was fought in large part because the American political system could not accommodate regional differences, especially regarding slavery. Yet slavery had been abolished in the British empire without force a generation earlier. World War II was caused in part because the Great Powers failed to provide a fair and equitable peace after World War I, which itself represented the complete bankruptcy of great power diplomacy. Was it not World War I and its consequences that gave Hitler an opportunity in Germany?

I am not arguing that all wars are unnecessary: some must be fought. I would place the Civil War and World War II in that category, given the immediate political debacle preceding them. But we must try to learn from history the full nature of war so that if we do feel a war must be fought, we shall sanction it soberly and for the gravest motives, with our eyes open to the full understanding of what we are asking of our troops, and with profound awareness of what the consequences may be for them and for the humanity of which we are all a part.

10

The Necessity of Force: The Civil War, World War II, and the American View of War

RUSSELL F. WEIGLEY

T HE Civil War and the Second World War are the greatest wars of the United States, measured by almost every dimension of involvement—numbers engaged, casualties suffered, and impact upon the nation's image of war and subsequent military history. The War of the American Revolution, the Indian Wars, and the Vietnam War were of longer duration, but they did not involve the degree of unified national commitment and participation of the 1860s and 1940s wars. While without the Revolution there would be no United States of America, so that the war of 1775–83 was of unique importance in that respect, still the achievement of American independence represents the remarkable accomplishment of relatively small minorities of the population as active political leaders and committed soldiers of the Revolutionary cause—in contrast to the major participation of millions in the war efforts of 1861–65 and 1941–45.

In asserting that the Civil War and the Second World War rank as our greatest wars not only in their physical dimensions but also in their impact upon our image of war and therefore upon subsequent military history, we must pause, however, to consider in addition the Vietnam War. Until the late 1960s, there could hardly be any question of the accuracy of the statement that the two great wars molded the national conception of the nature of war itself. While I believe that the statement remains essentially true, nevertheless any consideration of the Civil War and Second World War in their relation to the American image of war in the final years of the twentieth century must grapple also with how the Vietnam War altered the perceptions inherited by us from our earlier great wars.

From the Civil War and the Second World War, the people of the United States drew a positive conception of the use of war as an instrument of national purpose. Each of the great American wars spawned its full share of the horrors of war. Some 623,026 American fighting men died in the Civil War; 110,100 federal soldiers and 1804 navy men killed in action or mortally wounded, while 250,122 federal soldiers and 3000 navy personnel died of disease, accidents, or other causes; 94,000 Confederates were killed or mortally wounded in action, while 164,000 died of disease or other causes. At least 471,427 on both sides were wounded, for total Civil War casualties of 1,094,453. In the United States armed forces of World War II, some 292,131 were killed or mortally wounded; 115,185 died of other causes, for a total of 407,316 deaths; another 670,846 were wounded, to make up 1,078,162 total casualties. Beyond the obvious costs of deaths and wounds among the fighting men, furthermore, the Civil War especially brought the horrors of property destruction and confiscations to much of the South, and also to a few areas of the North where Confederate armies raided—along with the psychic damage suffered by civilians in the path of invading armies. To nineteenth-century Americans, loss of houses, farms, livestock, crops, and business property could be a form of death. In spite of all that, however, the perception of war emerging from the two great American conflicts was by no means a perception of war as sheer unmitigated horror.

Instead, the results of both of the great American wars have seemed worth the costs paid for them. While no lesser judge than God could truly essay weighing 623,000 mostly white deaths against the value of freedom for some 3,950,000 African-Americans and their descendants released from the bonds of slavery, on balance the purposes for which the victors fought the Civil War must seem just, and the consummation in the advancement of human freedom worth fighting for. As for the other principal war aim of the Union—the one that preceded the emancipation of the slaves—the preservation undivided of the American experiment in democracy, there is little doubt that few Southerners would dispute the positive value of the outcome today. How and when slavery in North America would have ended without the Civil War is problematic enough, and the unbroken preservation of the Union seems gain enough, that the American Civil War can readily be pronounced a conflict whose results warranted its toll, albeit that toll was high. Thus have the American people mainly perceived the Civil War.

The Second World War was less directly costly to the United States. There were somewhat fewer casualties, and those out of a population of 135,000,000 in contrast to an 1860 population of 30,000,000. No part of the continental United States suffered invasion or physical devastation from the war. The main purpose for which the war was fought was as just as the aims of the Civil War: to eliminate the Führer, Adolf Hitler, and his evil regime in Germany was to assure the survival of Western civilization against a tide of barbarism. It is hard to imagine how a thriving democracy could have been maintained in the United States if this country had not intervened in the war to forestall the complete domination of the Eurasian land mass by the Axis powers, with only the Western hemisphere left free from Axis domination, and the fate of much of Latin America uncertain after such a disruption of the world balance of power—yet North American isolation of that kind would have been the likely outcome if the United States had not entered the war.

Perhaps the provocation that impelled Japan to attack Pearl Harbor—the petroleum embargo of July 26, 1941, that signaled the end of Japan as a great power unless the Japanese could find a substitute source of oil—was slightly less clearly warranted than American resistance to Hitler; the Japanese empire was not governed by a regime quite so indisputably monstrous as Hitler's. Nevertheless, the atrocities that accompanied Japanese conquests in eastern Asia and the western Pacific were heinous enough, and it was the partnership of Japan with Germany that posed the threat that all of Eurasia would stand as one against not only the national interests of the United States but all the basic values of the Western world. So the American people have perceived this country's participation in the Second World War as, like the Civil War, an endeavor worthy of the costs it entailed.

Together, then, the Civil War and the Second World War pointed the American people to an assessment of war as an instrument of national policy that was overwhelmingly positive. War is not to be actively sought after—the deliberate pursuit of war was one of the aspects of his policy that made Hitler monstrous—but certainly war sometimes becomes an acceptable means to worthy ends that could not assuredly be attained without it.

The Vietnam War has called gravely into question these perceptions and conclusions left by the two greatest American wars. The American opposition to the Vietnam War began with the premise that when the United States entered upon its major military intervention in Vietnam in 1965, the war going on there between the Republic of Vietnam in the South and the so-called Democratic Republic of Vietnam in the North was a Vietnamese variant of the Civil War, in which foreign intrusion by the United States served no vital interest of this country. Worse, American intervention represented an unwarranted, imperialistic interference in another people's efforts toward self-determination and an immoral use of overwhelmingly destructive American military power against a people sadly lacking in the means to protect themselves from that power. So emotionally intense did the opposition to the Vietnam War become, however, that resisting a particular war grew into a condemnation among many Americans of virtually all war waged by the United States, on the ground that American military strength so overmatched that of any other nation—except possibly the Soviet Union—that employing it was inherently unfair and unjust. Moreover, so deep were the suspicions that the Vietnam War engendered concerning almost all the objectives of American foreign and military policy and of the integrity of the United States government that, to many, any war entered upon by the United States must by definition have repressive, reactionary, anti-democratic purposes.

Thus the Vietnam War produced among many Americans a reversal of the legacy from the two great American wars whereby the waging of war seemed on the whole an acceptable endeavor likely to yield positive results. Out of the war in Southeast Asia came the so-called Vietnam syndrome, palsying the will of the United States to engage in virtually any war whatever. Even those Americans who did not accept the conclusions of the anti-Vietnam War movement hesitated to face the risks of popular anti-war sentiment by entering upon any commitment of American military force beyond so minuscule an enterprise as the invasion of Grenada, Operation URGENT FURY, on October 25, 1983. Even for those who had not come to regard any American war as intrinsically immoral, even for the chieftains of the American armed forces, Vietnam left a fear that no war could command adequate public support and that, consequently, any war was likely to repeat the Vietnam pattern of American failure. So probably most Americans, including many of the country's military leaders themselves, perceived invoking war as, more often than not, an unacceptable instrument of policy. Most of the likely war scenarios came to appear as entangling the United States in either the immoral or the unwinnable, or both.

In early 1991, the triumph of the United States and the associated powers in the Persian Gulf War and particularly in the rapidly triumphant Operation DESERT STORM ground war operations of February 24–28 could briefly be understood as overcoming the Vietnam syndrome. It had required considerable courage on the part of President George Herbert Walker Bush and his administration to fly in the face of the syndrome by promptly inaugurating Operation DESERT SHIELD to halt further Iraqi aggression following the August 2, 1990, invasion of Kuwait. It required courage again to turn from a defensive posture to the military offensive and active war with Operation DESERT STORM, beginning with aerial attacks on Iraq and Kuwait on January 16, 1991. The ensuing swift victory nipped in the bud a new Vietnam-like American anti-war movement, and of course it also brought prompt relief from fears among those otherwise supportive of action against Iraq but anticipating a campaign of bloody stalemate in the Kuwait desert. Nevertheless, any proclamation of the demise of the Vietnam syndrome in the wake of the Persian Gulf War was premature. The American response to the crisis in Bosnia and Her-cegovina in 1992–94 reflected post-Vietnam doubts and suspicions of almost any American use of military force returned practically to full vigor.

Against the possibility of military intervention in Bosnia, it was some of the very military leaders who had been architects of the triumph over Iraq who were in the forefront of the opposition, most notably General Colin L. Powell, Chairman of the Joint Chiefs of Staff until September 30, 1993. With its military leaders opposed, the Bush administration dem-onstrated toward Bosnia nothing like the decisiveness of its Persian Gulf War policy. After President William Jefferson Clinton took office on Janu-ary 20, 1993, unwavering decision-making in foreign and military affairs came still more to be in short supply. General Powell's attitude seemed to be that as the country's ranking professional military officer he was willing to employ military force only when he was assured of the means to score a prompt and clear-cut victory. No crisis fraught with complexities that might interfere with the possibility of rapid and unambiguous victory need apply for his attention. Neither should any whose geographical setting would permit less than the kind of unobstructed unleashing of American weaponry that had been possible in the deserts of Kuwait and Iraq. Moun-tainous terrain was particularly unacceptable as a setting for American military action. So much for the end of the Vietnam syndrome. Under the post-Persian Gulf regime, the crucial question governing American mili-tary action was evidently not whether American national interests were at stake, or whether the values of humanity or justice might touch the only remaining superpower's sense of international responsibility; the crucial question was whether the circumstances were convenient for the Ameri-can military and unlikely to offer any source of embarrassment.

The military's desire to undertake no employment of force unless clear-cut victory could be assured, and therefore not to employ force at all unless it received authorization to strike with overwhelming power, cut in two directions to inhibit any American resort to military force whatever. On the one hand, approval of the use of overwhelming power was likely to be hard to come by because of considerations of expense, the geographic and other conditions discouraging all-out involvement in such possible arenas as Bosnia or Somalia, and the fact that the drawdown of military strength after 1991 and the end of the Cold War made deployable American military force on the scale of the Persian Gulf simply no longer readily available. On the other hand, military insistence that if force be employed at all it ought to be overwhelming touched some of the most sensitive of the national nerves rendered uneasy by the memory of the Vietnam War.

For the misgivings about war as an instrument of policy that grew out of the Vietnam experience involved particularly the tendency of overwhelming force to become excessive force, destroying not only military targets but civilian lives and property as well, and thus probably violating the canons of the international law of war as well as the precepts of morality. The questions arising out of Vietnam about the possibly excessive use of force in large-scale aerial bombing or in an attempting to pacify guerrilla-infested villages redounded in turn, furthermore, to become questions even about the conduct of the two great wars hitherto viewed mainly in positive terms, the Civil War and the Second World War. The effect was that after Vietnam, not even those two wars could be regarded by many Americans in as positive a perspective as before. The military means employed by Americans in 1861–65 and 1941–45 came in part to seem of dubious merit, which in turn darkened the entire perception of those wars and made American willingness to resort to military force in the future yet more problematic, especially if the force in question was to be of the overwhelming power on which the military leaders insisted.

National satisfaction that the Civil War and World War II were not only great wars but good wars had always been to at least some degree shadowed—though until Vietnam only lightly so—by misgivings over destructive episodes in both wars that ranged beyond the customary targeting of military personnel and equipment alone, leaving civilians safe.

At the heart of the international war conventions that had evolved over the centuries to limit the violence of war, and thereby to prevent warfare from becoming all-consuming, was the principle of non-combatant immunity. Under this principle, non-combatants were to be secure from military violence in their lives and, for the most part, also in their private property. By the second half of the nineteenth century, the principle was generally observed in wars among the states comprising European civilization, if only because observance was to the mutual advantage of all concerned. The shock provoked by German violation of the principle of non-combatant immunity—in addition to violation of more specific provisions of international maritime law—by means of unrestricted submarine warfare in World War I suggests the extent to which non-combatant immunity had come to be almost taken for granted. The destruction of non-combatant life by German submarines in the First World War was minuscule compared with the toll extracted by the conduct of various belligerents in World War II, but in 1917 unrestricted submarine warfare appeared to much of the world as a barbarous departure from the civilized conduct of war.

The United States had not departed from the code by any means so drastically in the Civil War as Germany did in World War I. Still, the destruction of civilian property and the deliberate effort to undermine civilian morale through terrorization practiced by Major-General William Tecumseh Sherman in Georgia and South Carolina and by Major-General Philip H. Sheridan in the Shenandoah Valley of Virginia probably crossed to the wrong side of the boundary marking international legal protection of private property. Officially, the only property to be destroyed was that which contributed to the Confederate war effort. Houses and the personal possessions within them were supposedly exempt from destruction and molestation, and instances in which houses were deliberately razed appear to have been rare. But barns, grist mills, and other agricultural property went up in flames in large numbers, along with the crops within or outside of them, although their connection with the South's warmaking abilities was too indirect to make them appear legitimate exceptions to the rule of immunity for private property.

Moreover, Sherman's and Sheridan's manner of waging war against civilians entered into American military thought as an extension of that political aspect of military strategy that had historically considered such political targets as the enemy's capital city to be appropriate objectives of military operations. The Union's destructive marches opened the way for enlarging the sphere in which American soldiers saw civilians as possible military targets. It is speculative to suggest that Sherman's and Sheridan's attacks upon civilians made American airmen in World War II and thereafter more readily willing to bomb civilian objectives from the air. After all, Sherman and Sheridan did not wage war against civilians' lives. Nevertheless, making war against non-combatants emerged from the American Civil War as a strategy that American military leaders generally regarded as acceptable. Once that acceptance existed, the door was opened enough that a further opening into more ruthless attacks on civilians came at least within the boundaries of contemplation.

American military leaders generally could adopt such attitudes all the more readily because the idea of an all-encompassing war had not belonged to the North alone. In the Confederacy, Lieutenant-General Thomas J. "Stonewall" Jackson called for carrying destruction and fear to the North's civilians. While General Robert E. Lee never allowed Jackson to have his way in such an approach toward total war, Lee's own raid into Pennsylvania in the summer of 1863 was not so gentle as is sometimes thought. A major purpose was to replenish supplies at the expense of the North, and to that end Lee's Army of Northern Virginia conducted what amounted to a plundering expedition. Grains and livestock were seized wherever the army passed. Herds of cattle from Pennsylvania not yet otherwise dispersed grazed in Virginia as late as the autumn of 1863. Lee observed the forms of civilized war by offering Pennsylvania farmers payment either in Confederate States currency or in receipts to be paid by the Confederate Government after the war. The reality differed little from the effects of Sherman's marches.

Confederates as well as Yankees had called for still harsher measures against their adversaries. The usual American conception of war in the 1860s was one of an intensely and ruthlessly destructive enterprise. The objectives in the Civil War were by no means modest: the South believed it was fighting to preserve its very way of life; the North fought to stamp out all pretensions to independent sovereignty among the seceded states. With the purposes so large, untrammeled means appeared appropriate to the purposes. The Indian Wars had already nourished an American image of war that tended toward total war in aims and means. When in the late seventeenth and eighteenth century Europe had experienced an era of relatively limited war, limited in both objectives and methods, European settlers in North America and the North American Indians learned that their economic and social arrangements were too nearly incompatible to permit their communities to co-exist in close proximity. Both settlers and Indians had, therefore, escalated their conflicts against each other into wars of unlimited purposes. The Indians aspired, with increasing hopelessness to be sure, to push white and black settlers back into the sea. The settlers aimed to remove all Indians from their neighborhoods, and finally to drive the Native Americans so far to the westward that they could no longer have any particular effect on white and black communities, let alone threaten those communities' existence. With purposes running so deep, methods of war soon became indiscriminate, targeting whole populations rather than warriors alone, and making all species of property liable to destruction. Ferocity of means came all the more readily because the Indians did not possess a code of non-combatant immunity such as was emerging as part of the law of warfare in Europe. The Civil War then confirmed and enhanced the tendencies toward unlimited war already begun in North America by the Indian conflicts.

The American conduct of the Second World War further advanced these tendencies. Again the objectives of the war became exceedingly large ones, escalating into demands for the absolute submission of America's enemies. Such demands could be pursued yet more avidly than the North had pursued them in 1861–65 because the World War II adversaries appeared to be not only threats to the values and national interests of the United States but embodiments of downright evil. Against such enemies, the United States could well declare total victory to be its objective. To accompany such an objective, the American attitudes formed in the Indian Wars and the Civil War made unlimited means appropriate also.

The means approached the unlimited particularly in the strategic bomber offensives against Germany and Japan, the campaigns of aerial bombardment that exploited a more advanced technology to give new meaning to Sherman's and Sheridan's strategy of extending the targets of war beyond the enemy's armed forces to his economy and his people. At first the United States Army Air Forces attempted, nevertheless, to limit the targets of the aerial bombardment of Germany to those economic objectives that bore a direct relationship to the German war effort, and not to bomb the enemy population indiscriminately. The Americans at first chose this course rather than to follow the strategy of our British ally's Royal Air Force into promiscuous bombing of population centers. Thus the AAF attempted to avoid jettisoning the historic international law principle of non-combatant immunity. While target priorities varied during the course of the strategic bomber offensive against Germany, the AAF repeatedly returned to the enemy's petroleum industry as a target of special importance. During the final year of the war, the U.S. Strategic Air Forces destroyed Germany's mainly synthetic petroleum industry—nearly knocking it out and thereby paralyzing Germany in the autumn of 1944. The U.S. Army Air Forces relented because of inadequate intelligence regarding the severity of the enemy's oil shortage and in response to calls for aerial support of the ground campaign during the autumn 1944 deadlock. But it returned for the kill in the spring of 1945, to bomb so devastatingly that Germany would have had to surrender even if there had been no invasion on the ground, because Germany could not move tanks, guns, and trucks or fly aircraft or lubricate machinery.

In the course of the bombing of Germany, nevertheless, the Americans had also increasingly abandoned their scruples about attacking civilians, until by the end the American bomber offensive was scarcely distinguishable from the British in its destruction of non-combatant lives and property. Much of the cause lay in the very success of the bombing of military and quasi-military objectives; there were fewer and fewer such targets to strike. Meanwhile the expenses of building four-engined bombers and training their nine-man crews to high degress of skill were so great that the bombers and crews could not be allowed to remain idle, lest there be awkward questions in Congress and the press about the wisdom of the investments already made in air power. The Boeing B-17 Flying Fortresses and Consolidated B-24 Liberators had to be employed somehow, even if that meant violating the laws of war.

Against Japan, moreover, the AAF yet more readily abandoned restraints and adopted indiscriminate methods such as its leaders had professed to abhor when the RAF employed them against Germany. Intensive strategic bombing of Japan began November 24, 1944, with a strike of 111 bombers based on Saipan against Tokyo. It accelerated from bases also on Tinian and Guam, made possible by the capture of these islands in the Marianas group and by the new availability of the Boeing B-29 Superfortress. Even for the very-long-range B-29, however, the approximately 2000-mile round trip from the Marianas to Japan and back represented a decided straining of capacity. An aircraft damaged over Japan might well find the long trip home impossible and have to ditch in the Pacific Ocean. That was a main reason why the exceptionally costly battle for Iwo Jima was fought February 19–March 14, 1945: to provide an intermediate landing site for injured bombers, and also to offer a base within fighter escort range of Japan. By that time, however, the dangers of attempting precision bombing of military targets in Japan had assured a shift in American bombing methods, actually long in the planning, with the Twentieth Air Force persisting in the change long after Iwo Jima could be used.

To minimize the risks to aircraft, the Twentieth, charged with the bombing of Japan, turned from daylight to night attacks. Because of the difficulty of precision bombing at night, the AAF also turned to the indiscriminate bombing of whole cities that the British had practiced against Germany. The change could be rationalized in part with the argument that Japanese industry, differently organized from the German, was too much scattered throughout the cities, sometimes reaching into households, to permit effective precision bombing anyway. Yet the Twentieth Air Force also enhanced the indiscriminate nature of its raids by following the example set by the British incendiary attacks against Hamburg on July 24–August 3, 1943, and later invoked by Bomber Command against other German cities; the Americans launched firebomb strikes calculated to reduce Japanese cities into vast crematoria. The March 9–10, 1945, incendiary bombing of Tokyo took at least 84,000 lives, probably not many fewer than the toll in direct casualties of the August 6, 1945, atomic bombing of Hiroshima. The so-called conventional fire-bombing raids also prepared American consciences for the use of an atomic bomb against Hiroshima and another on August 9 against Nagasaki. The new weapon simply made it possible to accomplish with a single bomb and a single airplane what already was being done with thousands of bombs and hundreds of airplanes. Either way, the United States had followed Great Britain in discarding the international law principle of non-combatant immunity, and did so on a wholesale scale.

Yet the ability to use the atomic bombs to destroy two Japanese cities with just one airplane dropping one bomb against each of them precipitated a stirring of regret and doubt among Americans about the method their country had used to bring an end to the Second World War. For nearly a quarter-century following 1945 the prevailing American image of the United States conduct of World War II and the merits of having fought it remained generally positive, but feelings of guilt about having been the only nation to use atomic weapons in war became a source of gradually increasing pain to the American psyche. Misgivings about the atomic destruction of Hiroshima and Nagasaki surely prepared the way for misgivings during the Vietnam War about any aerial bombing of civilians whatever, although there was never much prospect of employing atomic and nuclear weapons in Vietnam during the American intervention. In the context of a new war whose entire rationale struck large numbers of Americans as questionable, aerial bombardment of civilians could only lend fuel to doubts about the wisdom and morality of the entire enterprise.

The United States government avoided in Vietnam any reversion to the indiscriminate aerial bombardment of the latter part of the war against Germany and Japan, seeking to assure both American and world opinion that the bombing of North Vietnam was confined to precision strikes against military or at least quasi-military targets, particularly hydroelectric dams and transportation bottlenecks. Still, almost any bombing of civilians now came to appear to be too much, so that while generalized doubts about the merits of aerial bombing received initial nurturing from the opposition to prosecuting the Vietnam War by any means, aerial or otherwise, opposition to the entire war nourished in turn an opposition to all aerial bombing. And as opposition to the Vietnam War increasingly raised questions among Americans about the appropriateness of resorting to any war whatever as an instrument of national policy, so opposition to aerial bombardment in Vietnam doubled back upon World War II to help generate a new questioning of the expediency, legality, and morality of strategic bombing even then.

By the time of the Persion Gulf War, the United States government felt obliged to take still greater pains to assure its people that the methods chosen to bomb Iraq caused almost zero civilian casualties and that bombs themselves had acquired guidance systems so sophisticated that they could scarcely fail to strike the military and quasi-military targets at which they were aimed. Any deaths or wounding of civilians had to be described now with the euphemism "collateral damage." Even so, questions about the aerial campaign against Iraq proved one of the principal sources of danger that a popular war might abruptly turn unpopular.

Moreover, so patently fragile was popular acceptance of the war against Iraq, so dependent the acceptance on the war's brevity, minimal casualty toll, and the uninterrupted nature of the successes, that far from exorcising the Vietnam syndrome of American public reluctance to resort to war in virtually any circumstances at all, the Persian Gulf War left the United States evidently even less willing to employ military force as an instrument of national policy after 1991 than before. A principal criterion for determining to embark upon military action now became the promise of the action to produce swift and almost complete victory with almost no casualties on the model of the Persian Gulf War. To assure fulfillment of the promise in conditions where it might be deemed to exist, any use of military force was to be overwhelming in scale in proportion to the strength of the projected adversaries. If no promise of rapid and cheap triumph existed, if a possible military action did not virtually guarantee the appearance of large and satisfactory results at low cost within a brief span of time, then in the early to mid-1990s the American government and public would probably judge the action unacceptable.

To that effect General Colin Powell as chairman of the Joint Chiefs of Staff spoke out publicly on the much-debated policy issue of American intervention in Bosnia and Hercegovina. He expressed what the *New York Times* described as "his philosophy that military force is best used to achieve a decisive victory and [on that basis] for the first time publicly explained his reluctance to intervene in Bosnia." He "assailed the proponents of limited military intervention to protect the Bosnians." According to the *Times*, "General Powell said: 'As soon as they tell me it [a military action] is limited, it means they do not care whether you achieve a result or not. As soon as they tell me [that an action will be] 'surgical,' I head for the bunker.'" As envisaged by Powell, a "surgical" action meant the opposite of overwhelming force, and while Powell claimed he did not insist that "you have to apply overwhelming force in every situation," he also argued that: "Decisive means and results are always to be preferred even if they are not always possible." Decisiveness in results implied also a clear definition before intervention began of the results to be desired. Only with such a definition, in terms acceptable to the military, could the achievement of the objectives with minimal casualties and within a limited time be envisaged and thus as much as possible assured.[1]

In the autumn of 1992 and through the following year, neither the Bush nor the Clinton administration could provide a clear definition of results that might be obtained through American military intervention in Bosnia, and thus there could be no assurance of the kind of rapid entry and exit that the military prescribed. The policy-makers of both administrations desired an end to the mutual slaughter of Serbs, Croats, and Bosnian Muslims, along with an independent state of Bosnia and Hercegovina; but no plan for military intervention could guarantee these desiderata. So no military action occurred, except light air strikes in conjunction with other North Atlantic Treaty Organization powers against Serb military positions and minimal air patrolling in support of United Nations relief efforts.

Given the post-Vietnam and post-Persian Gulf attitudes of both the public and the military, it is surprising that the Bush administration committed 28,000 troops to a United Nations effort to end starvation in Somalia, through Operation RESTORE HOPE, beginning December 9, 1992. But President Bush had staked his place in history on his foreign-policy reputation and on the establishment of a new and peaceful world order in the wake of the Cold War, while the persistent troublesomeness of Iraq in spite of the Persian Gulf War and the embarrassment of doing nothing to quell mass slaughter in Bosnia had raised grave doubts about that reputation and therefore engendered acute embarrassment. George Bush stood in much need of a last, redemptive foreign-policy triumph. Moreover, the initial terms of intervention in Somalia promised the kind of military intervention that General Powell was willing to support. All that was at first deemed necessary was a sufficient restoration of order and of avenues of communication within Somalia to permit food distribution to relieve widespread famine. The Somali people being fed again, an exit was expected in about a month.

The desire to paper over pusillanimity in Bosnia through a supposedly quick and easy triumph in Somalia evidently was desperate enough to forestall recognition that any long-term solution in Somalia would require a virtual trusteeship on the part of the United States or the

United Nations while a nation-building effort took place. Otherwise Somalia would remain fragmented into the suzerainties of various clan leaders, whose rivalries did much to account for the breakdown of food distribution in the first place. This unpleasant truth began to become inescapably apparent before President Bush left office, as of course it should have been apparent before the operation commenced. The hoped-for early American departure did not occur because starvation persisted, particularly in the Somali capital of Mogadishu, and because the feuding clan chieftains continued to obstruct the movement of foodstuffs in many parts of the country. Therefore the Somali intervention passed on to President Clinton, who allowed his administration to be pushed by the United Nations Secretary-General Boutros Boutros-Ghali into a reluctant and cautious approach toward nation-building, specifically toward disarming the clan leaders.

Partly for reasons having to do with the Egyptian Secretary-General's own alliances in Middle Eastern politics, Boutros-Ghali's efforts were directed most forcefully toward the disarming of General Mohammad Farah Aidid's followers and in time toward the capture of that general himself. By May 1993 the American troop commitment was down to 4000, but participation in the United Nations' quarrel with General Aidid was threatening to draw the remaining Americans into a quagmire. On June 5, virtual war broke out between United Nations—including United States—forces and General Aidid. That day a clash between Aidid's men and Pakistani United Nations peacekeepers killed twenty-four of the Pakistanis. The subsequent gradual escalation of the fighting reached a climax on October 3, when U.S. Army troops, the 3rd Battalion, 75th Rangers, raiding into the Aidid stronghold of South Mogadishu, found themselves practically cut off from reinforcement for much of the day while they fought a pitched battle in which eighteen of them died and seventy-five were wounded, while a Sikorsky UH-60L Black Hawk helicopter pilot, Chief Warrant Officer Michael Durant, was shot down, captured, and subsequently held hostage for thirteen days.

Four days before the battle in South Mogadishu, on September 30, General Powell had retired from his post as chairman of the Joint Chiefs of Staff. By that time the Somali intervention scarcely could be regarded as meeting his prescriptions for military action, but having identified himself with Operation RESTORE HOPE he persisted in defending it. President Clinton had a harder time defending it after the October 3 casualties provoked a considerable public and Congressional outcry for withdrawal. To avoid a complete confession of failure, the President announced on October 7 a short-term reinforcement of Somalia by 1700 troops, including armored forces, the lack of which had supposedly contributed to the Rangers' lengthy isolation, with an additional 3600 Marines to stand offshore in case of need; but he also promised a withdrawal of all American combat troops by March 31, 1994, a movement that proceeded as scheduled.

In spite of the reinforcements, therefore, the effect of the American casualties of October 3, 1993, was to promise the Somali resistance against United Nations nation-building a date beyond which the Americans would presumably no longer provide muscle for the Secretary-General's policies. (Another effect was the long delay for concurrent proposals to use American military power to help restore the democratically elected President Jean-Bertrand Aristide to office in the nearby Republic of Haiti.) Thus the losses and embarrassments of Somalia reinforced the Vietnam syndrome yet again, to render further employment of American military power still more unlikely—even in the nearby Caribbean area.

Even without the casualties of October 3 in Somalia, General Powell had already continued until his retirement to resist efforts to find some sort of ground for American intervention to end the fighting and the killing in Bosnia. His successor as chairman of the Joint Chiefs of Staff, General John M. Shalikashvili, showed little more enthusiasm for the employment of American military power.

Given the constitutional dubiety of General Powell's activities in policy-making, it is remarkable that he remained one of the most popular and least criticized of American military leaders since World War II—probably the most popular since the Vietnam War. Surely his presiding over the successful Persian Gulf War had much to do with this public acceptance. But it is almost certainly also true that his considerable immunity to criticism derived also from the circumstances that in his foreign-policy initiatives, his views coincided with those of a segment of the articulate public that usually would have been most ready to attack a military chieftain who strayed beyond the customary boundaries of military authority: the liberals and in general the left. General Powell sought to keep the United States out of war. So did the political left wing. On avoidance of military interventions in the early 1990s, the judgments of the country's highest-ranking soldier converged with those of the groups that would ordinarily have supplied his most vocal critics. And because General Powell evidently represented the opinions of a large body of high-ranking military men, the convergence on foreign- and military-policy issues was that of the nation's military leadership with its liberal political and media leaders.

The latter groups were not so likely to approve of possible entry into war even if the war should be assuredly winnable in short order and with minimal casualties and other costs. If the agreement between the military and the liberals on avoidance of military actions was therefore less than total, it nevertheless overlapped enough to spare Powell from left-wing dissent. After all, the conditions that he attached to his approval of military actions pretty much barred any such actions whatever, once his misjudgment about the ease of terminating the Somali intervention had reinforced his larger reluctance to embark upon adventures. Once the experience of Somalia had been digested, the chances that new scenarios would afford opportunities for complete military triumph swiftly and at low cost became almost nil.

General Powell and his military supporters were in favor of militry actions that would be practically without risk. According to this new standard for invoking military power, the United States might never have entered even the Second World War. Certainly when President Franklin D. Roosevelt's embargo on petroleum exports to Japan on July 26, 1941, provoked Japan into attacking Pearl Harbor the following December 7, there could be no guarantees of a quick victory and few casualties. The outlook was for a prolonged war with high casualties, both of which came to pass. Still less would General Powell's principles permit the North to embark on the Civil War. The power of the United States in December 1941 was such that even the destruction or disabling of the battleships of the Pacific Fleet at Pearl Harbor and the subsequent loss of the Philippine Islands could not generate real doubt of eventual American victory; but in 1861 the North obviously could feel much less assurance that it would win the war, let alone assurance about the war's duration and cheapness. The Confederacy's confidence in ultimate victory had to be still smaller. As did that of the North American colonies when they entered into war against the British mother country in 1775.

Did General George Washington refuse to go to war because he could not feel certainty about winning, and about winning in overwhelming, swift, and uncostly fashion at that? Obviously he did not. Would any truly great military commander—a Robert E. Lee, a Ulysses S. Grant, a George C. Marshall—have refused to fight unless he knew he could not lose? Is not a willingness to run risks for the sake of cherished values and interests close to the heart of what defines greatness in a human being—or in a nation?

To stand on the battlefield of Gettysburg while also commemorating the fiftieth anniversary of pivotal events in American participation in the Second World War does not entail the glorification of war. It does, however, call for a recollection of the utility and sometimes the necessity of waging war for the sake of national interests and values that cannot otherwise be protected, and to do so although the risks be high and the outcome uncertain. Without war, the independence of the United States could in all probability not have been achieved. Without the Civil War, the emancipation of the slaves in the American South and the consequent larger fulfillment of the ideals of the American Revolutionary War also in all probability could not have been attained; the roots of American slavery were planted deep enough that it is hard to envisage how they could have been pulled free without the violence of Gettysburg and the other battles of 1861–65. Without the Second World War, the evils of Nazism might command power still. Yet none of these wars was fought without risk.

And without a willingness to resort on occasion to war, and in circumstances that may require accepting risks, no great power can retain its greatness. Nor can the United States in particular hope to go on fulfilling the responsibilities attendant upon its wealth and might, responsibilities all the larger because of the special commitment of this nation, alone among the great powers, to the protection and advancement of freedom and democracy.

Not every occasion for the use of military force can as self-evidently combine force with the interests of justice as did the Civil War after it became a struggle against slavery or the Second World War as a crusade against Hitler. On occasion, military force may have to be employed in pursuit of ends that represent considerably less than a total good as well as in the face of risk. The Korean War of 1950–53 comes readily to mind. Against the possibility of an exchange of atomic bombardments should the war have become enlarged, or simply against the immense probable costs of an all-out conflict with the People's Republic of China, the United States in the Korean War had to settle for objectives a good deal more modest than the total defeat of its enemies. Waged for limited aims, the Korean War had to be fought also with limited means, among other reasons to ensure that the aims would not be driven to uncontrollable escalation by escalating means. Nevertheless, the Korean War was worth the costs and the risks that it entailed. The argument could be made that simply saving the Republic of Korea as an Asian outpost of national self-determination and potentially of democracy was enough to make the contest worthwhile. Beyond that, however, establishing the principle that the United States would not accept an expansion of Communist power brought about by overt military aggression laid down an important ground rule for the remainder of the Cold War, without which the dangers that the Cold War might turn hot could have been considerably worse than they were.

The occasional utility of and necessity for a great nation's accepting the risks and costs of war is central to the ongoing significance of the events that occurred at Gettysburg 131 years ago, especially as we view those events today from the perspective of the fiftieth anniversary of the other great American war. The battle of Gettysburg encompassed many acts of gallantry and glory, but it entailed more of pain, anguish, and death than of glory. Nevertheless, the results secured through the Union's victories at Gettysburg and throughout the Civil War would appear to justify extremely grave costs. The pre-Vietnam American consensus that the Civil War and the Second World War were essentially good wars did not spring from illusion.

Epilogue
Two Casualties of War

DON E. FEHRENBACHER

ON New Year's Eve, 1944, I was still in Tennessee but getting ready to leave the next day. Two months of duty at Smyrna Army Air Field had come to an end with orders transferring me elsewhere. I did not know then that eighty-two years earlier, my great-grandfather had been there within a few miles of Smyrna, like me an Illinoisan deposited in Tennessee by the whims of war. Unlike me, however, he never left. New Year's Eve, 1862, was the last day of his life.

Thirty-three-year-old George W. Outman had enlisted the summer before in the 73rd Illinois, a new infantry regiment organized and commanded by a Methodist preacher named James F. Jaquess. After falling sick and spending a good many weeks in an army hospital, Outman returned to duty in time to become one of the casualties at Stones River, arguably the bloodiest battle of the war. According to his company commander (who described him as a man 5 feet, 9¹/₂ inches tall, with a light complexion, blue eyes, and brown hair), he was killed "by a musket ball passing through the center of the breast."

To his wife and three children back home in Bureau County, the shocking news brought not only grief but the threat of poverty, even though a widow's pension of eight dollars a month was eventually awarded by a grateful government. For my grandmother, a little girl of four who could scarcely comprehend what had happened, life became harder that sad winter and harder still seven years later when her mother died while trying to relocate the family in Kansas. If her father had survived the war, she would have grown up differently and perhaps married differently. My very existence, it seems, is connected to a single deadly moment in Tennessee on the last day of 1862. The generational effects of the Civil War are so vast and problematic as to be beyond the reach of conventional scholarship, but they are none the less real.

My own route to Tennessee was much more circuitous than that of my great-grandfather. Never having stepped inside an airplane or traveled far enough by any other means to see a mountain, desert, or ocean, I was pulled out of college in February 1943 and, after fourteen months of training in Missouri, Michigan, Texas, and Arizona, found myself one day navigating a Liberator (B-24), with ten men aboard, across the Atlantic from Labrador to Northern Ireland. Our ultimate destination was the American air base at Wendling in East Anglia, home of the 392nd Bombardment Group of the Eighth Air Force. From there, beginning on May 23, we flew thirty combat missions over Germany and Occupied Europe, including one that gave us a splendid view of the D-Day armada. Of course we had adventures, such as fighter attacks, engines on fire, flak holes in the fuselage, and at least one emergency landing, but we came through unscathed—all of us, that is, except Robert Farrar.

Farrar, a youngster from Conway, Massachusetts, was our ball-turret gunner, guarding the vulnerable underside of the airplane. With German fighter opposition declining in the summer of 1944, the turret was removed, and Farrar consequently did not complete his thirty missions along with the rest of us on August 24. Whatever his forebodings at being thus left behind, they proved to be justified; for his plane went down soon after he began to fly with another crew. As was so often the case in that eerily remote air war, death took the outward form of mere disappearance, a failure to return to base. The terror and pain of his last moments were unrecorded and only dimly imaginable.

George Outman and Robert Farrar died eighty-two years apart and on different continents. Locus of conflict is, of course, the fundamental difference between the earlier and later wars of the United States. The Civil War was the nation's most intensive war—the last one fought on home ground, and the only one fought entirely against a domestic foe. Even within that framework, it was remarkably concentrated. About 40 percent of the 10,000 separate "military actions" of all kinds took place in Virginia and Tennessee, and most of the major battles were fought in those two states or very close to their borders. Spiritually as well as physically, it was an inward-directed, visceral struggle, one in which not only the survival but the constitutional form and moral character of the nation were at stake. Today, it remains both the one major disruption and the supreme reaffirmation of the constitutional order designed to secure, among other things, the blessings of "domestic tranquillity."

The Second World War was, in contrast, America's most extensive war, the only one fought on a global scale. A powerfully centrifugal force, it so expanded the role of the United States in world affairs as to constitute a kind of revolution, to which the American people, after half a century, are still adjusting. George Outman's war and Robert Farrar's war are America's two greatest wars because of their costs in effort expended and lives lost, because of the gross evils they destroyed, and because they are, along with the Revolution and the Constitutional founding, the major defining events in American history.

George Outman is one of the world's countless soldiers who is utterly silent. No bundle of letters, no diary, nothing in his handwriting has survived to provide traces of the man that he was. As a mere corporal, he is not mentioned in the 128 volumes of *The Official Records* of the war. His name is not inscribed anywhere that I know of. Certainly, neither his nor Robert Farrar's name will be found on any monument to American war dead in Washington. Their memorials are, one might say, less visible but more functional, being embedded in the very structure of the enduring nation and the world we live in.

Notes

ACKNOWLEDGMENTS

1. Ulysses S. Grant, *Personal Memoirs of U. S. Grant* (New York: Webster, 1885), 1:250; and Infra, 37.

2. Ibid., 38.

3. James Bryce, *The American Commonwealth*, 2 vols. (London and New York: Macmillan, 1880), 1:8; and infra, 5.

4. Carl N. Degler's comments in Erich Angermann, *Challenges of Ambiguity: Doing Comparative History* (Providence, R.I., and Oxford, Eng.: Berg, 1991; published for the German Historical Institute, Washington, D.C.), 21.

5. Infra, 144; Previously published in Gabor S. Boritt, ed., *Lincoln, the War President: The Gettysburg Lectures* (New York: Oxford University Press, 1992), 148.

ONE: TOWARD SUMTER AND PEARL

1. Roy P. Basler et al., eds., *The Collected Works of Abraham Lincoln*, 9 vols. (New Brunswick: Rutgers University Press, 1953–55), 8:101, (hereafter *CWL*).

2. James Bryce, *The American Commonwealth*, 2 vols. (London and New York: Macmillan, 1888), 1:8.

3. Peter Brock, *Radical Pacifists in Antebellum America* (Princeton: Princeton University Press, 1968), 187.

4. John Maynard Keynes, *The Economic Consequences of the Peace* (New York: Harcourt, Brace and Howe, 1920), 5.

5. Gabor S. Boritt, ed., *Lincoln, the War President: The Gettysburg Lectures* (New York: Oxford University Press, 1992), 8.

6. Ibid.

7. Adrienne Koch and William Peden, eds., *The Life and Selected Writings of Thomas Jefferson* (New York: The Modern Library, 1944), 698.

8. Ibid., 278.

9. John Hope Franklin, *The Militant South* (Boston: Beacon Press, 1964), 3.

10. Elting E. Morison, *Turmoil and Tradition* (Boston: Atheneum, 1960), 313.

11. Peter Allt and Russell K. Alspach, eds., *The Variorum Edition of the Poems of W. B. Yeats* (New York: Macmillan, 1940), 402.

12. David M. Potter, *The Impending Crisis* (New York: Harper, 1976), 121.

13. Basler et al., eds., *CWL*, 2:453.

14. James D. Richardson, ed., *A Compilation of the Messages and Papers of the Presidents*, 20 vols. (New York: Bureau of National Literature, 1917), 7:3168.

15. James G. Randall and David Donald, *The Civil War and Reconstruction* (Boston: Heath, 1961), 148.

16. Basler et al., eds., *CWL*, 4:271.

17. Parker's exact words were not recorded at the time. Some historians use verbatim the order attributed to him; some paraphrase it closely and don't use quotation marks; some ignore it. One, Willard M. Wallace, *Appeal to Arms* (New York: Harper, 1951), quotes it as unauthenticated, but adds, "The thought could not have been entirely absent from his mind." The point here is that, exact or not, Parker's alleged order is fixed in the American tradition, as evidenced by its inclusion without cavil in the 1992 edition of John Bartlett (Justin Kaplan, ed.), *Familiar Quotations* (Boston: Little, Brown, 1992), 333.

18. James MacGregor Burns, *Roosevelt: The Soldier of Freedom* (New York: Harcourt Brace Jovanovich, 1970), 28.

19. Hadley Cantril, ed., *Public Opinion 1935–1946* (Princeton: Princeton University Press, 1951), 975.

TWO: GRANT AND EISENHOWER

1. William S. McFeeley, *Grant: A Biography* (New York: Norton, 1981), xv.

2. *New York Times,* June 13, 1945, p. 3.

3. Ulysses S. Grant, *Personal Memoirs of U. S. Grant,* 2 vols. (New York: Webster, 1885), 1:38–39.

4. Stephen E. Ambrose, *Eisenhower: Soldier, General of the Army, President-Elect, 1890–1952* (New York: Simon and Schuster, 1983), 49.

5. Grant, *Memoirs*, 1:145–46.

6. Ibid., 1:250.

7. Ibid., 1:307–8.

8. Stephen E. Ambrose, *Eisenhower: Soldier and President* (New York: Simon and Schuster, 1990), 81–82.

9. Ibid., 95.

10. Ibid., 94.

11. Ibid., 116.

12. Dwight D. Eisenhower, *Crusade in Europe* (New York: Doubleday, 1948), 249.

13. Grant, *Memoirs*, 2:178, 188.

14. Dwight D. Eisenhower, *At Ease: Stories I Tell to Friends* (Garden City: Doubleday, 1967), 275.

15. McFeeley, *Grant*, 165.

16. Grant, *Memoirs*, 2:226.

17. Ambrose, *Eisenhower: Soldier and President*, 138–39.

18. Grant, *Memoirs*, 1:356.

19. Ambrose, *Eisenhower: Soldier and President*, 153.

20. Ibid., 128.

21. Dwight D. Eisenhower to John S. D. Eisenhower, May 11, 1944, John Eisenhower Papers, Eisenhower Library, Abilene, Kansas.

22. Ibid., 207.

23. Stephen E. Ambrose, *Halleck: Lincoln's Chief of Staff* (Baton Rouge: Louisiana State University Press, 1962), 102.

24. Ambrose, *Eisenhower: Soldier and President*, 172–73.

25. Grant, *Memoirs*, 2:495.

26. Ambrose, *Eisenhower: Soldier and President*, 200.

27. Ibid., 253.

28. Ibid., 236.

THREE: MILITARY INTELLIGENCE: UNMASKING THOSE FEARSOME APPARITIONS

The author thanks Edwin C. Fishel and William B. Feis, who are authorities on Civil War military intelligence, and Edward J. Drea, an expert on World War II intelligence, for critiquing the initial draft of this essay.

1. Although codes and ciphers are technically different, I have used the words interchangeably. Also, technically the words "break" and "read" mean different things to cryptanalysts but, again, I have used them interchangeably.

2. Michael Howard and Peter Paret, eds. and trans., Carl von Clausewitz, *On War* (Princeton: Princeton University Press, 1976), 118.

3. Diane T. Putney, *ULTRA and the Army Air Forces in World War II: An Interview with Associate Justice of the U.S. Supreme Court Lewis F. Powell, Jr.* (Washington, D.C.: Office of Air Force History, 1987), 189.

4. Military Intelligence Division, U.S. War Department, *German Military Intelligence, 1939–1945* (Frederick, Md.: University Publications of America, 1984), 277.

5. U.S. War Department, *The War of the Rebellion: A Compilation of the Official Records of the Union and Confederate Armies,* (hereafter *OR*), 128 vols. (Washington: GPO, 1880–1901), vol. 25, pt. 2, pp. 827–28.

6. E. Porter Alexander, "The Great Charge and Artillery Fighting at Gettysburg," in Robert U. Johnson and Clarence C. Buel, eds., *Battles and Leaders,* 4 vols. (New York: Yoseloff, 1956 reprint), 3:358.

7. E. P. Alexander, *Military Memoirs of a Confederate: A Critical Narrative* (New York: Scribner, 1907), 172–73.

8. Rachael Sherman Thorndike, ed., *The Sherman Letters: Correspondence Between General Sherman and Senator Sherman from 1837 to 1891* (New York: De Capo, 1969 reprint), 187, 193–94.

9. John Y. Simon, ed., *The Papers of Ulysses S. Grant,* 18 vols. to date (Carbondale and Edwardsville: Southern Illinois University Press, 1967–   ), 13:57–60 (a map is on 58–59).

10. Clifford Dowdey, ed., and Louis H. Manarin, assoc. ed., *The Wartime Papers of R. E. Lee* (New York: Bramhall, 1961), 819.

11. Ibid., 693.

12. John McEntee to Colonel George Sharpe, Aug. 31, 1864, Record Group 393, *The Records of United States Army Commands, 1821–1920,* Part I, Entry 3980, National Archives, Washington, D.C.

13. *OR*, vol. 25, pt. 1, p. 228.

14. John B. Jones, *A Rebel War Clerk's Diary* (New York: Sagamore, 1958), 469, 486.

15. William B. Feis, "Neutralizing the Valley: The Role of Military Intelligence in the Defeat of Jubal Early's Army of the Valley, 1864–1865," *Civil War History* 39 (Sept. 1993): 212.

16. Kenneth Strong, *Intelligence at the Top: The Recollections of an Intelligence Officer* (Garden City: Doubleday, 1969), 180–81.

17. *War Diary.* SI Branch, OSS London. Vol. 4: Proust, p. 20, in vol. 2 of John Mendelsohn, ed., *Covert Warfare: Intelligence, Counterintelligence, and Military Deception During the World War II Era,* 18 vols. (New York: Garland, 1989).

18. Military Intelligence Division, *German Military Intelligence,* 283.

19. Rear Admiral Robert N. Colwell, "Intelligence and the Okinawa Battle," *Naval War College Review* 38 (March–April 1985): 82.

20. E. B. Sledge, *With the Old Breed at Peleliu and Okinawa* (New York: Oxford University Press, 1990 paperback edition), 89.

21. Intelligence Directive Number 8, Supreme Headquarters, Allied Expeditionary Force, May 7, 1944, p. 2, in vol. 9 of Mendelsohn, *Covert Warfare.*

22. Ronald H. Spector, *Eagle Against the Sun: The American War with Japan* (New York: Free Press, 1985), 452.

23. Andrew Lossky, "Estimates of Enemy Strength," *Military Review* 25 (Aug. 1947): 21.

24. Quoted in Allison Gilmore, " 'We Have Been Reborn': Contributions of Japanese Prisoners to the Allied Propaganda War in the Southwest Pacific," unpublished article. My thanks to Professor Gilmore for sharing with me the results of her pathbreaking research on Allied psychological warfare against Japan.

25. Stephen E. Ambrose, "Eisenhower and the Intelligence Community in World War II," *Journal of Contemporary History* 16 (1981): 157.

26. F. H. Hinsley and Alan Stripp, eds., *Codebreakers: The Inside Story of Bletchley Park* (New York: Oxford University Press, 1993), 156.

27. Edward J. Drea, *MacArthur's ULTRA: Codebreaking and the War Against Japan, 1942–1945* (Lawrence: University Press of Kansas, 1992), 7–8.

28. Ronald Lewin, *The American Magic: Codes, Ciphers and the Defeat of Japan* (New York: Farrar Straus Giroux, 1982), 8.

29. Synthesis of Experiences in the Use of Ultra Intelligence by U.S. Army Field Commands in the European Theater of Operations, pp. 16 and 20, in vol. 1 of Mendelsohn, *Covert Warfare;* Strong, *Intelligence at the Top,* 181–82.

30. Howard and Paret, *On War,* 140.

31. Ronald H. Spector, ed., *Listening to the Enemy: Key Documents on the Role of Communications Intelligence in the War with Japan* (Wilmington: Scholarly Resources, 1988), 135.

32. Drea, *MacArthur's ULTRA,* 186.

33. Peter Calvocoressi, *Top Secret Ultra* (New York: Ballantine, 1981, paperback), 111.

34. Michael Howard, *British Intelligence in the Second World War.* Volume Five. *Strategic Deception* (New York: Cambridge University Press, 1990), 9.

35. William B. Breuer, *Hoodwinking Hitler: The Normandy Deception* (Westport, Conn.: Praeger, 1993), 191.

36. Howard, *British Intelligence,* 185–86.

37. Appendix No. 1 to informal Report to Joint Security Control: Enemy Reactions to FORTITUDE April–June 1944, unpaginated, in vol. 15 of Mendelsohn, *Covert Warfare.*

38. Ronald Lewin, *Ultra Goes to War: The First Account of World War II's Greatest Secret Based on Official Documents* (New York: McGraw-Hill, 1978), 339.

39. Thomas Parrish, *The Ultra Americans: The U.S. Role in Breaking the Nazi Codes* (New York: Stein and Day, 1986), 228.

40. F. H. Hinsley et al., *British Intelligence in the Second World War: Its*

Influence on Strategy and Operations, 3 vols. in 4 parts (London, 1979–88), vol. 3, pt. 2, p. 438.

FOUR: BATTLE IN TWO WARS: THE COMBAT SOLDIER'S PERSPECTIVE

The author thanks Thomas W. Collier, his colleague at the University of Michigan, for the advice and assistance that he so generously offered in this project.

1. James Jones, *WWII* (New York: Grosset and Dunlap, 1975), 62.

2. Charles R. Cawthon, *Other Clay* (Niwotco: University Press of Colorado, 1990), xx; Douglas Edward Leach, *Now Hear This* (Kent, Ohio: Kent State University Press, 1987), xii.

3. James D. Horan and Gerold Frank, *Out in the Boondocks* (New York: Putnam, 1943), 137; Ernie Pyle, *Brave Men* (New York: Holt, 1944), 27.

4. Horan and Frank, *Boondocks,* 136; Richard Tregaskis, *Guadalcanal Diary* (New York: Random House, 1943), 29; Edith Morton Eustis, compiler, *War Letters of Morton Eustis to His Mother* (New York: Spiral, 1945), 227, 121, 171; Carlton McCarthy, *Detailed Minutiae of Soldier Life in the Army of Northern Virginia* (Richmond: Randolph and English, 1888), 34–35.

5. John William De Forest, *A Volunteer's Adventures* (New Haven: Yale University Press, 1946), 62; Don M. Wolfe, ed., *The Purple Testament* (Garden City: Doubleday, 1947), 143; Patrick O. Sheel and Gene Cook, eds., *Semper Fidelis* (New York: Sloane, 1947), 50.

6. Joseph T. Durkin, S. G., ed., *John Dooley, Confederate Soldier, His War Journal* (Washington, D.C.: Georgetown University Press, 1945), 38.

7. John O. Casler, *Four Years in the Stonewall Brigade,* 2nd ed. (Girard, Kansas: Appeal, 1906), 291; Russell Davis, *Marine at War* (Boston and Toronto: Little, Brown, 1961), viii–ix; Lester Atwell, *Private* (New York: Simon and Schuster, 1958), 149; Ralph G. Martin, *The G. I. War* (Boston and Toronto: Little, Brown, 1967), 399.

8. Lewis Mumford, *Green Memories* (New York: Harcourt, Brace, 1947), 306–7.

9. Leander Stillwell, *The Story of a Common Soldier of Army Life in the Civil War, 1861–1865* (Eire, Kansas: Hudson, 1920), 56; Richard Hall, *Stanley: An Adventurer Explored* (London: Collins, 1974), 128; David Lamb, "Bill, Willie, and Joe," in *MHQ: The Quarterly Journal of Military History,* vol. 1, no. 4 (Summer 1989), 40.

10. Robert J. Houston, *D-Day to Bastogne, a Paratrooper Recalls World War II* (Smithtown, N.Y.: Exposition, 1980), 10; T. Grady Gallant, *On Valor's Side* (Garden City: Doubleday, 1963), 227.

11. John D. Billings, *The History of the Tenth Massachusetts Battery of Light Artillery in the War of the Rebellion 1862–1865* (Boston: Arakelyan, 1909), 231; William Nathaniel Wood, *Reminiscences of Big I* (Jackson, Tenn.: McCowat-Mercer, 1956), 39; Ira Dodd, *The Song of the Rappahannock* (New York: Dodd, Mead, 1898), 78; Pyle, *Brave Men*, 247.

12. William W. Blackford, *War Years with Jeb Stuart* (New York: Scribner, 1945), 263–64, 268–69.

13. Ibid., 268.

14. Eugene B. Sledge, *With the Old Breed at Peleiu and Okinawa* (San Francisco: Presidio, 1981), here in 1983 Bantam edition, p. 75; Atwell, *Private*, 50; Walter Bernstein, *Keep Your Head Down* (New York: Viking, 1945), 149.

15. Alfred Bellard, *Gone for a Soldier* (Boston: Little, Brown, 1975), 64; William B. Dreux, *No Bridges Blown* (Notre Dame and London: University of Notre Dame Press, 1971), 232; George Wilson, *If You Survive* (New York: Ivy, 1986), in Ballantine Books edition, pp. 111–12.

16. Mumford, *Green Memories*, 325; Sledge, *With the Old Breed*, 75, 77, 65; Atwell, *Private*, 49; Bernstein, *Head Down*, 149.

17. Atwell, *Private*, 23; Blackford, *War Years*, 263; Wilson, *If You Survive*, 112.

18. Wilbur F. Hinman, *The Story of the Sherman Brigade* (Alliance, Ohio: by the author, 1897), 165–66.

19. Beirne Lay, Jr., *I've Had It: The Survival of a Bomb Group Commander* (New York: Harper, 1945), 24; Ernie Pyle, *Last Chapter* (New York: Holt, 1946), 44; John Muirhead, *Those Who Fall* (New York: Random House, 1986), 123; John B. George, *Shots Fired in Anger* (Plantersville, S.C.: Small Arms Technical Publishing Co., 1947), 123; James Jones, *Whistle* (New York: Scribner, 1978), in Dell Book edition, p. 25.

20. Eustis, *War Letters*, 142; Masaya Umezawa Duus, *Unlikely Liberators* (Honolulu: University of Hawaii Press, 1987), 109; Orval Faubus, *In This Faraway Land* (Conway, Ark.: River Road Press, 1971), 338; Robert G. Carter, *Four Brothers in Blue* (Austin: University of Texas Press, 1978), 297; Audie Murphy, *To Hell and Back* (New York: Holt, 1949), 264.

21. Stephen M. Weld, *War Diary and Letters of Stephen Minot Weld 1861–1865*, 2nd ed. (Boston: Massachusetts Historical Society, 1979), 396; Murphy, *To Hell and Back*, 46.

22. James T. Miller papers, James S. Schoff Civil War Collection, William L. Clements Library, University of Michigan, Ann Arbor; Weld, *War Diary*, 244; James A. Connolly, *Three Years in the Army of the Cumberland* (Bloomington: Indiana University Press, 1959), 253; Carter, *Four Brothers*, 484; John F. Brobst, *Well, Mary: Civil War Letters of a Wisconsin Volunteer* (Madison: University of Wisconsin Press, 1960), 93.

23. Edwin P. Hoyt, *The G. I.'s War* (New York: McGraw-Hill, 1988), 283–84; Mary Livermore, *My Story of the War* (Hartford, Conn.: Worthington, 1890), 185.

24. George P. Hunt, *Coral Comes High* (New York and London: Harper, 1946), 111; Grady P. Arrington, *Infantryman at the Front* (New York: Vantage Press, 1959), 74; Robert Stiles, *Four Years Under Marse Robert* (New York and Washington: Neale, 1903), 311.

25. John Muirhead, *Those Who Fall* (New York: Random House, 1986), 107.

FIVE: GENDERING TWO WARS

1. Robert E. Lee, *The Wartime Papers of Robert E. Lee* (Boston: Little, Brown, 1961), 913.

2. Sarah Morgan Dawson, *A Confederate Girl's Diary* (Bloomington: Indiana University Press, 1960), 343, entry for March 31, 1863.

3. Howard Peckham and Shirley Snyder, eds. *Letters from Fighting Hoosiers* (Indianapolis: Bloomington Indiana War History Commission, 1948), 231.

4. Dennis D. Nelson, *The Integration of the Negro into the U.S. Navy* (New York: Farrar, Straus and Young, 1951), 52–53.

5. George H. Roeder, *The Censored War: American Visual Experience During World War Two* (New Haven: Yale University Press, 1993), 103.

6. Henrietta Barr quoted in Marilyn Mayer Culpepper, *Trials and Triumphs: Women of the American Civil War* (East Lansing: Michigan State University Press, 1991), 97.

7. Ibid.

8. Wilbur Fisk, *Hard Marching Every Day: The Civil War Letters of Private Wilbur Fisk, 1861–1865* (Lawrence: University Press of Kansas, 1992), 184.

9. U.S. War Department, *The War of the Rebellion: A Compilation of the Official Records of the Union and Confederate Armies*, 128 vols. (Washington: GPO, 1880–1901), ser. 4, vol. 2, pp. 769–70.

10. Albert Kirwan, *The Confederacy* (New York: Meridian, 1959), 281.

11. New York Dept. of Labor, *Home Duties of Working Women in New York State* (Division Industrial Relations, Nov. 1945), 7.

12. Ibid., 5.

13. Agnes E. Meyer, *Journey Through Chaos* (New York: Harcourt, Brace, 1943), 226.

14. *Boston Evening Gazette* May 4, 1861, p. 2.

15. *OR*, ser. 1, vol. 16, pt. 2, p. 895.

16. Culpepper, *Trials and Triumphs*, 30–31.

17. Bell Irvin Wiley, *Confederate Women* (Westport, Conn.: Greenwood Press, 1975), 152.

18. *American Annual Cyclopedia, 1862* (New York, 1863), 240.

19. Lloyd Lewis, *Sherman: Fighting Prophet* (New York: Harcourt, 1932), 355.

20. *American Annual Cyclopedia, 1862*, 241.

21. John Lynch, Aug. 9, 1862, quoted in Matthew J. Gallman, *Mastering Wartime: A Social History of Philadelphia During the Civil War* (New York: Cambridge University Press, 1990), 71.

22. D'Ann Campbell, "Paradise or Purgatory: Servicewomen in the Pacific" (unpublished paper given at SUNY, Binghamton, April 1992), 5.

23. Howard Coffin, *Full Duty: Vermonters in the Civil War* (Woodstock, Vt.: Countrymen Press, 1993), 261.

24. William Dorsley Pender, *The General to His Lady: The Civil War Letters of William Dorsey Pender to Fanny Pender* (Chapel Hill: University of North Carolina Press, 1965), 260.

25. J. Roderick Heller III and Carolynn Ayres Heller, eds., *The Confederacy in on Her Way up the Spout: Letters to South Carolina, 1861–1864* (Athens: University of Georgia Press, 1992), 119.

26. Bell Irwin Wiley, *The Life of Johnny Reb* (Indianapolis: Bobbs-Merrill, 1943), 214.

27. Helen McKee, Nov. 19, 1943, in Judy Barrett Litoff and David C. Smith, eds., *We're in This War, Too: World War II Letters from American Women in Uniform* (New York: Oxford University Press, 1994), 132.

28. Roy P. Basler et al., eds. *The Collected Works of Abraham Lincoln*, 9 vols. (New Brunswick: Rutgers University Press, 1953–55), 7:499.

29. James G. Randall and David Donald, *Civil War and Reconstruction* (Boston: Heath, 1969), 472.

SIX: FIGHTING ON TWO FRONTS: WAR AND THE STRUGGLE FOR RACIAL EQUALITY IN TWO CENTURIES

1. Ira Berlin, Joseph P. Reidy, and Leslie S. Rowland, eds., *The Black Military Experience* (Cambridge, Eng.: Cambridge University Press, 1982), 385–86.

2. Philip McGuire, ed., *Taps for a Jim Crow Army: Letters from Black Soldiers in World War II* (Lexington: University Press of Kentucky, 1993), 64–65.

3. For a full discussion of the relation of black soldiers to army discipline, punishment, and justice see, Berlin, Reidy, and Rowland, eds., *Black Military Experience*, chap. 9.

4. Ulysses Lee, *The United States Army in World War II, Special Studies: The*

Employment of Negro Troops (Washington: Office of the Chief of Military History, United States Army, 1966), 315–20, quote on p. 317.

SEVEN: WAR AND THE CONSTITUTION: ABRAHAM LINCOLN AND FRANKLIN D. ROOSEVELT

1. Tyler Dennett, ed., *Lincoln and the Civil War in the Diaries and Letters of John Hay* (New York: Dodd, Mead, 1939), 121 (hereafter *Hay Diaries*).

2. Roy P. Basler et al., eds., *The Collected Works of Abraham Lincoln*, 9 vols. (New Brunswick: Rutgers University Press, 1953–55), 3:29, 4:264 (hereafter *CWL*).

3. *Franklin D. Roosevelt, Public Papers and Addresses . . . 1933* (New York: Random House, 1938), 14–15.

4. F. D. Wormuth and E. B. Firmage, *To Chain the Dog of War: The War Power of Congress in History and Law* (Dallas: Southern Methodist University Press, 1964), 30.

5. Basler et al., eds., *CWL*, 1:452.

6. C. C. Tansill, ed., *Documents Illustrative of the Formation of the Union of the American States* (Washington: GPO, 1927), 115.

7. Jefferson to W. C. Claiborne, Feb. 3, 1807; to James Brown, Oct. 27, 1808, Andrew A. Lipscomb, ed., Albert Ellery Bergh, managing ed., *The Writings of Thomas Jefferson*, 20 vols. (Washington: Thomas Jefferson Memorial Association of the United States, 1905), 11:151, 12:183.

8. Jefferson to J. B. Colvin, September 20, 1810, ibid., 12:418–422.

9. A. D. Sofaer, *War, Foreign Affairs and Constitutional Power* (Cambridge, Mass.: Ballinger, 1976), 377–79.

10. Basler et al., eds., *CWL*, 4:426.

11. Adams in the House of Representatives, May 25, 1836, quoted in C. A. Berdahl, *War Powers of the Executive in the United States* (Urbana: University of Illinois Press, 1921), 15.

12. Basler et al., eds., *CWL*, 6:408; 5:421, 6:29–30, 428.

13. Dennett, ed., *Hay Diaries*, 205.

14. Basler et al., eds., *CWL*, 7:281.

15. Ibid., 6:263, 267.

16. B. R. Curtis, "Executive Power" (1862), reprinted in B. R. Curtis, ed., *A Memoir of Benjamin Robbins Curtis, LL.D. with Some of His Personal and Miscellaneous Writings* (Boston: Little, Brown, 1879), vol. II.

17. Louis J. Jennings, *Eighty Years of Republican Government in the United States*, 2nd ed. (New York: Scribner, 1868), 36.

18. James Bryce, *The American Commonwealth*, 2 vols. (Chicago: Sergel, 1891), 1:51, 61.

19. Henry Adams, "The Sessions, 1869–1870," *North American Review* (July 1870), in Henry Adams, *The Great Secession Winter of 1860–61 and Other Essays,* edited by George E. Hochfield (New York: Sagamore, 1958), 195.

20. Quoted by A. J. P. Taylor, *Essays in English History* (Harmondsworth: Penguin, 1976), 13.

21. Basler et al., eds., *CWL*, 7:281.

22. 2 Black 635.

23. Churchill to Roosevelt, June 15, 1940, Warren F. Kimball, ed., *Churchill and Roosevelt: The Complete Correspondence,* 3 vols. (Princeton: Princeton University Press, 1984), 1:51.

24. W. L. Langer and S. E. Gleason, *The Challenge to Isolation* (New York: Harper, 1952), 539.

25. Roosevelt to Churchill, May 16, 1940, Kimball, ed., *Churchill and Roosevelt,* 1:38.

26. R. H. Jackson, "Acquisition of Naval and Air Bases in Exchange for Over-Age Destroyers," *Official Opinions of the Attorneys-General of the United States* (Washington: GPO, 1941), xxxix, 484–96; cf. also his concurring opinion in *Youngstown Co. v. Sawyer* (1952).

27. E. S. Corwin, letter in the *New York Times,* Oct. 13, 1940.

28. *New York Times,* April 25, 1941.

29. See C. A. Beard, *American Foreign Policy in the Making 1932–1940* (New Haven: Yale University Press, 1946) and *President Roosevelt and the Coming of the War 1941* (New Haven: Yale University Press, 1948).

30. Robert A. Taft, *A Foreign Policy for Americans* (Garden City: Doubleday, 1951), 31.

31. Henry L. Stimson and McGeorge Bundy, *On Active Service in Peace and War* (New York: Harper, 1948), 368.

32. Roosevelt to Grenville Clark, July 15, 1941, Roosevelt Papers, Franklin D. Roosevelt Library, Hyde Park, N. Y.

33. Roosevelt to R. H. Jackson, May 21, 1940; to T. H. Eliot, Feb. 21, 1941, Roosevelt Papers.

34. Cabell Phillips, "No Witch Hunts," *New York Times Magazine,* Sept. 21, 1941.

35. Francis Biddle, *In Brief Authority* (Garden City: Doubleday, 1962), 238.

36. Archibald Cox, *The Court and the Constitution* (Boston: Houghton Mifflin, 1987), 194–95.

37. *West Virginia Board of Education v. Barnette,* 319 U.S. 624.

38. American Civil Liberties Union, *Annual Report,* 1944.

39. Roosevelt, *Public Papers,* 364.

40. Annual Message, January 6, 1941, Roosevelt, *Public Papers,* 670.

41. *Ex parte Milligan,* 4 Wall. 2, 125 (1866).

42. Adams, "The Session, 1869–1870," 194–95.

43. Basler et al., eds., *CWL*, 8:152; Roosevelt, *Public Papers*, 365.

44. Basler et al., eds., *CWL*, 6:267.

45. *Korematsu v. U.S.*, 323 U.S. 14 (1944).

EIGHT: TO PRESERVE A NATION: ABRAHAM LINCOLN AND FRANKLIN D. ROOSEVELT AS WARTIME DIPLOMATISTS

The author thanks his colleagues Lawrence F. Kohl and Forrest McDonald for reading this essay and offering many useful suggestions.

1. "Four Freedoms" Speech, Jan. 6, 1941, Samuel I. Rosenman, ed., *The Public Papers and Addresses of Franklin D. Roosevelt*, 13 vols. (New York: Harper, 1938–50), 9:663.

2. Lincoln, quoted in T. J. Barnett to Samuel L. M. Barlow, Sept. 25, 1862, cited in Howard Jones, *Union in Peril: The Crisis over British Intervention in the Civil War* (Chapel Hill: University of North Carolina Press, 1992), 175.

3. Quotes in Eric Larrabee, *Commander in Chief: Franklin Delano Roosevelt, His Lieutenants, and Their War* (New York: Harper, 1987), 644.

4. Edward M. Bennett, *Franklin D. Roosevelt and the Search for Victory: American-Soviet Relations, 1939–1945* (Wilmington, Del.: Scholarly Resources, 1990), xxi; contemporary (Owen D. Young) quoted in Frank Freidel, *FDR: A Rendezvous with Destiny* (Boston: Little, Brown, 1990), 106.

5. Roy P. Basler et al., eds., *The Collected Works of Abraham Lincoln*, 9 vols. (New Brunswick: Rutgers University Press, 1953–55), 7:23 (hereafter *CWL*).

6. Basler et al., eds., *CWL*, 1:278, 6:500, 5:478, 6:156. Gabor S. Boritt first analyzed Lincoln's aversion to war. See "War Opponent and War President," in Gabor S. Boritt, ed., *Lincoln, the War President: The Gettysburg Lectures* (New York: Oxford University Press, 1992), 179–211.

7. Roosevelt on war quoted in Edgar B. Nixon, ed., *FDR & Foreign Affairs: January 1933–January 1937*, 3 vols. (Cambridge: Harvard University Press, 1969), 3:377–84; Roosevelt to Churchill quote in Nathan Miller, *FDR: An Intimate History* (Garden City: Doubleday, 1983), 464.

8. Basler et al., eds., *CWL*, 5:350; Roosevelt quoted in Warren F. Kimball, *Swords or Ploughshares? The Morgenthau Plan for Defeated Nazi Germany* (New York: Lippincott, 1976), 96.

9. Gabor S. Boritt, "The Voyage to the Colony of Linconia: The Sixteenth President, Black Colonization, and the Defense Mechanism of Avoidance," *The Historian* 37 (Aug. 1975): 628, 627; Basler et al., eds., *CWL*, 5:388; James M. McPherson, *Abraham Lincoln and the Second American Revolution* (New York: Oxford University Press, 1991), 85.

10. James M. McPherson, "American Victory, American Defeat," in Gabor

S. Boritt, ed., *Why the Confederacy Lost* (New York: Oxford University Press, 1992), 36, 39; Garry Wills, *Lincoln at Gettysburg: The Words That Remade America* (New York: Simon & Schuster, 1992), 183.

11. Boritt, "War Opponent," 200.

12. Basler et al., eds., *CWL*, 1:75, 2:255, 3:376, 5:537.

13. James G. Randall, *Constitutional Problems Under Lincoln*, rev. ed. (Urbana: University of Illinois, 1951), 513–14; Basler et al., eds., *CWL*, 7:281; Roosevelt quoted in Warren F. Kimball, *The Juggler: Franklin Roosevelt as Wartime Statesman* (Princeton: Princeton University Press, 1991), 7.

14. Basler et al., eds., *CWL*, 2:501, 5:537.

15. Wills, *Lincoln at Gettysburg*, 88; Basler et al., eds., *CWL*, 2:276.

16. Kenneth M. Stampp, "One Alone? The United States and National Self-determination," in Boritt, ed., *Lincoln, the War President*, 140.

17. Basler et al., eds., *CWL*, 6:428, 5:421.

18. Ibid., 6:408, 4:426.

19. Ibid., 4:532, 3:306, 263.

20. Ibid., 6:149–50, 408–9.

21. Richard Hofstadter (first historian), *The American Political Tradition and the Men Who Made It* (New York: Knopf, 1948), 132; James G. Randall (second historian), *Lincoln the President: Springfield to Gettysburg*, 2 vols. (New York: Dodd, Mead, 1945), 1:161; Basler et al., eds., *CWL*, 6:29.

22. Basler et al., eds., *CWL*, 5:422–23; Thomas A. Bailey, *The Art of Diplomacy: The American Experience* (New York: Appleton-Century-Crofts, 1968), 132.

23. *Times* (London), Oct. 7, 1862, p. 8.

24. Basler et al., eds., *CWL*, 6:30, 7:507, 435, 8:333; Stampp, "One Alone? The United States and National Self-determination," 143.

25. Basler et al., eds., *CWL*, 7:23.

26. Ibid.

27. Wills, *Lincoln at Gettysburg*, 54, 38.

28. Ibid., 75, 76; Basler et al., eds., *CWL*, 1:367.

29. Ibid., 2:405–7.

30. McPherson (first historian), *Lincoln and Second American Revolution*, 64; Basler et al., eds., *CWL*, 3:303; Robert W. Johannsen (second historian), *Lincoln, the South, and Slavery: The Political Dimension* (Baton Rouge: Louisiana State University Press, 1991), 7, 21–22; Basler et al., ed., *CWL*, 2:130.

31. Ibid., 2:266, 3:16, 3:315.

32. Ibid., 4:438, 5:537.

33. Webster's speech, Jan. 27, 1830, Charles M. Wiltse, ed., *The Papers of Daniel Webster: Speeches and Formal Writings* (Hanover, N.H.: University Press of New England, 1986), 1:347–48; Basler et al., eds., *CWL*, 7:281.

34. First Roosevelt quote, in U.S. Department of State, *Papers Relating to the Foreign Relations of the United States, 1943* (Washington: GPO, 1963), 3:38 (here-

after *FRUS*); second Roosevelt quote, in U.S. Department of State, *Bulletin 10* (Jan. 1, 1944): 7; Kimball (first historian), *Juggler*, 186; James MacGregor Burns (second historian), *Roosevelt: The Soldier of Freedom* (New York: Harcourt Brace Jovanovich, 1970), 609.

35. Atlantic Charter, Aug. 14, 1941, Rosenman, ed., *Public Papers*, 10:314.

36. Quoted in Robert Dallek, *Franklin D. Roosevelt and American Foreign Policy* (New York: Oxford University Press, 1979), 139.

37. Roosevelt, "Quarantine Address," Oct. 5, 1937, *FRUS, Japan, 1931–1941*, 2 vols. (Washington: GPO, 1943), 1:383; Robert A. Divine, *Roosevelt and World War II* (Baltimore: Johns Hopkins, 1969), 23.

38. Roosevelt to White, in Elliott Roosevelt, ed., *F.D.R.: His Personal Letters, 1928–1945*, 4 vols. (New York: Duell, Sloan and Pearce, 1950), 2:968.

39. Rosenman, ed., *Public Papers*, 9:259.

40. U.S. Department of State, *Peace and War: United States Foreign Policy, 1931–1941* (Washington: GPO, 1943), 565.

41. Quotes in Robert Sherwood, *Roosevelt and Hopkins: An Intimate History*, rev. ed. (New York: Grosset & Dunlap, Universal Library, 1950), 191.

42. U.S. Department of State, *Peace and War*, 607; Beard quoted in William L. Langer and S. Everett Gleason, *The Undeclared War, 1940–1941* (New York: Harper, 1953), 278.

43. Diary entry for April 10, 1941, in Henry L. Stimson and McGeorge Bundy, *On Active Service in Peace and War*, 2 vols. (New York: Harper, 1947), 2:368.

44. U.S. Department of State, *Peace and War*, 741–43.

45. Charles C. Tansill, *Back Door to War: The Roosevelt Foreign Policy, 1933–1941* (Chicago: Regnery, 1952). See also Charles A. Beard, *President Roosevelt and the Coming of the War, 1941* (New Haven: Yale, 1948).

46. Roberta Wohlstetter, *Pearl Harbor: Warning and Decision* (Stanford: Stanford University Press, 1962), 3.

47. Kimball, *Juggler*, 41.

48. Warren F. Kimball, ed., *Churchill & Roosevelt: The Complete Correspondence*, 3 vols. (Princeton: Princeton University Press, 1984), 1:559; Yalta Conference Protocol of Proceedings, Feb. 1945, *FRUS, The Conferences at Malta and Yalta, 1945* (Washington: GPO, 1955), 977–78.

49. Divine, *Roosevelt and World War II*, 97, 93.

50. Kimball, *Juggler*, 61, 63.

51. Ibid. (first historian), 45; Burns (second historian), *Soldier of Freedom*, viii.

52. Divine, *Roosevelt and World War II*, 98.

53. Rosenman, ed., *Public Papers*, 9:670; *supra*, 165.

54. Basler et al., eds., *CWL*, 8:152; Rosenman, ed., *Public Papers*, 11:365.

NINE: RETELLING THE TALE: WARS IN COMMON MEMORY

1. W. W. Howe, "The New Birth," in Frank Moore, ed., *The Rebellion Record*, vol. 1 (New York: Putnam, 1861), 31; anonymous Congressman quoted in Alan Brinkley et al., *American History*, 8th ed. (New York: McGraw-Hill, 1991), 795.

2. *Rolling Stone*, 523 (April 7, 1988): 36.

3. Philip Caputo, *A Rumor of War* (New York: Ballantine, 1978), xiv–xv; John Hellmann, *American Myth and the Legacy of Vietnam* (New York: Columbia University Press, 1986), 164.

4. Quoted in Studs Terkel, *"The Good War": An Oral History of World War II* (New York: Ballantine, 1985), 189.

5. Quoted in Ernest B. Furgurson, *Chancellorsville 1863: The Souls of the Brave* (New York: Knopf, 1992), 230.

6. Quoted in Charles Royster, *The Destructive War: William Tecumseh Sherman, Stonewall Jackson, and the Americans* (New York: Vintage, 1993), 271.

7. Peter Svenson, *Battlefield: Farming a Civil War Battleground* (Boston: Faber and Faber, 1992), 196 for Dabney; Stephen W. Sears, ed., *For Country, Cause & Leader: The Civil War Journal of Charles B. Haydon* (New York: Ticknor & Fields, 1993), 248, 249, 251.

8. Joseph Heller, *Catch-22* (1961; New York: Dell, 1990 reprint), 442.

9. Lillian Ross, *Picture* (New York: Limelight, 1984), 26, 28.

10. Cindy S. Aron, "'To Barter Their Souls for Gold': Female Clerks in Federal Government Offices, 1862–1890," *Journal of American History* 67 (March 1981): 847.

11. Sean Hennessey, "Oral History Interview with His Mother, May 1991," transcript in possession of the author; Whitelaw Reid, *After the War* (New York: Moore, Wilstach & Baldwin, 1866), 224, 360.

12. J. Glenn Gray, *The Warriors: Reflections on Men in Battle* (1959; New York: Harper, 1970 reprint), 174, 23–24; Terkel, *Good War*, 108.

13. *North American Review* (Oct. 1867), 580–81; Betty Rosenbaum, "The Relationship Between War and Crime in the U.S.," *Journal of Criminal Law and Criminology* 30 (1940): 725; Audie Murphy, *To Hell and Back* (New York: Holt, 1949), 188; Police chief quoted in John D. Seelye, "The American Tramp: A Version of the Picaresque," *American Quarterly* 15 (1963): 543.

14. Terkel, *Good War*, 273; Richard Holmes, *Acts of War: The Behavior of Men in Battle* (New York: Free Press, 1985), 402.

15. Dixon Wecter, *When Johnny Comes Marching Home* (1944; Westport, Conn.: Greenwood, 1976 reprint), 183; Terkel, *Good War*, 235, 130.

16. John William De Forest, "Chivalrous and Semi-Chivalrous Southrons," *Harper's New Monthly Magazine* (Jan. 1869), 192.

17. Victoria Bynum, "Reshaping the Bonds of Womanhood: Divorce in Reconstruction North Carolina," in Catherine Clinton and Nina Silber, *Divided Houses: Gender and the Civil War* (New York: Oxford University Press, 1992), 327; Judy Barrett Litoff et al., *Miss You: The World War II Letters of Barbara Woodall Taylor and Charles E. Taylor* (Athens: University of Georgia Press, 1990), 209.

18. Edith Abbott, "The Civil War and the Crime Wave of 1865–70," *Social Service Review* 1 (1927): 220; Bell Irvin Wiley, *Confederate Women* (Westport, Conn.: Greenwood, 1975), 162, 163.

19. Wecter, *Johnny,* 170; Jean Attie, "Warwork and the Crisis of Domesticity in the North," in Clinton and Silber, *Divided Houses,* 257.

20. Karen Anderson, *Wartime Women: Family Relations and the Status of Women During World War II* (Westport, Conn.: Greenwood, 1981), 163.

21. Shirley A. Leckie, *Elizabeth Bacon Custer and the Making of a Myth* (Norman: University of Oklahoma Press, 1993), 52; Abbott, "Crime Wave," 222; Wecter, *Johnny,* 233.

22. William Graham Sumner, "What Our Boys Are Reading," *Scribner's Monthly* (March 1878), 684.

23. Richard M. Ugland, "The Adolescent Experience During World War II: Indianapolis As a Case Study," unpublished Ph.D. thesis, Indiana University, 1977, p. 261.

24. Wecter, *Johnny,* 168.

25. Earl Schenck Miers, *When the World Ended: The Diary of Emma LeConte* (New York: Oxford University Press, 1957), 21–22.

26. Quoted in Katharine M. Jones, *The Plantation South* (New York: Bobbs-Merrill, 1957), 121–22.

27. Michael C. C. Adams, *Our Masters the Rebels: A Speculation on Union Military Failure in the East* (Cambridge: Harvard University Press, 1978), 1; Frank L. Owsley, *The Plain Folk of the Old South* (Baton Rouge: Louisiana State University Press, 1949), 2.

28. Reid Mitchell, *Civil War Soldiers* (New York: Viking, 1988), 107; Royster, *Destructive War,* 81.

29. Royster, *Destructive War,* 81, 87; Wiley, *Women,* 151.

30. Mitchell, *Soldiers,* 135–36.

31. Thomas Goodrich, *Bloody Dawn: The Story of the Lawrence Massacre* (Kent, Ohio: Kent State University Press, 1991), 158, 153.

32. *New York Times Book Review,* Feb. 24, 1991, and April 14, 1991.

33. James F. Rusling, "The Yankee As a Fighter," *United States Service Magazine* 4, 1 (1865): 27–43; James Russell Lowell, "Ode Recited at the Harvard Commemoration, July 21, 1865," *Atlantic Monthly* 16 (Sept. 1865): 369; *New York Herald,* May 24, 1865.

34. Robert G. Athearn, *William Tecumseh Sherman and the Settlement of the West* (Norman: University of Oklahoma Press, 1956), 99.

35. Paul Fussell, *Thank God for the Atom Bomb* (New York: Summit, 1988), 78; Ronald Schaffer, *Wings of Judgment: American Bombing in World War II* (New York: Oxford University Press, 1985), 128.

36. Wade Huntley, "Point of View," *The Chronicle of Higher Education*, March 31, 1993, A40.

37. William Pfaff, *The Wrath of Nations* (New York: Simon and Schuster, 1993), 173.

38. Bill McCloud, *What Should We Tell Our Children About Vietnam?* (Norman: University of Oklahoma Press, 1989), 26.

39. Ambrose Bierce, *In the Midst of Life* (New York: New American Library, 1961), 249; *New York Times*, June 30, 1864.

40. John William De Forest, *Miss Ravenel's Conversion from Secession to Loyalty* (1867; New York: Holt, 1955), 484.

41. McCloud, *Vietnam*, 87.

TEN: THE NECESSITY OF FORCE: THE CIVIL WAR, WORLD WAR II, AND THE AMERICAN VIEW OF WAR

1. Michael R. Gordon, "Powell Delivers a Resounding No On Using Limited Force in Bosnia," *New York Times*, Sept. 28, 1992, sec. A, p. 1, col. 4 ("his philosophy . . . in Bosnia), p. 5 ("As soon as . . . for the bunker"), p. 5, col. 1 ("you have to apply . . . in every situation"); Colin L. Powell, "Why Generals Get Nervous," ibid., Oct. 8, 1992, sec. A. p. 35, col. 4 ("Decisive results . . . not always possible").

For Further Reading
A Bibliography

ONE: TOWARD SUMTER AND PEARL
Robert V. Bruce

For an outstanding analysis of American ideas about union through the period covered here, see Paul C. Nagel, *One Nation Indivisible: The Union in American Thought, 1776–1861* (1964). An authoritative and well-written study of the "Era of Good Feelings" is George Dangerfield, *The Awakening of American Nationalism, 1815–1828* (1965); for key episodes in that period, see James M. Banner, *To the Hartford Convention* (1970) and Glover Moore, *The Missouri Controversy, 1819–1821* (1953). On the mood and culture of the ante-bellum South, see John Hope Franklin, *The Militant South* (1956); Clement Eaton, *The Freedom-of-Thought Struggle in the Old South* (1964); and Bertram Wyatt-Brown, *Honor and Violence in the Old South* (1986), a skillful condensation of a massive and masterly book by the same author. The latter stages of the period covered here are thoroughly and keenly analyzed in David M. Potter, *The Impending Crisis, 1848–1861* (1976), which won a posthumously awarded Pulitzer Prize. The outbreak of hostilities and the ensuing historical controversy are lucidly and convincingly discussed in Richard N. Current, *Lincoln and the First Shot* (1963).

The twentieth-century side of this story is admirably covered in Raymond J. Sontag, *A Broken World, 1919–1939* (1971), a volume in the series *The Rise of Modern Europe*. John Maynard Keynes, *The Economic Consequences of the Peace* (1920) is a brilliant polemic that contributed importantly to reaction against the Versailles Treaty and to the general disillusionment of the early postwar years. Adolf Hitler, who dominated the later years of the period, is well covered in Alan Bullock, *Hitler: A Study in Tyranny* (1964) and in Joachim C. Fest, *Hitler* (1974). For the American leader in those same years see Frank Freidel, *Franklin D. Roosevelt: A Rendezvous with Destiny* (1990) and James MacGregor Burns, *Roosevelt: The Lion and the Fox* (1956). The background of Japanese history and culture is treated in two books by Edwin O. Reischauer: *Japan: The Story of a Nation* (1981) and *The Japanese Today: Change and Continuity* (1988). The American position during the approach of war in Europe is examined in Arnold A. Offner, ed., *America and the Origins of World War II* (1971); Arnold A. Offner, *American Appeasement* (1969); and Wayne S. Cole, *Roosevelt and the Isolationists, 1932–1945* (1983), a definitive study. An excellent symposium with two dozen contributors is Dorothy Borg and Shumpei Okamoto, eds., *Pearl Harbor as History: Japanese-American Relations, 1931–1941* (1973). An important early episode is discussed in Armin Rappaport, *Henry L. Stimson and Japan, 1931–33* (1963). Later stages in the coming of war with Japan are ably recounted in Jonathan G. Utley, *Going to War with Japan, 1937–1941* (1985) and Waldo Heinrichs, *Threshold of War: Franklin D. Roosevelt and American Entry into World War II* (1988), covering the period from March 11 to December 7, 1941. The upshot at Pearl Harbor is viewed from both sides of the encounter in the exhaustive yet fascinating volume by Gordon W. Prange, *At Dawn We Slept* (1982).

TWO: GRANT AND EISENHOWER
Stephen E. Ambrose

There is a vast literature on Grant and Eisenhower. The most important works are *The Papers of Ulysses S. Grant*, John Y. Simon, ed., 18 vols. to date (1967–   ) and *The Papers of Dwight D. Eisenhower* (1970–   ), 12 vols. to date. The memoirs cited in the footnotes are valuable.

J. D. C. Fuller, *Grant & Lee: A Study in Personality and Generalship* (1933), began the revival of Grant's military reputation. Bruce Catton fully restored the general to his rightful place with *A Stillness at Appomattox* (1953), *U. S. Grant and the American Military Tradition* (1954), *Grant Moves South* (1960), and *Grant Takes Command* (1969). Recent biographies include William S. McFeely, *Grant: A Biography* (1981) and Brooks D. Simpson, *Ulysses S. Grant and the Politics of War and Reconstruction, 1861–1868* (1991). T. Harry Williams's "The Macs and the Ikes: America's Two Military Traditions," in *The Selected Essays of T. Harry Williams* (1983), first published in 1952, briefly compares, among others, Grant and Eisenhower. Finally, the *Personal Memoirs of U. S. Grant,* 2 vols. (1885–86) is indispensable.

On Eisenhower, I have produced a study of his generalship called *The Supreme Commander* (1970); a study of his decision to halt at the Elbe River in April, 1945 entitled *Eisenhower and Berlin, 1945* (1967); and a two-volume biography called *Eisenhower* (1983, 1985).

Russell Weigley's *Eisenhower's Lieutenants: The Campaign of France and Germany* (1981) follows the campaign from the invasion of France to the end of the war in detail and with great insight. Bernard Law Montgomery's *Memoirs* (1958) tells his side of the story of his disputes with Eisenhower. Forrest Pogue's *The Supreme Command* (1954) is the capstone volume in the U.S. Army's multi-volume history of the U.S. Army in Northwest Europe. Omar Bradley, *A Soldier's Story* (1951), the memoirs of Eisenhower's principal subordinate, is a good example of how not to write memoirs. Walter B. Smith, *Eisenhower's Six Great Decisions* (1956), by Eisenhower's Chief of Staff, is an outstanding and perceptive memoir.

THREE: MILITARY INTELLIGENCE: UNMASKING THOSE FEARSOME APPARITIONS
Peter Maslowski

Although some books have been written on Civil War spies, such as Alan Axelrod's *The War Between the Spies: A History of Espionage During the American Civil War* (1992), no monograph exists on the general subject of

Civil War military intelligence. The most sophisticated work appears in essays; for some of the best see Edwin C. Fishel, "The Mythology of Civil War Intelligence," *Civil War History* 10 (1964): 344–67, and "Myths That Never Die," *International Journal of Intelligence and Counterintelligence* 2 (1988): 27–58; William B. Feis, "A Union Military Intelligence Failure: Jubal Early's Raid, June 12–July 14, 1864," *Civil War History* 36 (1990): 209–35, "Neutralizing the Valley: The Role of Military Intelligence in the Defeat of Jubal Early's Army of the Valley, 1864–1865," *Civil War History* 39 (1993): 199–215, and "The Deception of Braxton Bragg: The Tullahoma Campaign, June 23–July 4, 1863," *Blue & Gray Magazine* 10 (1992): 10–21, 46–53; and Peter Maslowski, "Military Intelligence Sources during the American Civil War: A Case Study," in Walter T. Hitchcock, ed., *The Intelligence Revolution: A Historical Perspective. Proceedings of the Thirteenth Military History Symposium, U.S. Air Force Academy* (1991), 39–70. In addition, the entries relating to the Civil War (and to World War II) in G. J. A. O'Toole, *The Encyclopedia of American Intelligence and Espionage: From the Revolutionary War to the Present* (1988) are exemplary.

Tim Travers, *The Killing Ground: The British Army, the Western Front and the Emergence of Modern Warfare, 1900–1918* (1987) explains the shift in warfare from a human-centered and qualitative to a machine-centered and quantitative paradigm. Three books written by army officers who knew nothing about ULTRA but explain the intelligence cycle and discuss World War II humint sources are Stedman Chandler and Robert W. Robb, *Front-Line Intelligence* (1946); Robert R. Glass and Phillip B. Davidson, *Intelligence is for Commanders* (1948); and Irving Heymont, *Combat Intelligence in Modern Warfare* (1960). For the OSS, see Anthony C. Brown, ed., *The Secret War Report of the OSS* (1976); William Casey, *The Secret War Against Hitler* (1988); Bradley F. Smith, *The Shadow Warriors: O.S.S. and the Origins of the C.I.A.* (1983); and Joseph E. Persico, *Piercing the Reich: The Penetration of Nazi Germany by American Secret Agents during World War II* (1979). John Prados tells the tale of the *Chanticleer* and the *Nachi* in "The Spies at the Bottom of the Sea," *MHQ: The Quarterly Journal of Military History* 6 (1994): 38–47. For aerial recon, see George W. Goddard, *Overview: A Life-Long Adventure in Aerial Photography* (1969); Andrew J. Brooks, *Photo Reconnaissance*

(1975); Roy M. Stanley, II, *World War II Photo Intelligence* (1981); and Peter Mead, *The Eye in the Air: History of Air Observation and Reconnaissance for the Army, 1785–1945* (1983).

Carl Boyd explained MAGIC in *Hitler's Japanese Confidant: General Oshima Hiroishi and MAGIC Intelligence, 1941–1945* (1993). The public was unaware of ULTRA until one of Bletchley Park's participants, F. W. Winterbotham, wrote *The Ultra Secret* (1974). Since then other participants have discussed breaking enemy codes, including Patrick Beesly, *Very Special Intelligence: The Story of the Admiralty's Operational Intelligence Centre, 1939–1945* (1977); Edward Van Der Rhoer, *Deadly Magic: A Personal Account of Communications Intelligence in World War II in the Pacific* (1978); W. J. Holmes, *Double-Edged Secret: U.S. Naval Intelligence Operation in the Pacific during World War II* (1979); Gordon Welchman, *The Hut Six Story: Breaking the Enigma Codes* (1982); Edwin T. Layton, *"And I Was There": Pearl Harbor and Midway—Breaking the Secrets* (1985); F. H. Hinsley and Alan Stripp, eds., *Codebreakers: The Inside Story of Bletchley Park* (1993). As for the Double Cross System, Jual Pujol tells his story in *Operation Garbo: The Personal Story of the Most Successful Double Agent in World War II* (1985).

The discussion of ULTRA in the Southwest Pacific Area relies heavily on Edward J. Drea's model monograph, *MacArthur's ULTRA: Codebreaking and the War against Japan, 1942–1945* (1993). For Europen ULTRA the indispensable starting point is the multi-volume *British Intelligence in the Second World War* (1979–90). F. H. Hinsley authored the first three volumes, which are subtitled *Its Influence on Strategy and Operations;* Hinsley and C. A. G. Simkins co-authored volume 4, *Security and Counterintelligence;* and Michael Howard wrote volume 5, *Strategic Deception.* Michael I. Handel, ed., has much to say in *Strategic and Operational Deception in the Second World War* (1987). Ralph Bennett, a historian who worked at Bletchley Park, wrote *Ultra in the West: The Normandy Campaign of 1944–45* (1979) and *Ultra and Mediterranean Strategy* (1989). David Kahn's *Seizing the Enigma: The Race to Break the German U-Boat Codes, 1939–1943* (1991) is excellent, as are Ronald Lewin's *Ultra Goes to War: The First Account of World War II's Greatest Secret Based on Official Documents* (1978) and *The American Magic: Codes, Ciphers and the Defeat of Japan* (1982).

For those who want to sample many important sigint documents first-hand, consult Ronald H. Spector, ed., *Listening to the Enemy: Key Documents on the Role of Communications Intelligence in the War with Japan* (1988); James L. Gilbert and John P. Finnegan, eds., *U.S. Army Signals Intelligence in World War II: A Documentary History* (1993); and John Mendelsohn, ed., *Covert Warfare: Intelligence, Counterintelligence, and Military Deception During the World War II Era*, 18 vols. (1989).

FOUR: BATTLE IN TWO WARS: THE COMBAT SOLDIER'S PERSPECTIVE
Gerald F. Linderman

Notwithstanding the limitations mentioned in the text, soldier letters and soldier narratives remain the building blocks of those larger interpretations of battle experience that historians are beginning to construct.

Two interesting collections of letters are those of Union soldier Robert G. Carter and G.I. Morton Eustis. For the volume *Four Brothers in Blue* (1978), Carter, who began his military career as a private in the 22d Massachusetts, provided the narrative that connects his letters and those of his three brothers, all of whom saw combat during the Civil War. *The War Letters of Morton Eustis to His Mother* (1945) illuminates the changing attitudes of the son of a socially prominent family from his enlistment in 1941 as a private in the 101st Cavalry to his death in 1944 as a first lieutenant in France.

Neither war lacks first-rate soldier narratives. For the Union side, see John Beatty, *Memoirs of a Volunteer, 1861–1863* (1946); Rice C. Bull, *Soldiering* (1977); and—a memoir of striking candor—Alfred Bellard, *Gone for a Soldier* (1975). On the Confederate side, there are William Dame's *From the Rapidan to Richmond and the Spottsylvania Campaign* (1920) and Carlton McCarthy's *Detailed Minutiae of Soldier Life in the Army of Northern Virginia* (1888). Among the most impressive World War II soldier accounts are Lester Atwell's *Private* (1958); Eugene B. Sledge's *With the Old Breed at Peleliu and Okinawa* (1981); and Harold P. Leinbaugh and John D. Campbell's *The Men of Company K* (1985).

In recent years there have begun to appear Civil War studies attempting to integrate diary, letter, and soldier-narrative source materials and to draw from them conclusions of a high order regarding the nature of the combat experience 1861–65. See Reid Mitchell's *Civil War Soldiers* (1988) and this author's *Embattled Courage: The Experience of Combat in the American Civil War* (1987).

In the literature of World War II, such books as Lee Kennett's *G.I.: The American Soldier in World War II* (1987), while very valuable, are often based on military and academic survey projects whose questions do not always strike to the heart of the combat soldier's concerns. J. Glenn Gray's *The Warriors: Reflections on Men in Battle* (1959) is a brilliant and provocative volume that claims for its principal propositions an applicability to front-line soldiers whose experience was different from that of the author, an intelligence officer engaged in interrogating prisoners of war. Ernie Pyle's excellent books—*Here Is Your War* (1943) and *Brave Men* (1944)— offer the lineaments of representative reactions to battle, but the task of providing an integrated, comprehensive view of the American combat soldier's experience continues to challenge historians and other writers interested in exploring World War II.

FIVE: GENDERING TWO WARS
D'Ann Campbell and Richard Jensen

For many years Bell Wiley stood apart from the drums and bugles historians by exploring the common soldiers of the Civil War and other aspects of social history. His most useful books remain *The Life of Billy Yank* (1952) and *The Life of Johnny Reb* (1943). Social history themes were well represented in Allan Nevins's magisterial four-volume history *The War for the Union* (1959–71). As wave after wave of "new social history" swept over scholarship in the last quarter-century, it appeared that the Civil War was immune. No longer. Gerald Linderman has studied many facets of *Embattled Courage: The Experience of Combat in the American Civil War* (1987). James McPherson used letters to discover *What They Fought For, 1861–1865* (1994). Reid Mitchell has two useful studies: *Civil War Soldiers: Their Expectations and Experiences* (1988) and *The Vacant Chair* (1993). Wiley's research has been replicated by James Robertson in *Soldiers Blue and Gray* (1988). Their research has taken them to scores of local and state archives, which eagerly sought out and reserved collections of letters from the war—letters emblematic of their communities' commitment to the war effort. Women occupied only the outer fringes of the war years until Mary Massey's rich overview, *Bonnet Brigades*, appeared in 1966. More recently, George Rable has explored the crises faced by Southern women in remarkable detail in *Civil Wars* (1989); and biographies of women leaders, such as Dorothea Dix and Clara Barton, and of servicewomen, such as *An Uncommon Soldier* (a private with the New York State Volunteers) edited by Lauren Cook Burgess (1994), increase in number each year. Regional specialists like Stephen Ash and Vernon Burton have explicated the social history of particular areas, and a new cohort of women's historians have turned their attention to nurses. Tying together soldiers and womenfolk, psychology and ideology, are the influential and penetrating essays of Drew Gilpin Faust collected in *Southern Stories: Slaveholders in Peace and War* (1992).

Homefront themes have always been prominent in World War II historiography. Historians have, however, concentrated on the economy, labor, women war workers, national politics, and the media, largely ignoring the soldiers. The one title on soldiers, by Lee Kennett, *G.I.: The American Soldier in World War II* (1987), is a promising start, but the shelf-space is short in contrast to the long row of Civil War books. Curiously, we know more about women soldiers and women veterans than about the men. Mattie Treadwell's 1954 official history of *The Women's Army Corps* is outstanding. Beginning with her book *Women at War with America: Private Lives in a Patriotic Era* (1984), D'Ann Campbell has published a series of chapters and essays on military women, including a re-analysis of questionnaires she gathered from women veterans. Social historians have been generally antiwar and have avoided military themes. Women's historians also tend to be pacifist, but it is hard for them to ignore the institutional breakthroughs represented by the WAC, WAVES, and nurses. Letters to and from servicemen are only now being deposited in archives (over half the servicemen are still alive, as are most of the spouses). A few gatherings have appeared in print. As demonstrated in *Since You Went Away: World War II Letters from American Women on the Home Front* (1991), and most recently in *We're in This War, Too: World War II Letters from American Women in Uniform* (1994), Judy Barrett Litoff and David C. Smith have been indefatigable collectors, and thanks to their efforts we can work with rich sources. Harold P. Leinbaugh and John D. Campbell, *The Men of Company K: The Autobiography of a World War II Rifle Company* (1985), have demonstrated the potential of oral history.

The best sociological traditions are represented by studies by Reuben Hill, *Families Under Stress: Adjustment to the Crises of War Separation and Reunion* (1949). A strikingly original source on what soldiers thought are the surveys undertaken for the army by sociologist Samuel Stouffer and a brilliant team of scholars. Stouffer's book *The American Soldier* (1949) is well known; much less familiar are the original data sets, held by the Roper Center at Yale, Williams College, and the University of Connecticut. Roger Fosdick's *A Call to Arms: The American Enlisted Soldier in World War II* (unpublished Ph.D. dissertation, Claremont Graduate School, 1984) and Campbell's papers have scratched the surface of the Stouffer data sets—but they are too quantitative for most historians, too old for most sociologists, and yet too rich and too revealing to be ignored for much longer.

SIX: FIGHTING ON TWO FRONTS: WAR AND THE STRUGGLE FOR RACIAL EQUALITY IN TWO CENTURIES
Ira Berlin

The fullest study of black soldiers in the Civil War is series 2 of *Freedom: A Documentary History of Emancipation, 1861–1867, The Black Military Experience* (Cambridge, Eng., 1982), edited by Ira Berlin, Joseph P. Reidy, and Leslie S. Rowland. It has the advantage of bringing together both contemporary documents and informed commentary on all aspects of the soldiers' experience. Documents relating to the experience of black Civil War soldiers can be found in the other volumes of the *Freedom* series as well. A number of valuable secondary sources address the soldiers' experience. The most important are Benjamin Quarles, *The Negro in the Civil War* (Boston, 1953); Dudley Taylor Cornish, *The Sable Arm: Negro Troops in the Union Army, 1861–1865* (New York, 1956); James M. McPherson, *The Negro's Civil War: How American Negroes Felt and Acted During the War for Union* (New York, 1965); and Leon F. Litwack, *Been in the Storm*

So Long: The Aftermath of Slavery (New York, 1979), chap. 2. Joseph T. Glatthaar, *Forged in Battle: The Civil War Alliance of Black Soldiers and White Officers* (New York, 1990) is a close study of relations of black soldiers and white officers. Glatthaar's essay "Black Glory: The African-American Role in Union Victory," in Gabor S. Boritt, ed., *Why the Confederacy Lost* (New York, 1992), makes a strong case for the importance of black soldiers to Union success. Three important nineteenth-century studies are by William Wells Brown, *The Negro in the American Rebellion* (Boston, 1867); George W. Williams, *A History of Negro Troops in the War of the Rebellion, 1861–1865* (New York, 1988); and Joseph T. Wilson, *The Black Phalanx: A History of the Negro Soldiers of the United States in the Wars of 1775–1812 and 1861–65* (Hartford, 1888). Mary F. Berry, *Military Necessity and Civil Rights Policy: Black Citizenship and the Constitution, 1861–1868* (Port Washington, N.Y., 1977), an important and often overlooked book, connects the service of black soldiers to the legal and constitutional changes of the Reconstruction era. Basic documents for the Civil War era can be found in Bernard C. Nalty and Morris J. MacGregor, eds., *Blacks in the Military: Essential Documents* (Wilmington, Del., 1981), chap. 2.

The literature on black soldiers in World War II is not nearly as full. An essential beginning can be made with Ulysses Lee, *The Employment of Negro Troops* (Washington, D.C., 1966); with A. Russell Buchanan, *Black Americans in World War II* (Santa Barbara, 1977), chaps. 5–9; and with Bernard C. Nalty, *Strength for the Fight: A History of Black Americans in the Military* (New York, 1986), chaps. 10–12 offering informed overviews. A close look at the special role of black airmen is Alan M. Osur, *Blacks in the Army Air Force During World War II* (Washington, D.C., 1977). The navy is addressed in Lawrence D. Reddick, "The Negro in the United States Navy During World War II," *Journal of Negro History* 32 (1947): 201–19. The question of segregation is given full treatment by Richard M. Dalfiume, *Desegregation of the U. S. Armed Forces: Fighting on Two Fronts, 1939–1953* (Columbia, Mo., 1969); and Morris J. MacGregor, Jr., *Integration of the Armed Forces, 1940–1965* (Washington, D.C., 1981). Also useful are Lee Nichols, *Breakthrough on the Color Front* (New York, 1954) and Richard J. Stillman, *Integration of the Negro in the U.S. Armed Forces*

(New York, 1968). Nalty and MacGregor, eds., *Blacks in the Military: Essential Documents*, chaps. 5–6, presents the documents for World War II. The letters of black soldiers have been collected in Philip McGuire, ed., *Taps for a Jim Crow Army: Letters from Black Soldiers in World War II* (Lexington, Ky., 1993). Of special value for the perspective of African-American communities during the World War II years is C. L. R. James et al., *Fighting Racism in World War II* (New York, 1980).

SEVEN: WAR AND THE CONSTITUTION: ABRAHAM LINCOLN AND FRANKLIN D. ROOSEVELT
Arthur M. Schlesinger, Jr.

The bibliographical notes of Chapter Eight introduce the reader to the literature on Lincoln and FDR. This can be supplemented by a few works focusing on constitutional questions in particular. Mark E. Neely's Pulitzer-Prize winning *The Fate of Liberty: Abraham Lincoln and Civil Liberties* (1991) is the best book on the subject. J. G. Randall's classic *Constitutional Problems Under Lincoln* (rev. ed. 1951) remains quite useful. Good general accounts are Harold Hyman, *A More Perfect Union: The Impact of the Civil War and Reconstruction on the Constitution* (1973) and Harold Hyman and William M. Wiecek, *Equal Justice Under the Law: Constitutional Development, 1835–1875* (1982).

For F.D.R. see E. S. Corwin, *Total War and the Constitution* (1947), which emphasizes departures from ordinary ways; and a pair of books by Clinton Rossiter: *Constitutional Dictatorship: Crisis of Government in the Modern Democracies* (1948) and *The Supreme Court and the Commander in Chief* (1951). Roger Daniels, *Concentration Camps U.S.A.: Japanese Americans and World War II* (1971) and Peter Irons, *Justice at War* (1983) are revealing.

Among general works see A. D. Sofaer, *War, Foreign Affairs and Constitutional Power* (1976) and F. D. Wormuth and E. B. Firmage, *To Chain the Day of War: The War Power of Congress in History and Law* (1984).

EIGHT: TO PRESERVE A NATION:
ABRAHAM LINCOLN AND
FRANKLIN D. ROOSEVELT AS
WARTIME DIPLOMATISTS
Howard Jones

Research on Lincoln begins with Roy P. Basler et al., eds., *The Collected Works of Abraham Lincoln*, 9 vols. (1953–55), *Supplements* (1973, 1991). The broadest diplomatic study is Jay Monaghan, *Diplomat in Carpet Slippers: Abraham Lincoln Deals with Foreign Affairs* (1945). An account of the foreign interventionist issue that rests on archival work in England and the United States is Howard Jones, *Union in Peril: The Crisis over British Intervention in the Civil War* (1992). On Seward, see Norman B. Ferris, *Desperate Diplomacy: William H. Seward's Foreign Policy, 1861* (1976).

James M. McPherson analyzes the President's wartime policies in *Abraham Lincoln and the Second American Revolution* (1991). He also offers valuable insights into Lincoln's wartime leadership in "American Victory, American Defeat," in Gabor S. Boritt, ed., *Why the Confederacy Lost* (1992). In another essay, McPherson shows that the essence of Lincoln's national strategy was unconditional surrender. See "Lincoln and the Strategy of Unconditional Surrender," in Gabor S. Boritt, ed., *Lincoln, the War President: The Gettysburg Lectures* (1992), 29–62.

Kenneth M. Stampp shows how Lincoln first spoke of the war's goal as preservation of the Union but then finally justified the struggle as a moral cause against slavery. See his essay, "One Alone? The United States and National Self-Determination," in Boritt, ed., *Lincoln, the War President*, 121–44. For a thought-provoking analysis of Lincoln's intentions at Gettysburg, see Garry Wills, *Lincoln at Gettysburg: The Words That Remade America* (1992). A provocative study of Lincoln's attitude toward blacks is LaWanda Cox, *Lincoln and Black Freedom: A Study in Presidential Leadership* (1981). See also her essay, "Lincoln and Black Freedom," in Gabor S. Boritt, ed., *The Historian's Lincoln: Pseudohistory, Psychohistory, and History* (1988), 175–96. Robert W. Johannsen sees Lincoln as heavily political in motive, even though moved also by moral considerations. See *Lincoln, the South, and Slavery: The Political Dimension* (1991).

A defense of both Presidents' policies in this volume, Arthur M. Schlesinger, Jr., "War and the Constitution: Abraham Lincoln and Franklin D. Roosevelt," first appeared in Boritt, ed., *Lincoln, the War President*, 145–78. Boritt shows Lincoln's hatred of war in an essay entitled, "War Opponent and War President," ibid., 179–211. For Roosevelt's papers and speeches, see Samuel I. Rosenman, ed., *The Public Papers and Addresses of Franklin D. Roosevelt*, 13 vols. (1938–50). The most complete documentation involving the two Atlantic wartime leaders is in Warren F. Kimball, ed., *Churchill and Roosevelt: The Complete Correspondence*, 3 vols. (1984). For other documents, see U.S. Department of State, *Peace and War: United States Foreign Policy, 1931–1941* (1943). Robert E. Sherwood has presented a sympathetic study of the President's policies in *Roosevelt and Hopkins: An Intimate History* (1948).

The best broad survey of Roosevelt's foreign policy is Robert Dallek, *Franklin D. Roosevelt and American Foreign Policy, 1932–1945* (1979), which sees its subject as a realistic statesman who continually adjusted his military and diplomatic policies to domestic pressures. A masterfully written study of the wartime leader as inept strategist is James MacGregor Burns, *Roosevelt: The Soldier of Freedom* (1970). According to Warren F. Kimball in *The Juggler: Franklin Roosevelt as Wartime Statesman* (1991), the President's policies always remained balanced on a tightrope. A solid general study that has resulted from a lifetime of work is Frank Freidel, *FDR: A Rendezvous with Destiny* (1990).

For critical studies of Roosevelt's hesitancy to accept his responsibilities as world leader, see Robert A. Divine's two works, *Roosevelt and World War II* (1969) and *The Reluctant Belligerent: American Entry into World War II* (1979). Dorothy Borg deals with the complexities of the President's diplomacy in "Notes on Roosevelt's 'Quarantine Speech,'" *Political Science Quarterly* 72 (Sept. 1957). Those leading the "revisionist" assault on Roosevelt include Charles A. Beard in two works, *American Foreign Policy in the Making, 1932–1940* (1946) and *President Roosevelt and the Coming of the War, 1941* (1948), and Charles C. Tansill, *Back Door to War: The Roosevelt Foreign Policy, 1933–1941* (1952). Roosevelt's defenders include Roberta Wohlstetter, who shows how Japan's success at Pearl Harbor resulted from intelligence failures by the United States. See her study, *Pearl Harbor: Warning and Decision* (1962). Gordon W.

Prange's massively researched study, *At Dawn We Slept: The Untold Story of Pearl Harbor* (1981), demonstrates that the Pearl Harbor attack resulted from a series of administrative errors by the United States and a dogged determination by the Japanese to strike a critical blow at America's strongest Pacific position.

NINE: RETELLING THE TALE: WARS IN COMMON MEMORY
Michael C. C. Adams

On the nature of myth, Keith Walden, *Visions of Order* (1982) and Haydon White, "The Historical Text As Literary Artifact," in R. H. Canary and H. Kozicki, eds., *The Writing of History* (1978). The concept of the good war is discussed in Michael C. C. Adams, *The Best War Ever* (1994) and in Richard Polenberg, "The Good War? A Reappraisal of How World War II Affected American Society," *Virginia Magazine of History and Biography* 100:3 (July 1992). Studs Terkel's *"The Good War": An Oral History of World War II* (1985) gives candid first-hand recollections. A good starting place for Civil War myth-making is Thomas L. Connelly, *The Marble Man* (1977). On images of Vietnam: John Hellmann, *American Myth and the Legacy of Vietnam* (1986); Bill McCloud, *What Should We Tell Our Children About Vietnam?* (1989); and H. Bruce Franklin, *M.I.A. or Myth-making in America* (1993).

Richard Holmes, *Acts of War* (1985) is good on the over-all nature of combat. For the Civil War, see Reid Mitchell, *Civil War Soldiers* (1988); Gerald F. Linderman, *Embattled Courage* (1987); and Stephen W. Sears, *Landscape Turned Red* (1983). World War II combat was analyzed by Samuel A. Stouffer et al., *The American Soldier* (1965) and S. L. A. Marshall, *Men Against Fire* (1947); also by E. B. Sledge, *With the Old Breed* (1981) and William Manchester, *Goodby Darkness* (1980).

Thomas De Quincey wrote *Confessions of an English Opium Eater* (1822, 1856). Soldiers' addiction is discussed in Dixon Wecter, *When Johnny Comes Marching Home* (1976). On World War II: Paul Fussell, *Wartime* (1989) and John Costello, *Virtue Under Fire* (1985), also good on sexual mores. Civil War drug reliance is discussed in Judith Lee Hallock, *Braxton Bragg and Confederate Defeat* 2 (1991) and James Lee

McDonough and James Pickett Jones, *War So Terrible* (1987). On veterans' maladjustment, Betty Rosenbaum, "The Relationship Between War and Crime in the U.S.," *Journal of Criminal Law and Criminology* 30 (1940): 722–40. On the Civil War: Edith Abbott, "The Civil War and the Crime Wave of 1865–70," *Social Service Review* 1 (1927): 212–34; and John D. Seelye, "The American Tramp: A Version of the Picaresque," *American Quarterly* 15 (1963): 535–53. James Jones, *WWII* (1975), for the later conflict.

On government-business expansion in the Civil War: Robert Cruden, *The War That Never Ended* (1973) and Robert V. Bruce, *1877: Year of Violence* (1989). For World War II: Paul A. C. Koistenen, *The Military-Industrial Complex* (1980); and for postwar conformity: William H. Whyte, Jr., *The Organization Man* (1956) and David Riesman et al., *The Lonely Crowd* (1961). On war's costs: Keith L. Nelson, ed., *The Impact of War on American Life* (1971); Maris A. Vinovskis, ed., *Toward a Social History of the American Civil War* (1990); and James L. Clayton, "Vietnam: The 200 Year Mortgage," *The Nation* 208 (May 26, 1969): 661–63.

On gender and the Civil War: Catherine Clinton and Nina Silber, *Divided Houses* (1992) and Mary Elizabeth Massey, *Bonnet Brigades* (1966). For World War II: D'Ann Campbell, *Women at War with America* (1984) and Susan M. Hartman, *The Home Front and Beyond* (1982). See also Chapter Five. On the failure to achieve racial equality, see Chapter Six; and C. Vann Woodward, "Equality: The Deferred Commitment," in *The Burden of Southern History* (1960); and James Baldwin, *The Fire Next Time* (1963). Social mores, including delinquency, are discussed in Eric H. Monkkonen, *The Dangerous Class* (1975), Philip Wylie, *Generation of Vipers* (1955), and James Gilbert, *A Cycle of Outrage* (1986).

On cultural antagonisms: William R. Taylor, *Cavalier and Yankee* (1963); W. Fletcher Thompson, Jr., *The Image of War* (1960); John Dower, *War Without Mercy* (1986). War's destructiveness is discussed in Charles Royster, *The Destructive War* (1993) and John Ellis, *Brute Force* (1990). On guerrilla war: Thomas Goodrich, *Bloody Dawn* (1991); Carl W. Breichan, *Sam Hildebrand* (1984); and Michael Fellman, "Women and Guerrilla Warfare," in Clinton and Silber, *Divided Houses*. Richard Hofstadter deals with *Social Darwinism in American Thought* (1955). On brutality to German prisoners in World War II: James Bacque, *Other*

Losses (1989). On terror bombing: Michael Sherry, "The Slide to Total Air War," *New Republic*, Dec. 16, 1981. See Sidney Blumenthal on the "Munich analogy" in *Our Long National Daydream* (1988).

On the draft: David R. Segal, *Recruiting for Uncle Sam* (1989). David L. Cohn, "Should Fighting Men Think?" *The Saturday Review of Literature*, January 18, 1947, and Martin Van Creveld, *Fighting Power* (1982) on the ideological profile of the GI. James W. Geary, *We Need Men* (1991), for the Civil War. On pessimism in World War II literature: Joseph J. Waldmeir, "American Literature, Politics, and the Last Good War," in Adam J. Sorkin, ed., *Politics and the Muse* (1989). Both the Lost Cause tradition and Ahab's quest are treated derisively in Gordon Forbes's World War II novel, *Goodbye to Some* (1961). The grunt on the knight's quest is in Philip Caputo, *A Rumor of War* (1978). For a Civil War view: Horace Porter, "The Philosophy of Courage," *Century Illustrated Monthly Magazine* 34 (May–Oct. 1888): 249ff; compare, "Oliver Stone on Moral Amnesia," National Public Radio (NP-870407.01-C), 1987.

Alan T. Nolan's views on Lee wasting his army are in *Lee Considered* (1991). Caleb Carr criticizes the generals in the *New York Times Book Review*, July 5, 1992. Also, on the legacy of Civil War generalship, see Russell F. Weigley, "American Strategy from Its Beginnings Through the First World War," in Peter Paret, ed., *Makers of Modern Strategy*, 2nd edition (1986).

TEN: THE NECESSITY OF FORCE: THE CIVIL WAR, WORLD WAR II, AND THE AMERICAN VIEW OF WAR
Russell F. Weigley

For the opening observations on numbers engaged and lost in American wars, the principal statistics are conveniently available in Everette B. Long with Barbara Long, *The Civil War Day by Day: An Almanac, 1861–1865*, Foreword by Bruce Catton (1971), 705–6 for Civil War armed forces; 710–11 for Federal casualties; 711 for Confederate casualties; 711–12 for other wars through the Korean War (particularly p. 712 for World War II casualty figures cited herein). The total numbers of Americans in service were greater in World War I, the Korean War, and the Vietnam War than in the Civil War, but casualties were fewer, and the impact on national life was smaller, except possibly for the Vietnam War as discussed herein. For numbers who served in the armed forces during the Vietnam War (a total of about 10,900,000), see Christian G. Appy, *Working-Class War: American Combat Soldiers and Vietnam* (1993), 28; for total American Vietnam War casualties (1,078,162), see Harry G. Summers, *Vietnam War Almanac* (1985), 111.

For the number of slaves in 1860 as given herein, see Long, *Civil War Day by Day*, p. 702. United States population figures for the Civil War and World War II are from United States Bureau of the Census with the cooperations of the Social Science Research Council, *Historical Statistics of the United States: Colonial Times to 1957* (1960), Series A 2, Total population residing in the United States, Estimated Population of the United States: 1790 to 1957, as of July 1, p. 7 (31,513,000 population in 1860; 35,701,000 in 1865); Series A 4, Total; A 5, Continental United States and Outlying Areas: 1880 to 1950, p. 7 (150,622,754 total population in 1940, with 131,663,275 residing in the continental United States).

For the international war convention, an outstandingly thoughtful discussion is Michael Walzer, *Just and Unjust Wars: A Moral Argument with Historical Illustrations* (1977), especially pp. 43, 135–59, 186–93. See also Sidney Axinn, *A Moral Military* (1989), especially pp. 70–73.

For Sherman's and Stonewall Jackson's methods of warfare, see Charles Royster, *The Destructive War: William Tecumseh Sherman, Stonewall Jackson, and the Americans* (1991); and also for Sherman: John F. Marszalek, *Sherman: A Soldier's Passion for Order* (1993). On Sheridan: Roy Morris, Jr., *Sheridan: The Life and Wars of General Phil Sheridan* (1992), especially pp. 205–9, and Bruce Catton, *A Stillness at Appomattox* (1953), 275–76, 287, 304–5. For Confederate warfare against property in Pennsylvania: Edwin B. Coddington, *The Gettysburg Campaign: A Study in Command* (1968), VII, "The Confederates Plunder Pennsylvania," 153–79, substantially published also as "Prelude to Gettysburg: The Confederates Plunder Pennsylvania," *Pennsylvania History* 30 (1963): 123–57. On this subject see also Royster, *Destructive War*, p. 37.

For the interpretation of Sherman's and Sheridan's methods of war in a standard post-Civil War American military textbook, see John Bigelow, Jr., *The Principles of Strategy Illustrated Mainly from American*

Campaigns (1894), "Sherman's March Through Georgia and the Carolinas, 1864," 144–47; "Sheridan's Devastation of the Shenandoah Valley, 1864," 147–49; "The People as a Military Objective," 228–33.

The argument that the Civil War confirmed an American propensity toward total war that had originated in conflicts with the Indians and thus prepared the country for World War II is presented succinctly in John W. Shy, *A People Numerous and Armed: Reflections on the Military Struggle for American Independence* (1976), 225–54, 291–94.

For American aerial bombing in World War II, see Bernard Brodie, *Strategy in the Missile Age* (1959), particularly on the oil campaign (pp. 109–15, 118–19); Ronald Schaffer, *Wings of Judgment: American Bombing in World War II* (1985); Michael S. Sherry, *The Rise of American Air Power: The Creation of Armageddon* (1987). Max Hastings, *Bomber Command* (1979), offers a British perspective that sometimes encompasses the Americans (see pp. 277, 328 for the oil campaign, pp. 205–8 for Hamburg). For the number of deaths resulting from the Tokyo raid of March 9–10, 1945, consult Sherry, *Rise of American Air Power*, 277, and his discussion of the evidence (p. 406, n. 76); the latter note also deals with the deaths caused by the atomic bombing of Hiroshima, which may have taken 130,000 lives directly.

On American bombing during the Vietnam War, the best critical work is Mark Clodfelter, *The Limits of Air Power: The American Bombing of North Vietnam* (1989). See also George C. Herring, *America's Longest War: The United States and Vietnam* (1986), 117, 119, 121, 124–26, 128–30, 146–51, 175–79, 199–200, 207, 216–17, 247–50, 253–54.

The books by Schaffer, Sherry, and Clodfelter are prime examples of the questioning attitude toward strategic bombing in World War II that the Vietnam War helped to generate.

The history of the intervention in Somalia is conveniently summarized in Sidney Blumenthal, "Letter from Washington: Why Are We in Somalia?" *The New Yorker* 49:35 (Oct. 25, 1993): 48, 50–54, 57–60; and in George J. Church, "Anatomy of a Disaster," *Time: The Weekly Newsmagazine* 142:16 (Oct. 18, 1993): 40–46, 48–50. For the events of October 3, 1993, see ibid., 42–44, 49, and Michael R. Gordon with Thomas L. Friedman, "Disastrous U.S. Raid Nearly Succeeded, Review Finds: Valorous Delay May Have Far-reaching Impact," *New York Times*, Oct. 25,

1993, sec. A, p. 1, cols. 1–2, p. 10, cols. 1–5. The withdrawal of combat troops from Somalia was completed March 25, 1994; Donatella Lorch, "What Began as a Mission of Mercy Closes with Little Ceremony," ibid., March 26, 1994, p. 1, cols. 5–6, p. 2, cols. 1–4; Rick Lyman, "With little ceremony, U.S. leaves Somalia," *The Philadelphia Inquirer*, March 26, 1994, sec. A, p. 1, cols. 2–3, p. 18, cols. 1–6.

Contributors

STEPHEN E. AMBROSE, Boyd Professor of History at the University of New Orleans, is Director of the Eisenhower Center and President of the National D-Day Museum in New Orleans. His books include *Halleck: Lincoln's Chief of Staff* (1962); *Eisenhower: Soldier and President,* 2 vols. (1983, 1990); and *D-Day June 6, 1944: The Climactic Battle of World War II* (1994).

MICHAEL C. C. ADAMS, Professor of History and Chair of the Department of History and Geography at Northern Kentucky University, is the author of *Our Masters the Rebels: A Speculation on Union Military Failure in the East 1861–1865* (1978), which won the Jefferson Davis award and was republished as *Fighting for Defeat* (1992); *The Great Adventure: Male Desire and Coming of World War One* (1990); and *The Best War Ever: America and World War II* (1994).

IRA BERLIN is Dean of Undergraduates and Professor of History, University of Maryland. He is the founder of the Freedmen and Southern Society Project and an editor of *Freedom: A Documentary History of Emancipation.* He also co-edited *Free at Last* (1992), the winner of the Lincoln Prize.

ROBERT V. BRUCE is Professor of History, Emeritus, Boston University. His books include *Lincoln and the Tools of War* (1956) and *The Launching of Modern American Science, 1846–1876* (1987), winner of the Pulitzer Prize.

D'ANN CAMPBELL is Professor of History and Dean of Arts and Sciences at Austin Peay State University in Tennessee. Her publications, including *Women at War* (1985), focus on women's roles on the homefront and in the military during American wars. RICHARD JENSEN, Professor of History at University of Illinois, Chicago, is author of several books and articles on American political, economic, and social history.

DON E. FEHRENBACHER is Coe Professor of History, Emeritus, Stanford University. His books include *Prelude to Greatness: Lincoln in the 1850s* (1962) and *The Dred Scott Case: Its Significance in American Law and Politics* (1978), the winner of the Pulitzer Prize.

HOWARD JONES is University Research Professor and Chair of the Department of History at the University of Alabama. His books include *Mutiny of the Amistad* (1987) and *Union in Peril: The Crisis over British Intervention in the Civil War* (1992), winner of Phi Alpha Theta's award for "Best Subsequent Book."

GERALD F. LINDERMAN, Professor of History, University of Michigan, has written *The Mirror of War: American Society and the Spanish-American War* (1974) and *Embattled Courage: The Experience of Combat in the American Civil War* (1987). He is presently working on a study of the American combat soldier's role in World War II.

PETER MASLOWSKI, Professor at the University of Nebraska-Lincoln, is the author of *Armed with Cameras: The American Military Photographers of World War II* (1993) and the co-author (with Allan R. Millett) of *For the Common Defense: A Military History of the United States of America* (1994, revised and enlarged edition).

ARTHUR M. SCHLESINGER, JR., Albert Schweitzer Professor of Humanities, City University of New York, won Pulitzer Prizes for both *The Age of Jackson* (1945) and *The Age of Roosevelt* (1957). His most recent book is *The Disuniting of America* (1992).

RUSSELL F. WEIGLEY is Professor of History at Temple University. His books include *The American Way of War* (1973), *Eisenhower's Lieutenants: The Campaign of France and Germany* (1981), and *The Age of Battles: The Quest for Decisive Warfare from Breitenfeld to Waterloo* (1991).

GABOR S. BORITT, Director of the Civil War Institute and Fluhrer Professor at Gettysburg College, author of *Lincoln and the Economics of the American Dream* (1978, 1994), editor and co-author of *Lincoln's Generals* (1994), is currently at work on a book on the Battle of Gettysburg.